T0301995

HEALTHCARE's OUT SICK - PREDICTING A CURE - Solutions that WORK !!!!

Predictive Analytic Modeling, Decision Making, INNOVATIONS, and Precision Medicine Necessary to Correct the Broken Healthcare Delivery System

Featuring

"Ask Dr. Dean"

Examples

HEALTHCARE's

OUT SICK - PREDICTING

A CURE - Solutions that

WORK !!!!

Predictive Analytic Modeling, Decision
Making, INNOVATIONS, and Precision
Medicine Necessary to Correct the
Broken Healthcare Delivery System

By
Gary Miner, Linda Miner, and
Darrell Dean

CRC Press
Taylor & Francis Group
Boca Raton London New York

CRC Press is an imprint of the
Taylor & Francis Group, an **informa** business
A PRODUCTIVITY PRESS BOOK

CRC Press
Taylor & Francis Group
6000 Broken Sound Parkway NW, Suite 300
Boca Raton, FL 33487-2742

First issued in paperback 2021

ISBN-13: 978-1-138-58109-8 (hbk)
ISBN-13: 978-1-03-217842-4 (pbk)
DOI: 10.4324/9780429506932

Publisher's Note

The publisher has gone to great lengths to ensure the quality of this reprint but points out that some imperfections in theoriginal copies may be apparent.

Library of Congress Cataloging-in-Publication Data

Names: Miner, Gary, author.
Title: Healthcare's out sick - predicting a cure - solutions that work !!!! : predictive analytic modeling, decision making, innovations and precision medicine necessary to correct the broken healthcare delivery system / Gary Miner, Linda Miner, Darrell Dean.
Description: Boca Raton : Taylor & Francis, 2019. | Includes bibliographical references. |
Identifiers: LCCN 2018048183 (print) | LCCN 2018051895 (ebook) | ISBN 9780429506932 (e-Book) | ISBN 9781138581098 (hardback : alk. paper)
Subjects: LCSH: Integrated delivery of health care--United States.
Classification: LCC RA971 (ebook) | LCC RA971 .M517 2019 (print) | DDC 362.1--dc23
LC record available at https://lccn.loc.gov/2018048183

Visit the Taylor & Francis Web site at
http://www.taylorandfrancis.com

and the CRC Press Web site at
http://www.crcpress.com

Contents

Foreword

by John Cromwell, MD
September 2018

The USA has a rich history in the science of quality improvement. As a surgeon, I'm extraordinarily proud that the modern concepts of continuous quality improvement in medicine began with the surgeon Dr. Ernest Codman in the early 20th century. Given this tradition, and the extraordinary advances in medicine, it is both puzzling and disconcerting that there are still mothers, fathers, sons, and daughters seeking medical care who die from our failure to safely deliver that care.

The healthcare industry is now far more massive than during Dr. Codman's time, with many more stakeholders chasing disparate goals and agendas. The necessity to realign the entire US healthcare system on "value-based" delivery of care rather than "volume-based" delivery of care is now broadly accepted, but the route to achieving that alignment is far from clear. All of this is happening in the midst of the fourth industrial revolution, in which massive advances in predictive analytics, machine learning, and artificial intelligence are becoming ubiquitously available.

I've had the fortune of knowing and collaborating with the senior authors, Gary and Linda Miner, for the past eight years and of admiring their ability to make challenging material easily digestible. I now have the chance to admire them for taking on the challenge of explaining how US healthcare is broken. They explore the broken and unsustainable facets of our current healthcare delivery system, and importantly, propose several strategies to use technological advances to favorably disrupt healthcare delivery and its sustainability.

I'm certain that if Dr. Codman were roaming modern-day hospitals, he would share the enthusiasm for the approaches presented in this volume. I congratulate the authors on making this complex subject both approachable and enjoyable to the non-technical reader.

John W. Cromwell, MD, FACS, FASCRS
Associate Chief Medical Officer | Director of
Surgical Quality and Safety
University of Iowa Hospitals & Clinics
Director, Division of Gastrointestinal, Minimally Invasive,
and Bariatric Surgery
Clinical Professor
University of Iowa Carver College of Medicine
Faculty, Interdisciplinary Graduate Program in Informatics
University of Iowa Graduate College

Foreword

by Daniel Robitshek, MD
October 2018

The conceptual pendulum in medical care has swung so often that the rope holding the weight of our nation's healthcare system is inexorably frayed. In the manufacturing world, the concept of systems driving function is obvious. Every system is perfectly designed to produce the results that it does. The same, however, is not true with healthcare. Of the eleven wealthiest first-world countries, the USA is ranked LAST in overall outcomes despite the fact that we spend over TWICE as much on healthcare as the next closest nation. The question is, *why is our healthcare system broken and what is the design flaw?* The ultimate dilemma is this: we as a nation need to decide what outcomes we want our future healthcare system to produce. Moreover, we need to understand how to RE-design the system to accomplish these outcomes.

I have known Dr. Darrell Dean for many years—as a colleague, a mentor, and a friend. Darrell has been involved for decades in almost every aspect of healthcare imaginable. His experience spans from a private, patient centered family practice, to his engagement in statewide population medicine; from primary caregiver for the most vulnerable elderly patients at local nursing homes to Director of Quality Improvement for a large healthcare system.

Dr. Dean understands the modern healthcare conundrum: the juxtaposition between the intimacy of the individual, unique doctor–patient relationship with the banality of our cold, imprecise, and ultimately broken massive healthcare system.

Please pay very close attention to all that Dr. Dean has to say. His expertise is not solely a by-product of his extensive experience. *He is innately wise.* He has been a source of wisdom for lay-people, patients, students, early career physicians, and experienced clinicians. He has compassionately provided support to patients and families walking through the last stages of life and he has boldly spoken truth to powerful leaders in the healthcare industry. He gets it!!! And, I am honored to call him my friend.

The contribution to the future mission, vision, and application of healthcare in the USA by Dr. Dean and co-authors Drs. Gary and Linda Miner through this superb and well-written treatise cannot be overstated. Indeed, I pray that its content becomes an integral part of the conversation that our country must undertake as we look to stabilize the swinging pendulum of our broken healthcare system once and for all.

Daniel Robitshek, MD, FACP, FACOI, SFHM
Associate Professor of Medicine, Medical College of Georgia
Assistant Professor of Internal Medicine, Philadelphia
College of Osteopathic Medicine
Director of Graduate Medical Education
Program Director, Internal Medicine Residency
Redmond Regional Medical Center
Rome, GA
Formerly:
Professor of Medicine and Health Sciences
University of California, Irvine School of Medicine
Full description of Awards and Honors can be found on his
faculty web page:
https://redmondresidency.com/staff/dr-daniel-robitshek/

Reviewer's Preface

by Thomas Hill, PhD
December 2018

This book offers up a manifesto for patients' interests, rights, and agency over all aspects of medical research and healthcare delivery. It is less of a detailed analysis of the incredible complexities—from the sometimes misplaced economic incentives to the rapid scientific advances that are difficult to absorb into the day-to-day practice of healthcare. Some readers may disagree with some or perhaps many of the proposals and opinions that are expressed. But the authors undeniably and passionately deliver a personal point-of-view informed by decades of experience as healthcare patients, researchers (Drs. Linda and Gary Miner), and providers (Dr. Darrell Dean). That is where this book offers a unique contribution.

The subject of healthcare is obviously complex, and Linda Miner, Gary Miner, and Darrell Dean make the case for patients to take ownership of their health and healthcare. They also strongly advocate personalized medicine enabled through modern genetics and predictive analytics, focused on the individual and her/his genetic makeup and specific life experiences and circumstances. Their preference for how best to make this affordable leans towards a mix of competitive private insurance and provider options, along with a single-payer (government-paid) system with sufficient bargaining power to force reasonable rates for catastrophic insurance.

Again, many might disagree with these suggestions and find the general notion of responsible patients keenly interested and highly educated about their treatment options and cost to be an unrealistic ideal. Also, the topic of a single-payer-system vs. competitive markets for health insurers (and providers) will remain hotly debated. However, it is hard to argue against the suggestion that informed patients actively promoting their own best possible health would make solving the healthcare challenge and lowering the cost of healthcare much easier.

So, enjoy this book and the stimulating thoughts about many different but relevant topics that it highlights. Also enjoy and take to heart the many useful tidbits of insight and advice from Dr. Dean that accompany the read, who also offers sound practical guidance on how to improve one's wellbeing, the wellbeing of Doctors, and the healthcare system in general.

The authors cite many personal experiences to illustrate their points. To add my own personal illustration of our healthcare "crisis": When our small dog lost his appetite and became lethargic one Friday, we took him to a vet who performed a basic examination, blood tests, and rehydrated our "little fellow"—all for a very reasonable fee. The vet then gave us his cell phone number and told us to call him if our dog is not better by Sunday. When was the last time your doctor gave you her/his personal phone number and encouraged you to call on a weekend if you're not feeling better? So how did we get to the point where my dog seems to get more personal and affordable healthcare than me, and how do we fix that? On the following pages, you will find Dr. Linda Miner's, Dr. Gary Miner's, and Dr. Darell Dean's insights and suggestions on how to "fix that."

Thomas Hill, PhD
Senior Director Advanced Analytics
EMAIL: thill@tibco.com
WEB: http://www.tibco.com/
Twitter: https://twitter.com/DrTomHill"@DrTomHill
LinkedIn: http://www.linkedin.com/in/DrThomasHill

Author's Preface

This book came about because of at least three forces in the authors' lives: (1) observing the rapidly rising costs of medical care during the past four decades, at rates much greater than the *cost of living* inflation rate, due largely to the fact that healthcare delivery was NOT transparent but instead the process more or less was *held secret* by the providers and payers; (2) observing and coping with medical errors that brought about the deaths of three of the senior authors' parents; and (3) the senior authors, trained in traditional statistics during their college and younger research years, fully embracing the *Modern Statistics—the Modern Predictive Analytics* during the last two decades and, in doing so, writing some of the most influential books on the use and practical value of predictive analytics. The primary value of Predictive Data Analytics (whether you use the term AI—Artificial Intelligence or Machine Learning to describe it) is that it can easily make *Accurate Predictions for the **individual***. Traditional statistics, for the most part, can only make inferences for **groups** or the **means** of populations. The ability of Predictive Analytics to make predictions for the individual patient—predictions that take into account all the uniqueness of a single individual, from their genetics and their environmental life experiences, so that the prediction is ***accurate for the individual***— is what is so powerful about these modern data analysis methods.

As such, Predictive Analytics holds the key to helping revolutionize healthcare delivery, in all aspects of the process, from a doctor's initial diagnosis to treatment, to recovery, to pharmaceutical use, to hospital/clinic administration tasks, to all the components of the payer's processes.

But, for this to happen, the healthcare establishment, e.g. the providers, researchers, and payers, have to embrace this new technology ... and they have been slow to do so, even though it has been readily available since the year 2000—almost 20 years ago. There seems to be great resistance among some in the medical establishment to embrace the new technology, instead resorting to what they have known as **Gold Standards** in an attempt to reassure themselves that they *know* how to use words in their communications such as "Data Analytics" and "Patient Centered Care" when they really have no understanding of what real "Data Predictive Analytics" or "Patient Centered Care" is all about. (The two senior authors have seen this firsthand, serving on *Medical Research Grant Review Panels* in Washington, DC, and also in observing the written and verbal communications coming from medical, pharmaceutical, and political people over the past few years.)

The senior authors have wanted to write this book for the past seven or eight years. Initially we wanted it to be released at the same time as our big volume, the 2015 *Practical Predictive Analytics & Decisioning Systems for Medicine* (Winters-Miner et al., 2015); however, time constraints did not allow us to write it at that time. We have kept computer folders filled with references, citations, and quotes for this book over the past eight years, and CRC Press has been asking us for the past four years to "write this book for them." Even back in 2014 we had communication with Kristine Mednansky of CRC Press/Taylor & Francis Group on this book. Then, in late May 2017, Don Karecki, formerly of KM Publishers, which he sold to the CRC Press/Taylor & Francis Group (Don had met us for breakfast in Tulsa, OK, a few years before asking us to write a book for CRC Press), emailed again and said, "It is time to do this—WILL YOU?" After several email exchanges with Don and Kristine, we finally agreed to do this book, even though we were in the last several months of finishing the 2nd edition of our 2009 award-winning book with lots of work on that still to do and VERY TIRED of WRITING BOOKS!!!! The 2nd edition of the *Handbook of Statistical Analysis and Data Mining Applications* took several months longer than originally planned but was finally released with an early 2018 copyright. Thus our way was freed to think only about this *Healthcare Solutions* book, which we finished writing on August 30, 2018. The main message of this book is encapsulated in the following diagram, the NEW MODEL OF HEALTHCARE (Figure 0.1).

The **Old Model**—what is currently the primary way of operating in healthcare delivery in the USA—is presented in

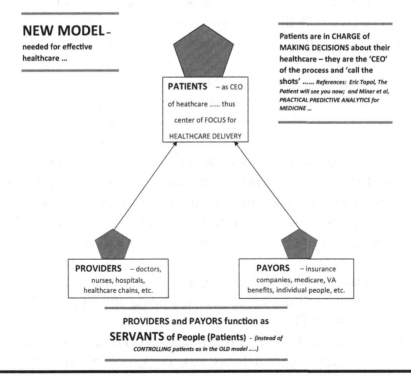

Figure 0.1 NEW MODEL: UMBRELLA PHILOSOPHY of EFFECTIVE HEALTHCARE SOLUTIONS for the USA.

another diagram in Chapter 2, and also both models are discussed again in Chapter 7.

A complete ***disruption*** or ***about-face*** has to happen with the old model to get to where the USA needs to go in order to provide healthcare to all at costs closer to 10% of the GNP (like other industrialized nations do ... and with better care than the USA now generally expereiences) instead of the close to 20% of the GNP that the USA now endures ... Disruption to find REAL TRUTH is the "name of the game" today.

Currently *Gold Standards* or standards of care, are used by doctors in providing what they have been taught to believe are the best solutions in healthcare delivery. But what those solutions really are is this (for many of the rules, if not most ...): INDOCTRINATED—PASSED-ON-RULES which may have little or no scientific proof for the most part.

Many doctors call the use of these *Gold Standards* EBM: Evidence-Based Medicine. Only reliance on three things will correct this misuse/misunderstanding and thus lead to ***Real EBM***:

1. Adding GENOMICS to the computations for diagnosis and treatments—this means the genetic differences in individual people (which thus also means the individual differences in response to medications and treatments).
2. Ruthlessly well-done PREDICTIVE ANALYTICS, where the INDIVIDUAL (and not the **mean** or **average** of a human population) is used in arriving at real truth. Thus the doctor can provide an **accurate prediction** just for an individual which tells the patient how they will react to any drug medication or treatment plan, and thus the patient can decide prior to receiving the drug, treatment, surgery, etc. whether the probability of it being effective for THEM is "WORTH IT."
3. All of which leads to **PRECISION MEDICINE**—the doctor and healthcare delivery staff being able to give information on how you as an individual, and not a group mean, will respond to a treatment plan.

What this means is this:

1. The medical healthcare delivery field has to do an *ABOUT-FACE* in how they THINK ABOUT and HOW THEY ACT in providing treatments for the INDIVIDUAL patient.
2. Medical research also has to do an *ABOUT-FACE*, which means firing their misuse of p-value/multiple p tests research and embracing fully modern PREDICTIVE ANALYTICS, including machine learning methods where the INDIVIDUAL is the focus (instead of the mean of the human population, which is currently still the case in a great amount of medical research, even though the modern PA methods have been available to medical research since about the year 2000, nearly 20 years ago!!!!).

In conclusion, we think it is a good thing that we did NOT produce this book back in 2015. The need for change in US healthcare delivery has not changed much from 2009 or 2015. However, others have seen the problems, and various ***disruptive models*** have been attempted, from Seattle's Qliance, which lasted for 10 years before dissolving last year (*https:// www.seattletimes.com/business/qliance-closes-after-10-year-effort-at-new-approach-to-basic-medical-care/*), to the Oak Street model (discussed in Chapter 7 *https://hbr.org/product/ oak-street-health-a-new-model-of-primary-care/717437-PDF-ENG*), to the current 2018 Amazon-JPMorgan-Berkshire Hathaway corporate delivery plan (discussed in Chapter 7— just being developed as this book is finished, thus we do not know its end result; *https://qz.com/1192693/amazon-jp-morgan-and-berkshire-hathaway-are-starting-a-healthcare-company/*). So many innovations and disruptions are being experimented with in various parts of the USA right now. Now is the ***Time for Change***. Most likely, the 2019 DC congressional year will see our legislatures really grappling with how to change healthcare delivery, so maybe this book coming out in

2019 is appropriate, and it was good that we were delayed in completing this book as NOW is the ***Right Time for Change*** ... hopefully the *Black Swan* solution (see end of Chapter 7) will come about and we can begin again with a successful healthcare delivery system for America.

Your Authors: Gary Miner, PhD
Linda Miner, PhD
Darrell Dean, DO

About the Authors

Dr. Gary D. Miner, PhD, received his BS from Hamline University in St. Paul, Minnesota, with biology, chemistry, and education majors; his MS in Zoology and Population Genetics from the University of Wyoming; and his PhD in Biochemical Genetics from the University of Kansas, as the recipient of a NASA Pre-Doctoral Fellowship. During the doctoral study years, he also studied mammalian genetics at the Jackson Laboratory in Bar Harbor, Maine, under a college training program on an NIH award; marine developmental embryology through a college training program at the Bermuda Biological Station in St. George's West, Bermuda, on an NSF award; and molecular techniques in developmental biology through a third college training program held at the University of California, San Diego, again on an NSF award. Following that, he studied as a postdoctoral student at the University of Minnesota in Behavioral Genetics, where, along with research in schizophrenia and Alzheimer's disease (AD), he learned "how to write books" from assisting in editing two book manuscripts with his mentor, Irving Gottesman, PhD (Dr. Gottesman returned the favor 41 years later by writing two tutorials for our 2012 *PRACTICAL TEXT*

MINING book). After academic research and teaching positions, Dr. Miner did another two-year NIH postdoctoral in
psychiatric epidemiology and biostatistics at the University
of Iowa, where he became thoroughly immersed in studying affective disorders and Alzheimer's disease. Altogether,
he spent over 30 years researching and writing papers and
books on the genetics of Alzheimer's disease (Miner, G.D.,
Richter, R., Blass, J.P., Valentine, J.L, and Winters-Miner, L.
*Familial Alzheimer's Disease: Molecular Genetics and Clinical
Perspectives.* Dekker: NYC, 1989; and Miner, G.D., Winters-
Miner, L., Blass, J.P., Richter, R., and Valentine, J.L. *Caring
for Alzheimer's Patients: A Guide for Family & Healthcare
Providers.* Plenum Press Insight Books: NYC). Over the years
he held positions, including professor and chairman of a
department, at various universities, including the University
of Kansas; the University of Minnesota; Northwest Nazarene
University; Eastern Nazarene University; Southern Nazarene
University; Oral Roberts University Medical School, where
he was Associate Professor of Pharmacology and Director
of the Alzheimer's Disease & Geriatric Disorders Research
Laboratories; and the Fuller Graduate School of Psychology &
Fuller Theological Seminary in Pasadena, California, where
for a period of time in the 1990s he was a visiting Clinical
Professor of Psychology for Geriatrics. In 1985 he and his
wife, Dr. Linda Winters-Miner (author of several tutorials in
the 2009, 2012, and 2015 scientific books on predictive analytics book), founded the Familial Alzheimer's Disease Research
Foundation (aka "the Alzheimer's Foundation"), which became
a leading force in organizing both local and international
scientific meetings and thus bringing together all the leaders
in the field of genetics of AD from several countries, which
then led to the writing of the first scientific book on the genetics of Alzheimer's disease; this book included papers by over
100 scientists coming out of the First International Symposium
on the Genetics of Alzheimer's Disease, held in Tulsa, OK,
in October 1987. During this time he was also an Affiliate

Research Scientist with the Oklahoma Medical Research
Foundation located in Oklahoma City, with the University of
Oklahoma School of Medicine. Dr. Miner was influential in
bringing all of the world's leading scientists working on genetics of AD together at just the right time when various labo-
ratories, from Harvard to Duke University and the University
of California–San Diego, to the University of Heidelberg,
Germany, and universities in Belgium, France, England, and
Perth, Australia, were beginning to find "genes" which they
thought were related to Alzheimer's disease. During the 1990s,
Dr. Miner was appointed to the Oklahoma Governor's Task
Force on Alzheimer's Disease and also was Associate Editor
for Alzheimer's Disease for *The Journal of Geriatric Psychiatry
& Neurology*, which he still serves on to this day. By 1995 most
of these dominantly inherited genes for AD had been discovered, and the one that Dr. Miner had been working on since
the mid-1980s with the University of Washington in Seattle was
the last of these initial five to be identified, this gene on chro-
mosome 1 of the human genome. At that time, having met
the goal of finding out some of the genetics of AD, Dr. Miner
decided to do something different, to discover an area of the
business world, and since he had been analyzing data for over
30 years, working for StatSoft, Inc. as a Senior Statistician and
Data Mining Consultant seemed a perfect "semi-retirement"
career. Interestingly (as his wife had predicted), he discovered that the "business world" was much more fun than the
"academic world," and at a KDD–Data Mining meeting in
1999 in San Francisco, he decided that he would specialize
in "data mining." Incidentally, he first met Bob Nisbet there,
who told him, "You just have to meet this bright young rising
star, John Elder!", and within minutes Bob introduced John to
Gary. As Gary delved into this new "data mining" field and
looked at statistics text books in general, he saw the need for
"practical statistical books" and started writing chapters and
organizing various outlines for different books. Gary, Bob,
and John kept running into each other at KDD meetings,

and eventually at a breakfast meeting in Seattle in August of 2005 decided they needed to write a book on data mining, and right there re-organized Gary's outline, which eventually became the *Handbook of Statistical Analysis and Data Mining Applications* (2009), published by Elsevier. Gary wishes to especially thank Dr. Irving Gottesman, his "mentor in book writing," who planted the seed back in 1970 while Gary was doing a postdoctoral with him at the University of Minnesota. Dr. Miner's latest book was published last year (2018 Copyright; 2nd Edition of the 2009 book): *https://www.amazon.com/Handbook-Statistical-Analysis-Mining-Applications/dp/0124166326/.* In more recent years, Gary has served as a merit reviewer for PCORI (Patient Centered Outcomes Research Institute), which awards grants for predictive analytics research into the comparative effectiveness and heterogeneous treatment effects of medical interventions.

Dr. Linda A. Winters-Miner, PhD, received a BS from the University of Kansas, with an education major; an MS in Education and Curriculum, also from the University of Kansas; and a PhD in Education with a minor in Educational Psychology and Statistics at the University of Minnesota, where she won a teaching assistantship which began her university teaching career. The following is a progression of her work and research interests.

- In progression over time: elementary teacher, college instructor, university professor, and university administrator.
- She pursued additional studies at the University of Iowa, where she was awarded a two-year postdoc in psychiatric epidemiology.

- With her husband, Gary, she became immersed in the study of affective disorders and Alzheimer's disease. In 1985, she and Gary founded the Familial Alzheimer's Disease Research Foundation, which became a leading force in organizing both local and international scientific meetings, bringing together all the leaders in the field of genetics of Alzheimer's from several countries, resulting in the first major book on the genetics of Alzheimer's disease.
- She coordinated the Tulsa site of one of the first drugs for Alzheimer's disease—the Parke Davis Cognex Study, Parke Davis, Tulsa, OK.
- Dr. Miner became a program director for three undergraduate programs (business and psychology) for adults and later three graduate programs (management science and business administration, and eventually including program director for MBA-Health Care, Southern Nazarene University, Tulsa). Besides program directing, and as a professor at SNU-Tulsa, Dr. Winters-Miner also taught research design and statistics and directed all the undergraduate business research projects.
- She served as a merit reviewer for PCORI (Patient Centered Outcomes Research Institute), which awards grants for predictive analytics research into the comparative effectiveness and heterogeneous treatment effects of medical interventions.
- Her research interests include brain laterality, Alzheimer's disease, disseminated intravascular coagulation (DIC), and she has co-authored and authored numerous articles and presentations.
- For ten years, Dr. Miner served as community faculty for research projects of the second-year residents in the Tulsa-based medical residency program (In His Image International). The research projects spanned many aspects of medical practice, according to the interests of

the students, including the medical interests of less developed nations.

■ She co-authored two books on Alzheimer's disease—*Molecular Genetics of Alzheimer's Disease*, which was the first book on the genetics of Alzheimer's, and a second book on Alzheimer's caregiving.

■ Dr. Miner was a contributor to the *Handbook of Statistical Analysis and Data Mining Applications* (co-authored by Drs. Robert A. Nisbet, Gary D. Miner, and John Elder), writing numerous predictive analytic tutorials for Nisbet et al. The book received the 2009 American Publishers Award for Professional and Scholarly Excellence (PROSE). The second edition has recently been published (2018), for which Dr. Miner again submitted revised tutorials.

■ Dr. Miner was also a contributor of tutorials to *Practical Text Mining and Statistical Analysis for Non-structured Text Data Applications*, which also received a PROSE award in February 2013.

■ She co-authored, and in fact was the lead author, for *Practical Predictive Analytics and Decisioning Systems for Medicine* (2015), Elsevier.

■ At present, she is a professor emeritus at Southern Nazarene University and teaches online classes in "Introduction to Predictive Analytics" and "Healthcare Predictive Analytics" for the University of California-Irvine.

Dr. Darrell L. Dean, DO, MPH, decided that he wanted to be a physician at age 10. That decision did not change until his first year of college, when he realized what was involved in that career path. On the suggestion of a nurse friend, he applied and was hired as an orderly at the hospital in the college town of Anderson, Indiana (Anderson College, now Anderson University). After one month as an orderly, his decision was that becoming a physician was the path that he was going to follow. If that decision did not pan out, he could never say that he wanted to be a doctor but did not try. He worked there on a full-time basis throughout the remainder of his college years, and the experience confirmed the goal of years before. Based on the advice of a family acquaintance of an osteopathic physician, he applied and was accepted to the Osteopathic University immediately following his college years, graduating from medical school in 1967 from Kansas City University of Medicine and Biosciences.

The next step in his career was a one-year internship in general medicine in an osteopathic hospital in Fort Worth, Texas. (That hospital is now closed.) Medical practice began immediately after his internship at an office in Hurst, Texas, with a contract with the hospital in Hurst, but it was short, due to receipt of a draft notice. One week after receipt of the notice, a follow-up letter notified him that he was eligible for an army commission. He accepted and served one year in Vietnam and one year in William Beaumont Army Hospital in El Paso, Texas.

Next, he practiced family medicine in multiple locations over the years, including:

a group practice (three physicians) at Wilcox Clinic in Wilcox, Arizona, for one year; a solo private practice in Decatur, Georgia, for 17 years; and a group practice in Taylorsville, Georgia, for eight years.

During his years of private practice, he held hospital medical staff positions as follows:

Northern Cochise General Hospital in Wilcox, Arizona, for one year; Doctor's Hospital in Tucker, Georgia, for five years; DeKalb Medical Center in Decatur, Georgia, for 12 years; Floyd Medical Center for 18 years.

After his solo practice in Georgia, he became the district health director for the Georgia Department of Public Health, with a district office in Rome, Georgia. That position included responsibility for public health, mental health, mental retardation, and substance abuse programs for a ten-county district in

Northwest Georgia for four years. During his work with public health, he achieved a master of public health degree from the Rollins School of Public Health at Emory University.

When he left public health, he again began a practice in family medicine in the small town of Taylorsville, Georgia, in the private office of another family medicine physician and his wife, who was an endocrinologist. He practiced there for eight years. One year after joining that practice Floyd Medical Center purchased the practice and he became an employee of the hospital.

After 5 additional years in traditional family practice, Floyd Medical Center moved him into a position as "Internal Consultant for Coding and Documentation." He spent one year with a hired consultant, who was employed due to an annual loss of $1.8 million per year due to inadequate physician documentation. The consultant trained him to locate and improve physician documentation. That training prepared him to address the loss and reduce the hospital financial loss to $300,000 per year over a two-year period.

Beginning in 2004, Floyd Medical Center developed a program for all quality and performance activity for all medical and surgical departments, for which he became medical director of clinical and operational performance until his retirement at the end of 2011.

In addition to the full-time position at Floyd Medical Center, in September 2010 he accepted the position of continuing medical education surveyor for the Medical Association of Georgia and CME committee chairman, and he has continued in the chairman position since retirement.

Also, since retirement, he has been employed in a part-time position as an attending physician with Senior Medical Systems for several Georgia nursing homes. He continues serving that role on a part-time basis.

Chapter 1

Medical (Madness)— Mistakes Throughout History

Introduction

Medicine and healthcare delivery in the USA is in a sick, chaotic, backward state today primarily because in the past either ***science was not used*** or if used it was mostly **bad science**. Interestingly, other entities in our society go bankrupt if they use the outdated processes and procedures that healthcare delivery embraces. Instead, to remain solvent these other entities, for the past twenty-five years, whether manufacturing, banking, or other commercial endeavors, have modernized technologies and faced realities with efficient and cost-effective workflows.

But not so for healthcare until only very recently—let us explain how this has happened—and we will try to do this in clear terms and simple analogies.

By "science was not used," we mean that doctors, and medical practitioners over the centuries would "try something," and if that something seemed to work with a patient, then it was thought to be "good" and used with future patients. The "something" tried was not only used on future patients by a particular doctor, but this doctor when training others transmitted this method to the new doctors as truth ... and so the diagnosis and the treatment became the standard practice, and carried down through decades or centuries until something else that seemed to work better was introduced. This method of medicine was to treat all patients based on a sample of one.

With the advent of the scientific method came major improvements to treatments and, more recently, a vast improvement to medicine was evidence-based medicine (EBM). The idea of EBM was highly commendable. Doctors wanted to have "evidence" that a treatment really worked or was really addressing the diseases in patients. Sometimes, however, some of the old treatments carried down by word of mouth and became part of this EBM. But other times researchers conducted studies to demonstrate or prove that a drug or treatment really worked. This started in earnest during the 20th century, particularly in the 1940s and 1950s. To document scientifically that methods were either true or false, medical people started using Fischerian p-value statistics (after Fischer had introduced this to agriculture studies in England in earlier decades), which we will call traditional p-value statistics from here on in this book. HOWEVER, most medical people were not fully trained in how to use ***traditional p-value statistics*** correctly; thus, what they thought was "good science" or "good EBM results" was incorrect up to 90% of the time (depending on the specific disease category and the statistical knowledge of the people reviewing scientific papers in various medical journals).

The medical scientific studies of the past century were to a large extent flawed in their scientific data analysis in one of two ways: (1) the **traditional p-value statistics** were used incorrectly, thus wrong conclusions were made, or (2) the traditional p-value statistics were used correctly, but not reported correctly because of bias of some sort in the writing of the research/author—i.e. the scientific researcher/author wanted to prove a particular theory and thus bent the correctly done statistics to try to prove what they wanted in order to be published.

And even if the traditional statistics were done correctly and reported correctly, almost all traditional statistics calculate information for the **mean of groups** of people and not for the **individual** person. This is an additional very big reason why medical research of the past is NOT accurate or relevant to YOU, an individual person. People are genetically different—heterogenous. What does this mean? People who are close to the average with respect to a certain trait or similar genetic profile might respond to a drug being tested, but people in the tails of the distribution, whether high or low, might not respond well to the medication. What is needed is research that is down to the level of the individual. (See Figure 1.1 for an illustration.)

Blood pressure drugs are particularly prone to this type of **scientific error**, as the genetic basis of high blood pressure is complex, probably involving many diverse groupings of genes. Thus, doctors must do a "trial and error" approach in prescribing blood pressure drugs. The doctor will try one; if it works, OK, but if not, then the doctor must try another with the patient. This must go on, sometimes for months, before a drug that works with a particular patient is found. A trial and error approach is backward; yesterday's mode of operation for most things in our world today. If medical researchers and healthcare delivery facilities use good individualized **predictive analytics**, they could eliminate a large part of these errors or hits and misses in prescribing treatments. Most of the rest of society's organizations and businesses are using predictive analytics (PA) today and have since about the year 2000 when these modern PA methods became widely available. Banks, insurance corporations, manufacturing companies, services, and nonprofits have all had to adapt to these PA methods during the past 18–25 years—if they did NOT, they probably went bankrupt and disappeared. So, most of the things and processes that society uses have had to use PA to survive in the real world ...

Suppose a drug company wanted to find out if its migraine medicine (B) was better than what was at present on the market, Medication A. It conducted a two-group experiment (a clinical trial) on whether Medication A or Medication B was more effective at bringing relief for migraine headaches. The higher the score, the better the outcome. Each of the dots in each group represents a person in the clinical trial. Each person in both groups had about the same level of migraines to begin with. They were randomly assigned to take Medication A or Medication B. At the end of the trial period the participants were medically assessed and the higher the score (more to the right) the more relief the participant seemed to get from the medication. Figure 1.1 shows the outcome of the study.

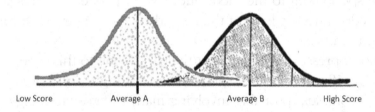

| Low Score | Average A | Average B | High Score |

Now if the drug company saw this result, it would rightly believe that Medication B provided the most relief—at least more than Medication A. They would like to put their medication on the market and have physicians prescribe it.

The problem in saying that Medication B should be given to everyone with migraines, based on this information, is that there are people both above and below the two averages (what statisticians say are in the tails of the distributions). Even though the results were significant, there were people who took medication A that found as much relief as people taking the "better" medication, Medication B. Likewise, there were people taking Medication B who had worse relief than some in the Medication A group. Prescribing for the mean does not work for all individuals. Perhaps Medication A works better for some people than Medication B. This is the problem with prescribing to the average. Something that is good for the average might not be good for the people "in the tails."

Figure 1.1 Medication A versus Medication B. (Figure by Linda Miner.)

ASK DR. DEAN:

Question 1: What types of mistakes have been made, prior to the 20th century, in healthcare delivery?
Answer: In reviewing the history of medical care from centuries ago, it is not possible to identify "medical mistakes" as such (that is, if we define "medical mistakes" as knowing what is "correct to do" but "not doing the 'correct' thing"). In early years, say 1600–1900, the number of "healers" who had a medical education was not large, but there were many people who treated injuries, illnesses, and various perceived conditions, even though they had no specific medical training. In fact, in those times past, treatments were based on unproven ideas and in retrospect were absolutely senseless. Some were remedies used as a result of trials by untrained "healers" who believed that the "treatment" would produce healing. The treatments might be used for a variety of conditions rather than any specific health problem. The people who availed themselves of these treatments had no knowledge of effective treatments, so whatever treatment was used was accepted. There was virtual ignorance about the cause of health problems and the effect of treatments, so adults and children could only look for help from family and friends who had some level of experience or seek help with those issues from a "healer." The treatments of the "healers" were possible due to the fact that there was very little control of healthcare providers by government in the 1700s to the 1900s.

In case of affliction due to infectious diseases, which were suffered by many, there was no known treatment, and they spread rapidly. Many people died as a result of the rapid spread of such infections. There were a number of these, such as diphtheria, yellow fever, smallpox, malaria, measles, and tuberculosis, which had no appropriate medicines or treatments. A typically recognized way to reduce the spread of such infections was isolation. If folks avoided the ill people, then they did not contract the infection, assuming they avoided them early in the illness.

Most of the medically educated healthcare providers (doctors) in those early times were from Europe, especially from Britain, though there were also providers who had apprenticed under a practitioner already working as a healthcare provider. Licensing of physicians began in Europe in 1760. In the USA, in 1877, Alabama became the first state to license doctors, and by 1890, 28 states had followed suit. By 1901 all states and territories except Alaska and Oklahoma had examining boards and a required license. Those states followed suit subsequently. In the USA, 160 medical schools were educating doctors by 1901.

... but medical practice seems NOT to dwell in the REAL WORLD!

Business and industry do not want a mismatching of products to the customer. Predicting what customers want and will buy is a constant practice of most businesses. *Only in medicine, do we accept mismatching and take what they tell us to use, then pay for it whether it works or not.* One wonders at the mind set - the belief that we cannot do better or - do we simply not want to do better? One perplexing indicator is the inability of healthcare/the medical domain to have data available to do the good PA research that is needed. Not even considering HIPAA, there are times when doctors, hospitals, and healthcare facilities hold onto the data they have and will not share it among facilities and the research world. In doing so they prevent progress both in cost efficiencies and in preventing bad outcomes.

The current healthcare delivery system in the USA is not sustainable ... it cannot continue as it is.

Where Have We Come from? How Have We Made Progress?

The history of how this has happened, including a brief history over the centuries prior to the USA being formed as a country, and more so of the healthcare "happenings" since about 1950 to the current day, will be described in more detail in this chapter.

Some of the other aspects of the current medical/healthcare delivery system in the USA, and around the world, will be discussed in additional chapters.

And in the final chapters, we will present the needed SOLUTIONS ... the "New Modern Medical—Healthcare Delivery Systems" that will have to happen to save the USA from complete bankruptcy and dissolution of its society.

We'll Start with a Personal Account (Actual Doctor Names Not Used)

I (Linda) remember crying in the middle of the night in my bed the day after my tonsillectomy. My dad stood over my bed with a worried expression, repeating, "It's going to be okay, honey. Stop crying, it's going to be okay." There was much scurrying and phone calls. My parents bundled me up into the back seat of the car. All the while, blood kept coming out of my mouth and running down my throat, making me gag and cry. My brother complained that I was getting it on the car! I went into a kind of stupor, lost in my crying as children do. The next thing I remembered was being on a table in the doctor's office. Old Doc Eicare was there in the corner near the sink with his young new partner, who later became our doctor, but whose name I cannot remember. I remember Old Doc Eicare, coming over to me holding his right hand upward by his other hand, saying, "Young lady, if you don't stop bleeding, I'll have to sew up your throat." That pronouncement frightened me greatly. Then he said, "Let's go to the other room and give her some time." He, the young doctor, and my family left me alone and turned off the light. Frightened as I was and still in a stupor, I willed myself to stop bleeding—and miraculously the bleeding stopped. *The reader might enjoy knowing that my brother (who was about 6 and I about 4) was the one with the chronically infected tonsils—mine were fine—but the hospital offered our folks a two for one price at the hospital, ignorant of the fact that my blood would not clot easily due to vitamin K deficiency. There were no tests in those days; just pull them in and yank out the tonsils—over in less than a day's hospital stay.*

The wisdom of Old Doc Eicare prevailed, despite that he was in such a hurry to get to me that night that he had slammed his thumb in his car door, necessitating a call to his assistant to stitch up his hand before he could properly attend to me.

As I grew up, being reasonably healthy, I didn't go to Old Doc Eicare again, but had I, I would have trusted him completely. Dr. Eicare retired, and I remember going to his successor—oh, I've just remembered his name—Dr. Logicsci. I didn't trust Dr. Logicsci as much but remember thinking his name suited him—with his sterile science, his hurry, and his authoritative pronouncements to his patients. My parents soon after signed me up with Dr. Logipeds, I believe the first female doctor in town, who was a pediatrician. She also was crisp, hurried, and had that same seemingly scientific stance.

Regardless of the wonderful intelligence of Dr. Logipeds, the times had changed most definitely. The Doc Eicares disappeared and were replaced by a new breed of time managers, more distant, more trusting in science journals and not so much in intuition; more left-brained, less right-brained.

At present, we are in a tumultuous era of change, but instead of becoming more scientific and clearer in our thinking, it seems we are becoming more lost. Medicine has become sicker but coated over with a veneer of pseudo-knowledge which doctors and their patients believe to be true. The love of objective truth has sometimes been lost in a lack of research acumen and a desire of some to publish to advance—as stated above, in misusing p value statistics (or perhaps not caring, in a desperate search for "significance") to advance one's career.

Historical Medical "Practices" That Seem Horrific Today

Snake oil sellers, determining one's personality and mental ability based on bumps on one's head (phrenology), conducting bloodletting to cure diseases to **adjust the humors**, operating in unsterile conditions, examining urine for signs of imbalances—such things belong in the horrors of history. Medicine has made tremendous advances in the past two hundred years or so. The more skilled we become at scientific research, the more the scientific discoveries, the faster those treatments and cures come. Where have we come from? The following are just a few interesting examples of historical methods of medical practice. Though we still have problems in our world, at least these horrors should not be repeated. We have made progress!

ASK DR. DEAN:

Question 2: In your experience working with Continuing Medical Education in hospitals and healthcare quality efforts, what are mistakes that have been fairly consistent over the past 40 years?

To some degree, hospital mistakes are about the same in number and type for all hospitals. Data has been produced that is, and should be, concerning to the medical profession generally. There needs to be a major, multi-disciplinary, comprehensive effort to address the various mistakes that are occurring. The work being done to reduce medical errors is commendable, but we need to have a more universal and comprehensive program that yields a pathway to correct the sources of error and the mistakes. It is not enough to study, analyze, and discuss the problem—we need to fix it. Is it fixable? There certainly are issues that are preventable, and there are behaviors that need correction.

Some issues that are common, especially in hospitals, are as follows:

Catheter-associated urinary tract infections
Lack of hand hygiene
Antibiotic use when not medically necessary
Medicine administration errors
Communication errors among hospital staff and physicians
Poor or inaccurate instructions for treatments

An important issue that can serve as an example is the occurrence of hospital-acquired Urinary tract infections. Urinary tract infections are the most common hospital-acquired infections, 80% of which are attributable to an indwelling urinary catheter. A significant percentage of hospital patients have a catheter inserted at some time during their hospital stay. These infections may develop at a rate of nearly 100% if the catheter is in place for as much as one week. In the last ten years the incidence of these infections has not changed, indicating that the problem of these infections persists.

Use of an indwelling catheter in hospital patients is typically not viewed by physicians and hospital staff as a significant procedure and is viewed as more of a nuisance than an important quality issue. If an infection occurs and persists it can lead to such complications as prostatitis, epididymitis, cystitis, pyelonephritis, and sepsis.

Hand hygiene is a very important practice in hospitals. This practice is recommended for reducing infections unrelated to the patient's admittance to the hospital. Many infections are caused by the transfer of infectious germs from hospital staff and doctors who do not sanitize their hands after each and every patient. The national average for appropriate hand hygiene is 40%. It needs to be 100% so that the infection rate of that issue is 0%. Hand hygiene is a vitally important action for all.

The issue of antibiotic use when it is not indicated is a vital issue nowadays. Antibiotics are very important for bacterial infections, but the reasons they are prescribed are often questionable. It is not good for a patient to pressure a doctor to prescribe an antibiotic when it is not necessary to deal with a viral infection. What is occurring is that some formerly useful antibiotics can no longer be used. Due to too frequent use, a medicine's effectiveness is lessened and it becomes useless as resistant strains of the bacteria have developed which no longer respond to it. Due to overuse, the number of antibiotics able to be used is reduced, and there are some medical scientists that are predicting that we could get to a time when there are no longer any useful antibiotics for any infections. If that were to happen, it would be disastrous.

Bloodletting, a Common Historical (but Gross) Treatment

Bloodletting went on for nearly 3,000 years. Initiated in the time of Hippocrates around 400 BC, it was thought that the body comprised four "humors." The elements of the universe were fire, water, earth, and air, and the humors were thought to correspond to those elements—"blood, phlegm, black bile, yellow bile" (Greenstone, 2010, par. 3, *http://www.bcmj.org/premise/history-bloodletting*). If those humors got out of balance, the person would become ill. To treat the illness, the patient was cut and allowed to bleed until the balance was restored. Theoretically, the patient would recover. "[W]hen Galen of Pergamum (129– AD 200) declared blood as the most dominant humor, the practice of venesection gained even greater importance" (Greenstone, 2010, par. 5). Galen was able to influence the increased use of bloodletting because he was a prolific writer. If one sees something in writing or hears it proclaimed enough times, the idea moves toward belief (we should all remember this when seeing ads on television for new medicines). Bloodletting became a "standard of care." Opening arteries, veins, stabbing thumbs, using suction cups, leeches … many methods were used.

Trepanning—Want a Hole in Your Skull?

Trepanning, or the boring of a hole in the head, was used even in the cave era. Cave paintings show such practices. The theory was that the hole would let out the evil spirits that brought headaches and other maladies (*https://www.topmastersinhealthcare.com/10-most-barbaric-treatments-in-modern-healthcare/*).

The Sad Story of King George III (1738–1820)

King George III was called the "mad king," not just because he was credited with losing the colonies. King George started exhibiting bizarre behaviors in his mid-30s. He talked fast and long, acted irrationally, was grandiose and at times delusional. Because of his manic-like episodes, the king was subjected to many medical treatments, including bloodletting. Another of those was "fire cupping" on his back to help draw out excess humors.

Although the process sounds painful, cupping is still used in traditional Chinese medicine. Its benefits seem to be "reducing pain intensity and providing positive short-term benefits" (Rushall, 2017, par. 3, *https://www.pacificcollege.edu/news/ blog/2014/09/20/many-benefits-chinese-cupping*). The studies Rushall refers to are not provided in the article, so it is not possible to understand the benefits. One wonders how it might work—perhaps focusing on the heat of the cup distracts one from the existing pain. I was able to find a literature review of the research on cupping for reducing hypertension (Myeong et al., 2010). Myeong et al. (2010) concluded that more research was needed, as the studies conducted were not free of bias and were not properly controlled. Evidently, cupping did not work for King George.

Various authors looking back at his documented symptoms have given several plausible explanations for King George's illness, which occurred in bouts from 1788 until his death, with the last ten years of his life being his sickest. One explanation or diagnosis involved bipolar disorder based on his writings during his "manic" periods (*BBC News*, April 15, 2013, *http://www.bbc.com/news/magazine-22122407*; Peters and Beveridge, 2010, *https://www.ncbi. nlm.nih.gov/pubmed/20503691*). Variegate porphyria was suspected due to the reported blue color of King George's urine and because some of the symptoms of porphyria are like untreated bipolar disorder. However, that hypothesis was initially withdrawn once it was realized that the medicine provided by one of his physicians was made from deep blue flowers, which colored his urine naturally. Another theory, poisoning, was raised when, in 2005, arsenic was found in a saved lock of his hair. A lock of King George's hair on display at the Science Museum in London was used for analysis.

(Seppa, N. (2005). King George III should have sued. *Science News, 168*(6), 94); (Cox et al., 2005, *https://pdfs.semanticscholar.org/e71f/5dd29ba98b360969e5f4af6298417832ad10.pdf.*)

A combination of poisoning and heritability brought back the porphyria theory. According to Crews (2008, *http://www.history.org/foundation/journal/spring10/king.cfm*), some descendants of the king were diagnosed with porphyria, indicating a gene had been passed down, and given his behaviors, King George was the likely donor. With the high levels of arsenic and lead, it was concluded that porphyria was a logical diagnosis for the king because arsenic and other heavy metals can trigger the porphyria gene to expression.

If modern scientists have had a hard time confirming a diagnosis, truly the physicians of his time were in the dark. They even had the advantage of the actual person in front of them. The poor king was tortured by the various "treatments" and suffered tremendously before his death after a final ten years of complete madness. According to Crews (2008, par. 11),

> "The king went from simple discomfort to intense distress. His decline began with stomach pain, cramps, and rashes. Initially, doctors attributed the symptoms to gout or wearing wet socks or eating peas, but the patient grew worse. His stomachaches became debilitating and left him doubled over. His feet swelled. His eyes turned yellow, and his urine was brown. Mental decline ensued."

And in paragraph 14 (Crews, 2008), "They turned to the nostrums of their age—bleeding, blistering, purging, and sedating. They kept him in an unheated room during winter. Nothing worked." Surprise!

One of the medicines the king's doctors gave him was tartar emetic (antimony potassium tartrate), which contained arsenic to induce vomiting. If, indeed, the king was given arsenic which then set off his genetic porphyria, then **it was treatment that exacerbated**, if not caused, the illness.

Later, we will consider how medical treatments today can cause further illnesses. We have learned much; we have much to learn.

ASK DR. DEAN:

Question 3: Why do you think these mistakes were made during the past 40 years?
Appropriate communication is critical in healthcare. If a doctor and hospital staff are not able to talk to each other in a way that yields understanding, many errors can occur and do. That applies to the hospital environment as well as the clinical setting outside the hospital. Research has shown that the physician's effective communication ability to explain, listen, and empathize has a dramatic effect on health outcomes. It also makes for better patient/physician relations and promotes better compliance with treatment instructions. Medication errors commonly occur when there is a lack of clear understanding by the person receiving the instruction, and that is made more problematic if the receiving person is unable to ask for clarification in the event that the instruction is unclear.

These issues have been consistent over the years of my involvement in the medical field. I am optimistic that the time will come when they are solved. I realize that these are not the only issues that need attention in medicine but are ones that have concerned me over time and based on my experience.

President Garfield—How His Doctors Killed Him

A sad account of past medical errors is that of James A. Garfield, newly elected 20th President of the United States, who was shot on July 2, 1881. The story is beautifully told in Candice Millard's book, *Destiny of the Republic,* published by Doubleday in 2011. If interested in knowing more, the reader is encouraged to read this fascinating book.

Garfield was shot twice at the Baltimore and Potomac Railway Station as he intended to travel to his wife (who was at their summer home) for a summer holiday. Garfield was shot by the mentally deranged Charles J. Guiteau, a minister, lawyer, and author, who was clearly disturbed. Guiteau, with his super-inflated ego and in a delusional state, was convinced that he should and would be appointed by Garfield to be the ambassador to France. After being rebuffed by White House staff one final time, Guiteau determined he would be doing the country a service by eliminating the source of his troubles.

The wounds today would likely not have been lethal. In fact, many soldiers in the Civil War were wounded similarly and lived with the bullets remaining in them for the rest of their lives. The problem for Garfield was that doctors (especially one) attempted many times to find and extract the bullets, introducing infection into Garfield's body.

Although this was the time of Joseph Lister (*https://www. britannica.com/biography/Joseph-Lister-Baron-Lister-of-Lyme-Regis*), most doctors were not convinced that germs were the cause of infections (or perhaps they had not all heard). The first day he was shot, there were ten physicians who showed up to treat the President. At least three found it necessary to stick their fingers into the wound, attempting to find the bullets (all without pain control or antiseptic measures). That subsequent introduction of bacteria was the beginning of the horrible, though sincere, treatment that Garfield received.

Dr. Doctor Bliss (yes, Doctor was his first name) was the main physician to assume treatment responsibilities and continued his care of the President back at the White House. He also did not follow antiseptic measures and did not believe in Lister's principles of sterile conditions.

Owing to Garfield's great physical fitness, he lingered with a horrible infection for 80 days after he was shot. If he had been treated today, he would have spent a few days in the hospital and would have recovered fully in just a few weeks. Instead, he languished in agony with the infection. His three-inch wound enlarged to over 20 inches as the doctors continued to try finding the bullets. The wound was described as "beginning at his ribs and extending to his groin. It soon became a super-infected, pus-ridden, gash of human flesh" (Markel, *https://www.pbs.org/newshour/health/dirty-painful-death-president-james-garfield*, par. 6). Dwindling from 210 pounds to 160 over that period of 80 days, sepsis finally took its toll and Garfield's life ended with a heart attack and a splenic artery aneurysm. Garfield's last words were, "This pain. This pain." Garfield died on September 19, 1881.

Guiteau stated: "The doctors killed Garfield, I just shot him" (Markel, *https://www.pbs.org/newshour/health/dirty-painful-death-president-james-garfield*, par. 11).

Medical practices for surgeons at the time, according to Millard (2011, pp. 157–158):

■ Doctors bragging about the "surgical stink" of their hospitals
■ Walking into surgery straight off the street without changing to clean clothes
■ Not washing their surgical coats—the thicker the layer of blood, pus and "crumblings, as they bent over their patients, the greater the tribute to their years of experience"
■ In the country, doctors frequently applied hot poultices of cow manure to open wounds

- Using wooden handles on surgical tools, which could not be sterilized
- Picking up instruments from the floor if they fell and continuing to use them
- Holding a knife in their teeth if they needed both hands
- Looping silk sutures through the buttonholes of their filthy lab coats

One last bit of misinformation was that in those days, doctors believed that patients could "be fed rectally" and gave Garfield beef broth enemas (Brian Resnick, Oct. 4, 2015, *https://www.the-atlantic.com/politics/archive/2015/10/this-is-the-brain-that-shot-president-james-garfield/454212/* par. 18). Poor man!

How anyone lived through injuries and surgeries of the past, with such practices, is a testament to our amazing human bodies.

Medicine and Surgery in Ancient Times

The first accounts of Egyptian medicine were from descriptions on papyri and are the earliest evidence of medical practice dating from about 3,000 BC onward. Karenberg and Leitz (2001) mentioned eight papyri from about 1,800 BC which listed various medical cases. Karenberg and Leitz (2001) indicated magic was often used to treat headaches, with spells recited over the victim. Demonic powers and supernatural causes were often cited as the causes of headaches—even injuries were suspected to be initiated supernaturally. Catfish (which were thought to be demonic) were cooked to ashes and those were rubbed on the head of the sufferer for four days, according to accounts by Karenberg and Leitz (p. 914).

In many ways, magic notwithstanding, Egyptians were pioneers of surgery and rightly theorized that the spinal cord transmitted information from the body to the brain, according to Fanous and Couldwell (2012, *https://www.ncbi.nlm.nih.gov/pubmed/22224784*). And as another example, embalmers were exposed to the body, and due to their removing brains during the mummification process, they were able to add to the knowledge that led to performing transnasal surgeries (Fanous and Couldwell, 2012).

Ganz and Arndt (2014) described treating skull fractures during the Roman Empire. However, according to the authors, rather than physicians, the heads of households were tasked with taking care of the medical issues of their family members. I loved my dad but cannot imagine him performing brain surgery on any of my family!

In terms of orthopedic surgeries, according to Blomstedt (2014), who studied several papyri accounts, ancient Egyptians were able to set bones and reduce displacements, but he found no credible evidence that they did therapeutic amputations. Most of the reductions seemed to be dislocated shoulders with subsequent wrapping of the joint in linens and treating with applications of grease and honey until the patient recovered. Hmmm … grease and honey—one wonders if they applied those if the skin was broken. And in fact, there were mummies found over the years that evidently died from open wounds or from a fracture of one kind or another. Infection was no doubt a problem for ancient peoples (Figure 1.2).

Anatomy—The Ins and Outs of Cadaver Dissection in Medical Training and Advancements or Lack Thereof

Egyptians started their processes of mummification about 2,600 BC (*https://www.si.edu/spotlight/ancient-egypt/mummies*). They removed the organs and must have gained an understanding of placement but not necessarily the function of each organ. Various papyri indicated they knew that blood vessels came from the heart to the body but thought all fluids of the body went through the heart. Evidently, they thought the brain had no important function, as they removed it and discarded it

Figure 1.2 Rendition from the tomb of Ipuy, showing a shoulder reduction procedure. (Websites viewed for drawing: *http://www.trauma.org/archive/history/egypt.html* **and** *https://www.pinterest.com/pin/229402174742644385/.*)

while storing the other entrails in jars placed with the body in the tomb.

Systematic study of anatomy started with the Greeks in about 5 BC (Elizondo et al., 2005), with names such as Hippocrates (from whence comes the Hippocratic Oath), Herophilus, and Galen. Galen was summoned to Rome by Marcus Aurelius, and his anatomy book was thus used by Romans as well. In fact, Galen's anatomy book, which had flaws—some of it was based on monkeys—was used through the Middle Ages. The study of medicine was mainly conducted in monasteries. It was during the Dark Ages that the dissection of human cadavers was deemed immoral and blasphemous, and all that physicians could study was what was done before (Elizondo-Omaña et al., 2005; Ghosh, 2015). Little wonder that strange theories and practices emerged, such as we saw with King George. Dissection and any new knowledge was stifled until the beginning of the Enlightenment in the 1400s, when the teaching practice was revived in medical training in Italy.

It wasn't until 1867 that Joseph Lister published two papers in *The Lancet* on germ theory (Pitt and Aubin, 2012). They also stated that in operations at that time, instruments were used from patient to patient. Lister made a huge impact on survival from surgeries. However, when Lister first introduced his ideas about germs he faced much opposition and skepticism from the medical community (Pitt and Aubin, 2012). Once it was observed that Lister's patients did not develop infections, his ideas gradually took over (too late for Garfield, however). Garfield's doctors believed they knew better. Skepticism is not uncommon even today whenever established practices are challenged.

In More Recent Times

Even into the mid-1900s, there were some bizarre treatments. Again referring to the article from Top Master's (sic) in Healthcare Administration (*https://www.topmastersinhealthcare. com/10-most-barbaric-treatments-in-modern-healthcare/*), we are reminded of treatments performed in our more recent history. Tonsillectomies are one mentioned. I can attest to that one, as I nearly lost my life over this procedure that did not need to be done for me. Bariatric surgeries caused a whopping 40% of issues within 6 months after surgery and 22% of problems within the hospital stay.

Psychiatry is an area where horrible things have been done to patients in the name of medicine. Insulin "therapy" was given to cause daily comas—why they thought this would help is beyond me—unless perhaps brain damage rendered the person unable to exhibit symptoms. The treatment was later (in the 1970s) found to be ineffective. Another horror was the use of a pick-like instrument shoved up the nose or into the corner of an eye to cut nerve fibers in the frontal lobes (hence, called a lobotomy). Frances Farmer was a well-known American actress in the 1930s who likely had bipolar disorder. Allegedly she had a transorbital lobotomy during one of her institutionalizations. This is portrayed in the 1982 movie *Frances* (*https:// en.wikipedia.org/wiki/Frances_(film)*) (Figure 1.3).

Linda Minor, 2018

Figure 1.3   Adapted from Frances Farmer photo, 1937 (photographer unknown). (*https://commons.wikimedia.org/wiki/File:Frances_Farmer_December_1937.png.***)**

Symphysiotomy

Symphysiotomies and closely related pubiotomies started in the 16th century. This is the practice of cutting the pelvic cartilage of a woman giving birth to a child to allow the child to come out easier. It was done in the United States up to the late 1800s before cesareans were performed to save the life of the child and the mother. The practice mostly died out on the United States but continued in Ireland up to the 1950s and in poor countries even to this day. The practice leaves the woman with horrible problems for the rest of her life—terrible back pain, problems walking, bladder and kidney infections, and so on. Evidently it was continued in Ireland because the C-section was considered dangerous for multiple pregnancies and Catholic women there were apt to have multiple

ASK DR. DEAN:

Question 4: Were some of these mistakes more prevalent in certain medical specialties?
In my opinion, these and other mistakes seem to be common, based on the fact that people tend to develop habitual behaviors that are repetitive and related to one's environment, habit patterns, education, and experience. I have not observed a difference in the specialties of doctors for the topics we are discussing here, but doctors do enter specific specialties based on their personality, skills, and interests, and thus there potentially could be some variation among specialties.

pregnancies. Actress Rita McCann had a pubiotomy performed in 1957 and describes the procedure in Cara Delay's web article (2016, The Torture Began (*https://nursingclio. org/2016/05/31/the-torture-began-symphysiotomy-and-obstetric-violence-in-modern-ireland/*).

Clearly, medical horrors are not only for long-past years. Today, procedures are performed that may in the future seem like similar torture. Today we are very concerned about medical mistakes, which happen more than we would like to admit. More of these types of mistakes are described in Chapter 4.

A couple of additional citations from history are presented below, in more of an outline—bulleted format along with the LINK so that the reader can go to that link and find more details if interested.

■ **10 SHOCKING MEDICAL MISTAKES (By John Bonifield, CNN and Elizabeth Cohen, CNN Senior Medical Correspondent;** *http://www.cnn. com/2012/06/09/health/medicalmistakes/index.html* Updated 10:16 AM ET, Sun June 10, 2012)—Medical errors kill more than a quarter million people every year in the United States and injure millions. Add them all up and "you have probably the third leading cause of death" in the country, says Dr. Peter Pronovost, an anesthesiologist and critical care physician at Johns Hopkins Hospital. The harm is often avoidable, and there are strategies you can use to help doctors and nurses get things right.

The following list of mistakes is from the citation/link above, i.e. *http://www.cnn.com/2012/06/09/health/medicalmistakes/ index.html*

1. Mistake: Treating the wrong patient
- *Cause*: Hospital staff fails to verify a patient's identity.
- *Consequences*: Patients with similar names are confused.
- *Prevention*: Before every procedure in the hospital, make sure the staff checks your entire name, date of birth, and barcode on your wrist band.

2. Mistake: Surgical souvenirs
- *Cause*: Surgical staff miscounts (or fails to count) equipment used inside a patient during an operation.
- *Consequences*: Tools get left inside the body.
- *Prevention*: If you have unexpected pain, fever, or swelling after surgery, ask if you might have a surgical instrument inside you.

3. Mistake: Lost patients
- *Cause*: Patients with dementia are sometimes prone to wandering.
- *Consequences*: Patients may become trapped while wandering and die from hypothermia or dehydration.
- *Prevention*: If your loved one sometimes wanders, consider a GPS tracking bracelet.

4. Mistake: Fake doctors
- *Cause*: Con artists pretend to be doctors.

- *Consequences*: Medical treatments backfire. Instead of getting better, patients get sicker.
- *Prevention*: Confirm online that your physician is licensed.

5. Mistake: The ER waiting game
- *Cause*: Emergency rooms get backed up when over-crowded hospitals don't have enough beds.
- *Consequences*: Patients get sicker while waiting for care.
- *Prevention*: Doctors listen to other doctors, so on your way to the hospital call your physician and ask them to call the emergency room.

6. Mistake: Air bubbles in blood
- *Cause*: The hole in a patient's chest isn't sealed air-tight after a chest tube is removed.
- *Consequences*: Air bubbles get sucked into the wound and cut off blood supply to the patient's lungs, heart, kidneys, and brain. Left uncorrected, the patient dies.
- *Prevention*: If you have a central line tube in you, ask how you should be positioned when the line comes out.

7. Mistake: Operating on the wrong body part
- *Cause*: A patient's chart is incorrect, or a surgeon misreads it, or surgical draping obscures marks that denote the correct side of the operation.
- *Consequences*: The surgeon cuts into the wrong side of a patient's body.
- *Prevention*: Just before surgery, make sure you reaffirm with the nurse and the surgeon the correct body part and side of your operation.

8. Mistake: Infection infestation
- *Cause*: Doctors and nurses don't wash their hands.
- *Consequences*: Patients can die from infections spread by hospital workers.

- *Prevention*: It may be uncomfortable to ask, but make sure doctors and nurses wash their hands before they touch you, even if they're wearing gloves.

9. **Mistake: Lookalike tubes**
   - *Cause:* A chest tube and a feeding tube can look a lot alike.
   - *Consequences*: Medicine meant for the stomach goes into the chest.
   - *Prevention*: When you have tubes in you, ask the staff to trace every tube back to the point of origin so the right medicine goes to the right place.

10. **Mistake: Waking up during surgery**
   - *Cause*: An underdose of anesthesia.
   - *Consequences*: The brain stays awake while the muscles stay frozen. Most patients aren't in any pain but some feel every poke, prod, and cut.
   - *Prevention*: When you schedule surgery, ask your surgeon if you need to be put asleep or if a local anesthetic might work just as well.

■ **HISTORY PROVES MANY DOCTORS' RECOMMEN-DATIONS ARE DISASTERS—many good specific examples of MISTAKES and MISTREATMENT** *(https://articles.mercola.com/sites/articles/archive/2008/09/23/history-proves-many-doctorsrecommendations-are-disasters.aspx).* A Gallup Poll from December of 2006 compared how people rated the *honesty and ethical standards* of people of various professions. Doctors were rated "very high" for honesty and ethics and were fourth from the top of the list at 69 percent, exceeded only by veterinarians, pharmacists, and nurses, who rated highest. In other words, 69 percent of people polled believed their doctors were honest and ethical.

If you, the reader, are interested in more evidence and stories like the above two, please find a short list of additional citations at the end of this chapter, following the "Reference Listing." We will discuss solutions to medical errors in the chapters that follow.

References

Blomstedt, P. (2014). "Orthopedic surgery in ancient Egypt." *Acta Orthopaedica, 85*(6), 670–676. Doi:10.3109/17453674.2014.950468

Crews, E. (2008). *The Poisoning of King George III < CW Journal:* Spring 10.

Elizondo-Omana, R.E., Buzman-Lopez, S., and Garcia-Rodriguez, Mde L., (2005, July). Dissection as a teaching tool; past, present, and future, *Anat Rec B New Anat, 285*(1), 11–5.

Fanous, A. A., and Couldwell, W. T. (2012). "Transnasal excerebration surgery in ancient Egypt." *Journal of Neurosurgery, 116*(4), 743–748. Doi:10.3171/2011.12.JNS11417

Ganz, J. C., and Arndt, J. (2014). "A history of depressed skull fractures from ancient times to 1800." *Journal of The History of the Neurosciences, 23*(3), 233–251. Doi:10.1080/09647 04X.2013.823267

Ghosh, S. K. (2015). "Human cadaveric dissection: a historical account from ancient Greece to the modern era." *Anatomy & Cell Biology, 48*(3), 153–169. Doi:10.5115/acb.2015.48.3.153

Greenstone, G. (2010, January/February). "The history of bloodletting," *CMJ, 52*(1), 12–14. Premise.

Karenberg, A., and Leitz, C. (2001). "Headache in magical and medical papyri of ancient Egypt." *Cephalalgia: An International Journal of Headache, 21*(9), 911–916.

Millard, C. (2011). *Destiny of the Republic.* Doubleday, NY.

Myeong Soo, L., Tae-Young, C., Byung-Cheul, S., Jong-In, K., and Sang-Soo, N. (2010). "Cupping for hypertension: A systematic review." *Clinical & Experimental Hypertension, 32*(7), 423–425. Doi:10.3109/10641961003667955

Rushall, K. (2017). *The many benefits of Chinese cupping, Pacific College of Oriental Medicine,* Blog, Par 3.

Pitt, D., and Aubin, J. (2012). "Joseph Lister: Father of Modern Surgery." *Canadian Journal of Surgery, 55*(5), E8–E9. Doi:10.1503/cjs.007112

Additional Resources for Chapter 1

These additional reference resources are for those readers that would like to explore both history and more recent issues of impediments to good healthcare delivery in the USA more thoroughly.

"10 Biggest Medical Scandals in History." (2013, February 20). Top Masters in Public Health Degrees. http://www.topmastersinpub-lichealth.com/10-biggest-medical-scandals-in-history/.

"10 Medical Errors that Changed the Standard of Care." (n.d.). Medscape. https://www.medscape.com/features/slideshow/med-errors.

"10 Most Famous Medical Mistakes of all Time." (n.d.). Masters in Health Care. http://www.mastersinhealthcare.com/blog/2011/10-most-famous-medical-mistakes-of-all-time/.

"10 Unbelievable Medical Mistakes." (2009, February 16) Oddee. https://www.oddee.com/item_96576.aspx.

"25 shocking medical mistakes." (2015, September 22). CNN. http://www.cnn.com/2015/09/22/health/gallery/25-shocking-medical-mistakes/index.html.

Cohn, J. (2007). *Sick: The Untold Story of America's Health Care Crisis – and the People Who Pay the Price.* Harper. https://www.amazon.com/Sick-Untold-Americas-Health-Crisis/dp/0060580453/ref=pd_bbs_sr_1/104-6819803-8751945?ie=UTF8&s=books&qid=1173816503&sr=1-1.

Edelberg, D."Case History: The Madness of Overmedication." (2017, October 2). WholeHealth Chicago. https://wholehealthchicago.com/2017/10/02/case-history-madness-overmedication/.

"History of Medical Errors." (n.d.). RadPhysics. http://www.radphys-ics.com/history-of-medical-errors.

"History of Medicine." Wikipedia. https://en.wikipedia.org/wiki/History_of_medicine.

"Medical Errors, Past and Present" (2007, November 27) abcNews. http://abcnews.go.com/Health/story?id=3789868&page=1.

Noah, T. (2007, March 13). "A Short History of Health Care." *Slate.* http://www.slate.com/articles/news_and_politics/chatterbox/2007/03/a_short_history_of_health_care.html.

Porter, R. (1999). *The Greatest Benefit to Mankind: A Medical History of Humanity.* (The Norton History of Science Series). New York: W. W. Norton & Company.

Spanberg, E. (2011, September 13). "Destiny of the Republic: A Tale of Madness, Medicine and the Murder of a President." *Christian Science Monitor.* https://www.csmonitor.com/Books/Book-Reviews/2011/0913/Destiny-of-the-Republic-A-Tale-of-Madness-Medicine-and-the-Murder-of-a-President.

Chapter 2

The "OUT OF CONTROL" SPIRAL:
(Cost to Patients—Costs to Medical Facilities—Spiral of "Tests"— Including "Un-Needed Tests"—Spiral of People/ Patients Demanding MORE—IMMEDIATE CURES … etc.) **OF THE PAST 40 YEARS and the Current Situation**

Chapter 1 examined the state of medical care—past problems and present problems. One huge problem with current healthcare is the COST! It turns out that the United States spends much more of its gross domestic product (GDP) on healthcare than other countries. To visualize this, please see Figure 2.1, which uses data from the Organization for Economic Cooperation and Development (OECD). Note that the United States spends nearly 18% of its GDP, whereas, for example, the United Kingdom spends less than 10% of its GDP.

Why does the United States spend more than all the other nations? (See Figure 2.2, also from OECD data.) This question is discussed in the following video (vlogbrothers, August 20, 2013) at the link provided: (*https://www.youtube.com/watch?v=qSjGouBmo0M*).

It is argued in the video that more than any other reason, our healthcare costs are exorbitant due to a lack of power to negotiate. In countries that use single (government) provider medical care, the government engages in tough negotiations. Regardless of our obesity, diabetes, usage of facilities, etc., in the USA the chief reason is that we are in no position to negotiate when our lives are at risk. The healthcare facilities, pharma, and so on, can

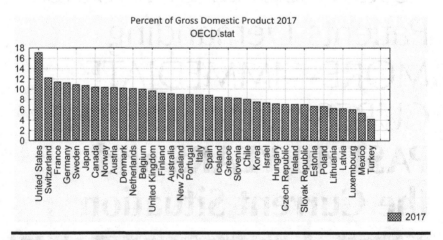

Figure 2.1 Graph from 2017 data from OECD released in 2018. (*https://stats.oecd.org/Index.aspx?DataSetCode=SHA.*) (Graph created by book author Linda Miner.)

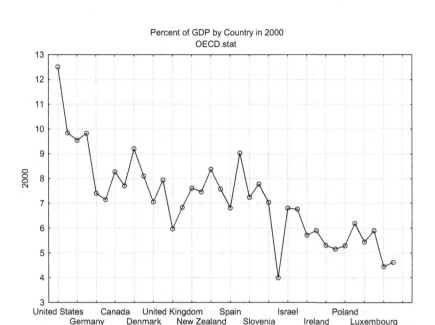

Figure 2.2 Graph with 2000 data from OECD released in 2018. (*https://stats.oecd.org/Index.aspx?DataSetCode=SHA.*) **(Graph created by book author Linda Miner.)**

charge what they wish, and we are forced to pay. The example of the power of negotiation given in the video was of hip replacement systems, awarded to the best company. The hip replacements had to be of top quality for the lowest price.

We have no central negotiation companies (Figure 2.3). We do not believe that we are as helpless as all that. Chapter 5 deals with our responsibility for our own health. We do have some power. We can communicate well, take care of ourselves, and we can seek out the best prices—for example, we do not have to get our MRI in the expensive hospital; we can seek out businesses that do it for less. We can discuss the need for each test recommended. Would an X-ray work as well as an MRI, for example? Do we really need to do what the healthcare professional says without question? No. Now, if we are seriously ill, it is much harder to negotiate for ourselves, and certainly the video makes an important point, but there is much that we can do for ourselves, and later chapters discuss these possible actions. Book

We could just X-Ray your back... hmmm.. but we have a payment due
on our new MRI machine.. so let's use that instead!

Figure 2.3   No one would ever think of doing such a thing as this!

author Gary's comparisons of models below show how our
responsibility for our own healthcare has changed (Figure 2.4).

The "Most Bitter Pill"—MEDICAL COSTS

Time Magazine in March 2013 presented a clear analysis of "Why
Medical Bills are Killing Us: How outrageous pricing and egregious profits are destroying our health care" (Brill, 2013). Several
personal stories showing how medical costs were "killing—devastating lives" of average US citizens were presented in this *Time*
magazine article. Some are summarized here, as follows.

Here's the case of a person we'll call Janice—The $21,000 Heartburn Bill

Janice was a 64-year-old former sales clerk, not yet
Medicare eligible (one has to be age 65). She felt some chest

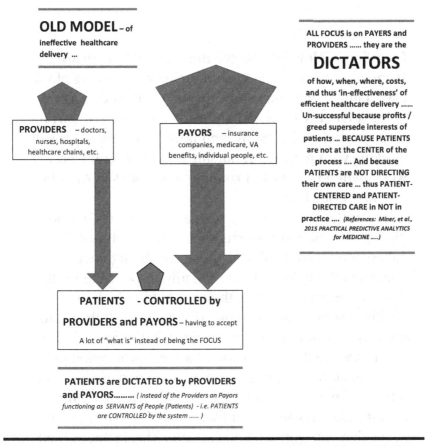

Figure 2.4   OLD MODEL by Gary Miner: Model of healthcare delivery in the USA during the past few decades ... NOT SUCCESSFUL—ever RISING COSTS for POORER CARE OF PATIENTS.

pains and called for an ambulance. She was taken four miles to the emergency room at Stamford Hospital, officially a non-profit institution. They conducted three hours of tests, and after a brief visit by a doctor, she was diagnosed with indigestion and sent home. **GOOD NEWS? NO**, when we look at the costs: $995 for the ambulance, $3,000 for the doctors, and $17,000 for the hospital, **TOTALING $21,000**. Since Janice had been out of work for a year and was not yet eligible for Medicare, she had no insurance. Where did these $$ figures come from? The hospital's CHARGEMASTER. A

ASK DR. DEAN:

Question 1: How do you see the "cost of healthcare" today from your perspective of being a practicing physician (family medicine) since the 1970s, involving developing a Quality Control Center for the northern part of Georgia during the 1990s, and now in your mid-70s still working with patients in nursing homes several days a week (when you are not running marathons in Atlanta, GA, and elsewhere)?

Answer: Before presenting relevant cost issues, the following information presents a complicated list of so-called healthcare facilities. These are the significant players in the field and are primarily responsible for the costs. It seems to me that they are held in high esteem, which in some ways may be appropriate, but there are important issues that need attention in the area of cost that influence the well-being of a huge proportion of the population. The cost issue needs broad attention to address the separate issue that people who need medical attention, regardless of their financial status, are able to receive appropriate medical care. This includes methods of payment that either are manageable at the time of care, or methods that allow them to negotiate the cost and meet the obligation in ways that do not include harassment.

VARIOUS TYPES OF HOSPITAL ENTITIES

Hospitals

Departments

Clinical—Emergency, Intensive Care, Coronary Care, Neonatal Unit, Neonatal Intensive Care, Pediatric Department, Pediatric Intensive Care, Physical Therapy, Surgery, Anesthesia, Maternity, Occupational Therapy,

General Medical Care Units, Rehabilitation, Respiratory Therapy, Sleep Laboratory, Nursing, Pathology, Quality Department, Radiology, Personnel Clinic, Chaplaincy

Support Services—Laboratory, Admissions, Nutrition and Dietetics, Central Supply, Medical Records, Information Systems (computers and hospital network), Human Resources (recruitment, hiring, employee benefits), Housekeeping and Maintenance

Financial—Billing and Collections

Administrative—Administrator, Assistant Administrator, Executive Committee, Board of Trustees, Chief Medical Officer, Chief Nursing Officer, Secretaries

CLINICS—Various Medical Clinics for different health issues, Doctor's Offices

Small—with 1 to 3–4 doctors
private or owned
Large—larger number of doctors
owned or independent
owned by a hospital, corporation, or other
privately owned by one or more doctors

Urgent Care Clinics
Clinics in Pharmacies, staffed by Nurse Practitioners
Public Health Department clinics, staffed by Nurses,
    Nurse Practitioners, Part-Time Doctors
Free Clinics
Specialty Clinics (different medical specialty focus)
Primary Care Clinics (Doctor's Offices)
School Clinics (for elementary, middle school, high
    school, colleges/universities) staffed by Nurses
Health Maintenance Organizations
Research Clinics

The above lists reveal the complicated business of healthcare, with a huge variety of issues that must be dealt with and that all require a portion of the cost of medical care. Admittedly, the costs necessary to maintain all of them may be higher than the absolute requirement, but there is a significant necessary cost for what these entities require.

> *(Editor's Comment: Does it really need to be this complicated? Maybe our "evolving business entities" came about because of the "old medical healthcare model" (the one we have presented in this book), where there were no "checks and balances"? Thus these complications may be part of the "chaos" of our current system? Simpler systems that are possible, within reach, and some of which are already operating in certain parts of the USA will be presented in Chapter 7.)*

The cost of supplies, maintenance, upkeep, and salaries is very high, most of which is at a reasonable level *(EDITOR'S NOTE: Is it really reasonable?)*. Perhaps some *(EDITOR'S NOTE: some? Maybe all?!!)* of those costs could be reduced. That concern needs to be addressed. The cost and methods of negotiation of specific medical devices and supplies need to be addressed and normalized so that the fees set for providing medical services to patients can be reduced.

There is much discussion about the level of healthcare costs and fees to patients. There definitely need to be changes made that include visibility of the fees charged for healthcare services so that those who avail themselves of the services are able to know ahead of time what the cost will be and can plan and prepare to pay what is necessary. That would be so much more preferable to the current system that leads to cost surprises. A further benefit would be the improved relationship between patient and provider.

Health insurance, while an important financial safety feature, is very confusing in the description provided to purchasers. There are many variables in the insurance company's descriptions and definitions that are not simply and clearly defined. Then, when a coverage decision is necessary following a medical event, there is further uncertainty about what amount of payment is available and what will be the co-payment amount. All of this uncertainty is distressing and unnecessary. If the charges were made clear, which clearly can be done, and the insurer was committed to assistance and the patient, the system would be infinitely more helpful and well-received, leading to a more productive and profitable business environment.

One of the possible ways of learning the cost of a medical procedure or service, since the costs of healthcare services are so vague and difficult to comprehend, is to comparison shop. However, there are only a relatively few such medical events that allow the leisure of time to comparison shop. And even if the patient does have the time to comparison shop, it is very difficult to find medical providers who will willingly provide accurate information—they are few and far between.

The lower cost of healthcare in other countries is often mentioned in presentations about our costs in the United States. To me, as a doctor practicing in the USA, that comparison is irrelevant, since the payment methods, as well as laws, can be different than ours. (However, maybe I should take a look at what is really going on around the world—authors Gary and Linda Miner will present that in the next chapter, Chapter 3).

Another factor that applies to the cost of healthcare in the USA is the amount and level of research that is performed here. Medical research is unbelievably expensive and does contribute to the overall cost of our healthcare. Research costs in other countries are much less and do not apply to the same degree as in the USA.

In considering the cost and use of medicines, there are several things that influence those costs. Perhaps the leading factor of the cost of medicines is that the sellers charge whatever they can get. It is a feature of the way business is done.

Factors that affect the use of medicines often take place at the point of service and in turn affect the overall cost of healthcare. Often medicines are prescribed for inappropriate reasons. Patient demand is one reason doctors comply. It is less time-consuming to write the prescription than to explain or refuse. Television ads are another inappropriate attraction, for people who view the ads. The description of the benefit of some medicines is very attractive, and even though the side effects and negatives are mentioned, that part of the ad is minor and easily ignored when the benefit is so colorfully described. If a person does ask their doctor to prescribe the advertised medicine, as suggested in the ad, the doctor may end up taking the time to defend the reason a particular medicine should not be used. When a new medicine is released, after research it is common for it to be used for treatment since the pharmaceutical company representatives are providing free samples for patients to doctors—the new medicine MAY be a better treatment of an illness, but not necessarily. Almost invariably the new medicine is much costlier than a prior medicine for the same indication.

Comments have been raised that doctors order unnecessary tests, X-rays, and studies that increase the cost to patients inappropriately. That is likely true at times. There are specific reasons for that to take place. Sometimes studies are ordered to obtain information about a symptom or health problem that is vague in its presentation, and tests, X-rays, and other studies may help clarify and reach a specific diagnosis. Sometimes the study does not add to the diagnosis even though the intent was appropriate in a particular case. Was the test inappropriate, since there was a negative result? I don't think so. On the other hand, there are situations where a test or study was done without a specific objective. A problem with that may be that some vague abnormality is seen. Then more studies or tests may need to be done to make sure it does not represent some problem. Often the follow-up test does not indicate a problem. The final conclusion is that if the initial, unnecessary test had not been done, considerable costs could have been avoided. Careful consideration is necessary before X-rays, MRIs, or CT scans, and tests of other types are ordered by a doctor.

There is an additional factor that is present concerning unnecessary testing. It is true that sometimes tests are done that, in truth, are not necessary for diagnostic reasons, but are performed as a protection from lawsuit. If a doctor is sued, a particular test may prove a complaint to be false, and if the test had not been done, the complaint may result in doubt and the suit lost.

"Chargemaster" is every hospital's internal price list; decades ago this was the size of a big city phone book, but today it is a massive computer file—and every hospital maintains one, apparently, and they are all different. If Janice had had insurance, the cost would have been a fraction of the $21,000, as each insurance company has negotiated prices for tests and

ASK DR. DEAN:

Question 2: Does the medical education of doctors-to-be prepare them to manage all the complicated issues that are presented to them in practice, following graduation? Answer: While that is difficult to answer overall, the answer is yes and no. Doctors are educated intensely and broadly, covering virtually all the illnesses and situations known. The final ability of an individual doctor is variable and depends on a variety of personal characteristics. The learning achieved following medical school, residency, etc., is applying that learning to patient presentations and experience. So, over time, the experience enhances the ability to successfully manage health problems, even the most complicated and severe. There is always additional help from specific specialists.

the cost of each item of medical care. For example, Janice had three blood tests (although only one was really needed), for which she was charged $199.50 each; but if she had had Medicare, that insurance would have only paid $13.94 for each of these tests, with no further charge to Janice. Each of the other tests and doctor encounters had similar highly "discounted" charges that Medicare paid. Patients without insurance are asked to pay directly, themselves, the full "Chargemaster" prices. Here is a reference for Chargemaster: *https://revcycleintelligence.com/features/the-role-of-the-hospital-chargemaster-in-revenue-cycle-management.* (Not much of a secret when it's on the Internet and one can Google it—but one has to know about it to Google it.)

This "Chargemaster" seems to be kept a secret, and hospitals hope that outsiders/patients pay no attention to it or the process that produces it. It appears that no hospital's chargemaster prices are consistent with those of any other hospital; furthermore, they do not seem to be based on anything objective—like real costs. In fact, there appears to be NO PROCESS, NO RATIONALE, behind this core document that is the basis for hundreds of millions of healthcare bills annually.

Here's the case of a person we will call Emilia—A Slip, a Fall, and a $9,400 Bill

- Emilia, now 66, is still making weekly payments on the bill she got in June 2008 after she slipped and fell on her face one summer evening in the small yard behind her house in New England. With her nose bleeding heavily, she was taken to the emergency room at a local hospital.
- Emilia was a school bus driver with limited income. But she would not budge when presented a $4,000 bill, so she got into a fight with the hospital when it refused to compromise at all on its chargemaster prices. Following are a few of the details:
- "I was there for maybe six hours, until midnight," Emilia recalls, "but most of it was spent waiting. I saw the resident for maybe 15 minutes, but I got a lot of tests."

ASK DR. DEAN:

Question 3: What is going to happen to the cost of drugs continually rising in price, sometimes increasing several times a year, and thus selling way above the "cost of living index"?

Answer: If medical and pharmaceutical costs are not reduced and based on specific criteria that are universally known, as in other industries, there will likely be federal intervention with price setting. That would be a very unpopular move among all in healthcare but will be necessary if the industry fails to change without that complex action.

- Emilia got three CT scans—of her head, her chest, and her face. The CT bills alone were $6,538. (Medicare would have paid about $825 for all three.) A doctor charged $261 to read the scans.
- Emilia got the same blood test that Janice (in the first story) got—the one Medicare pays $13.94 for, and for which Janice was billed $199.50 at Stamford. Emilia was charged 20% more: $239.
- Also on the bill were items that neither Medicare nor any insurance company would pay anything at all for: basic instruments and bandages and even the tubing for an IV setup. Under Medicare regulations and the terms of most insurance contracts, these are supposed to be part of the hospital's facility charge, which in this case was $908 for the emergency room.
- Emilia's total bill was $9,418.
- "When I got the bill, I almost had to go back to the hospital," Emilia recalls. "I was hyperventilating."
- Emilia had a health insurance policy that she thought would cover things. HOWEVER, it was from a Cigna subsidiary called Starbridge that insures mostly low-wage earners. That made Emilia one of millions of Americans who are routinely categorized as having health insurance but who really don't have anything approaching meaningful coverage.
- Starbridge covered Emilia for just $2,500 per hospital visit, leaving her on the hook for about $7,000 of a $9,400 bill.
- Emilia searched for various assistance programs but was turned down by all.
- Eventually the hospital sued her, and in a superior court where Emilia represented herself, a judge ruled that Emilia had to pay all but $500 of the original charges; the judge put her on a payment schedule of $20/week for six years. FOR EMILIA, THE CHARGEMASTER PRICES WERE ALL TOO REAL.

ASK DR. DEAN:

Question 4: Dr. Dean, I understand you interviewed 11 of your fellow physicians, asking them questions on several concerns—can you give us the results of this survey?
Answer: Survey Question 1: How much time do you spend with each patient? The range was 10 minutes to 30 minutes
Answer: Survey Question 2: What are the most common conditions encountered in your patients? The conditions are presented below in decreasing order of number of encounters—i.e. the first one, diabetes, is most commonly presented by a patient; and those from headache on down are only occasionally presented among this group of 11 doctors' patients:

1. Diabetes *(most commonly presented illness presented by patients among this group of 11 physicians)*
2. Hypertension
3. Hyperlipidemia
4. Depression
5. Anxiety
6. Upper respiratory symptoms
    The above six symptoms were presented frequently by many patients;
    those below were presented much less frequently by fewer patients:
7. Back pain
8. Headache
9. Stress
10. Hypercholesterolemia
11. Fatigue
12. ADD (Attention Deficit Disorder)
13. Joint pain
14. Congestive Heart Failure

15. GYN conditions
16. Osteoarthritis
17. Tendonitis

Answer: Survey Question 3: What are some unpleasant aspects of practicing as a doctor?

- staff that are untrained
- practice management
- patient demands
- managed care
- burnout of paperwork
- steps involved in referral
- prior approval
- selection of drugs based on cost and insurance company approval
- cost and barriers of prescriptions
- insurance coverage issues
- pre-authorizations
- time pressures
- reimbursement issues
- Electronic Medical Record
- paperwork
- prior authorization for procedures, etc.
- billing system

Answer: Survey Question 4: As a practicing physician, what is your specialty, gender, country of origin, and age?

- **SPECIALTY:** all were in Family Medicine (M.D. and D.O.)
- **GENDER:** some were female and some were male
- **COUNTRY OF ORIGIN:** USA, Mexico, Vietnam, and Spain
- **AVERAGE AGE:** 51

Here's the third case of a person we will call Steve— The One-Day, $87,000 Outpatient Bill

- Steve spent the day at an outpatient setting in the Midwest getting his aching back fixed.
- Steve's doctor intended to use a neurostimulator (implanted in the back to stimulate selected areas of the spine).
- Steve didn't ask how much the stimulator would cost because he had $45,181 remaining on the $60,000 annual payout limit his union-sponsored health-insurance plan imposed. "He figured, How much could a day at Mercy cost?" Palmer says. "Five thousand? Maybe 10?"
- Steve's bill for his day at Mercy contained all the usual and customary overcharges.
- Steve's bill for these basic medical and surgical supplies was $7,882.
- On top of that was $1,837 under a category called "Pharmacy General Classification" for things like antibiotics.
- BUT: The big-ticket item for Steve's single outpatient day was the stimulator (and that's where most of the medical center's profit comes from during this brief one-day visit). The bill for that was $49,237.
  - The medical center cost for this stimulator was about $19,000; thus, the center was making almost $30,000 profit on this, A PROFIT MARGIN OF 150%!
- Steve found out when he got his bill that he had exceeded the $45,000 that was left on his insurance policy's annual payout limit just with the neurostimulator. And his total bill was $86,951. After his insurance paid that first $45,000, he still owed more than $40,000, not counting doctors' bills.
  - NOTE: Under Obamacare, those limits were not allowed (or were not supposed to be allowed) in most health-insurance policies after 2013. But that still will

not be of much help for people like Steve, as it is one of the reasons that premiums skyrocketed under Obamacare along with high deductibles to the extent that the insurance is both unaffordable and basically worthless because of the high deductibles.

Here's the fourth case of a couple we will call Henry and Alice—Catastrophic Illness—and the Bills to Match

- Henry was dying of lung cancer. He and his wife Alice knew that they were only buying time. The crushing question was, how much is time really worth?
- Alice makes about $40,000 a year running a child-care center in her home.
- Henry kept saying he wanted every last minute he could get, no matter what.
- But Alice said, "I had to be thinking about the cost and how all this debt would leave me and my daughter."
- By the time Henry died at his home in Northern California the following November, he had lived for an additional 11 months.
- Alice had collected bills totaling $902,452.
- Henry and Alice didn't know that hospital billing people consider the chargemaster to be an opening bid.
- The couple knew only that the bill said they had maxed out on the $50,000 payout limit on a UnitedHealthcare policy they had bought through a community college.
- "We were in shock," Alice recalls. "We looked at the total and couldn't deal with it. So we just started putting all the bills in a box. We couldn't bear to look at them."
- Luckily, Alice found a **BILLING ADVOCATE** who felt so moved by their case that she waived most of her $100/hour advocate charges and was able to get this hospital system in California to negotiate discounts that amounted

to 85%. In fact, this particular hospital system averages getting only 18% of what it originally bills through its "Chargemaster" plan (but this is not the case with some other major hospital systems in the USA that collect between 50% to 65% of their "official charges").

■ HOWEVER, there was still an outstanding balance for Alice after Henry died. The advocate made a ton of deals with doctors, clinics, and other providers, but still Alice had paid out about $30,000 of her own money and still owed $142,000. And she was still getting letters and calls from bill collectors.

■ What to do? Take **BANKRUPTCY or NOT**?

'Bankruptcy or Not' is what only too many US citizens must struggle with each year because of overwhelming medical costs that are not covered by their insurance, or insurance that they just cannot afford. There must be a better system.

We will discuss these **BETTER SYSTEMS** that are found in all other major industrialized nations in Chapter 3, and in Chapter 7 we will present several solutions that are all realistic for the USA so that no one has to take bankruptcy to survive a medical crisis.

Reference

Brill, S. (2013, March 4). "Bitter Pill: Why Medical Bills are Killing Us: How outrageous pricing and egregious profits are destroying our health care". *Time Magazine.* http://content.time.com/time/subscriber/article/0,33009,2136864-2,00.html.`

Chapter 3

Successful Healthcare Delivery Systems Around the World: Today's Patient Safety Concerns and Poor Delivery Methods in the USA— What Is Needed in the USA Today to Provide Successful Delivery of Safe, Needed, and Cost-Effective Healthcare

Where Does the United States Stand in the World?

We always like to think of ourselves as number one, the best, with the best doctors, the best hospitals, and the most responsive care.

What is obvious if one examines data from around the world is that even though the United States spends more money on healthcare per capita than any other industrialized country, it certainly does not have the best healthcare.

In terms of expenditures, HealthTracker.org (Kamal and Cox, 12-20-17) provided data on our increases in spending. (*https://www.healthsystemtracker.org/chart-collection/ u-s-spending-healthcare-changed-time/#item-total- health-expenditures-increased-substantially-past-several- decades_2017*)

"Health spending totaled $74.6 billion in 1970. By 2000, health expenditures had reached about $1.4 trillion, and in 2016 the amount spent on health had more than doubled to $3.3 trillion. Total health expenditures represent the amount spent on healthcare and health-related activities (such as administration of insurance, health research, and public health), including expenditures from both public and private funds." For the full report, visit *http://www.who.int/whr/2000/ en/*. Please see Figure 3.1.

Data from OECD Health Data, 2018 (Figure 3.2), reveals that the United States spent a total of about 9% of its GDP on healthcare in the year 2000, while in 2017, the United States spent about 18%, which amounted to approximately $3.5 trillion! Assuming there were 325.7 million people in the United States in 2017, that amounts to approximately $10,746 per person for 2017 alone!

In terms of gross domestic product (GDP), as may be seen in Figure 3.2, the USA spends about 18% of its GDP for Healthcare. Other industrialized countries are between 6 and 10 percent of their GDPs.

So, in spending all this money, our healthcare should be much better than that of the rest of the world, right? Wrong!

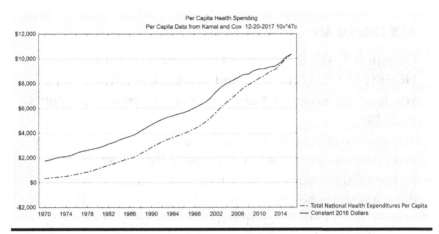

Figure 3.1   Linda Miner graph, using TIBCO-Statistica predictive analytic software, of Per Capita Healthcare Spending in the United States from 1970 to 2016 in Dollars and in Constant 2016 Dollars. Data were provided on the Healthsystemtracker.Org site from Kamel and Cox, 2017. (*https://www.healthsystemtracker.org/chart-collection/u-s-spending-healthcare-changed-time/#item-total-health-expenditures-increased-substantially-past-several-decades_2017***). The reader may find graphs and statistics on this interesting site.**

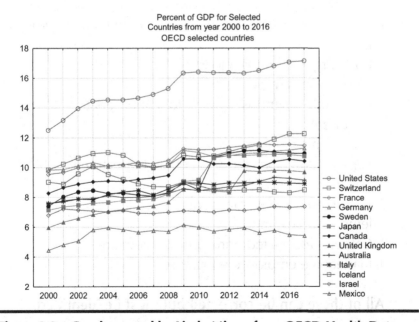

Figure 3.2   Graph created by Linda Miner, from OECD Health Data, 2018: ***https://stats.oecd.org/Index.aspx?DataSetCode=SHA.*

ASK DR. DEAN:

Question 1: What are important components of HOSPITAL QUALITY for good healthcare delivery that you have observed and desired in recent years, e.g. 1990s to 2019?

The quality of hospital healthcare is a broad concept. How that relates to each hospital is an issue that is determined by the unique issues and environment of each. Obviously, there are some healthcare issues that are universal but may be dealt with differently by various medical providers depending on the available resources (financial, physical, environment, personnel). There are also various types of hospitals. Some are more general while others specialize in specific health diagnoses and treatments. There is no "one size fits all," so to say.

Some of the quality problems that present in hospitals include:

1. Medication errors—wrong dose, wrong patient, wrong time
2. Post-surgery complications
3. Wrong site surgery
4. Inaccurate diagnosis, leading to inappropriate treatment
5. Communication errors
6. Sepsis—unrecognized soon enough, treatment not begun early enough
7. Instrument sterility—inadequate due to sterilizer problems, as an example
8. Catheter-associated urinary tract infections
9. Inadequate employee education

All of these can be corrected but must be identified.

These are just some examples of hospital quality problems. There are others that have been identified but are not included in the above list.

The main point about hospital quality is that it needs a continuous and detailed program that is constantly on alert. If the problems are identified, they can be solved, patient safety is improved, and quality of care is at its best.

The quality director of a hospital, in my opinion, should be a full-time physician who understands the importance of patient care quality in all its ramifications. Other characteristics of the quality director should include availability to other hospital staff, being open-minded and a good communicator, and being well-organized.

A strong quality program that works continually to identify and correct quality problems in the hospital develops an appropriate reputation that it is safe for patient care and is well thought of and supported in the community. That is the best indication of high quality, and that opinion is truthful in all respects.

Many hospitals seek quality validation by means of organizations that perform surveys and award hospitals that meet all the surveying organization's criteria. That is then taken to mean that the outside organization's "accreditation" verifies a high-quality institution. The problem with a requirement to meet the criteria of an outside surveyor is that a hospital may not have a problem with criteria developed by an outside organization that measures its performance. If a hospital meets a list of outside criteria, then they may not have the time to address the specific quality problems that exist in their hospital. They may spend time and focus on required quality measures while their own specific measures go undetected. In my opinion, each hospital's focus should be on the quality measures they discover by monitoring their clinical activities and patient outcomes. There is no reason not to consider outside data, findings, research, and suggestions found in other hospitals, but what is occurring in your hospital is of the highest importance. Each individual hospital needs to have a quality department that has developed a level of performance that can be on constant alert and understands how to identify quality issues. Then they need to be able to develop corrective actions and measure improvement.

The outside organizations that develop quality criteria based on cumulative data, research, and opinions of expert physicians and other folks that are considered healthcare experts come together to decide exactly what to require based on their collaborative opinions. Those requirements are then made a part of what a surveyed hospital's performance must meet to be accredited.

There are ten or more hospital accreditation organizations in the USA. They have developed standards that, if a hospital meets those specific standards, are then "accredited" by the organization's surveyors and are given a plaque stating that the hospital's quality of care meets the standards of the accreditation organization. The organization doing the survey charges the hospital $25,000 or more to review the requested information from the surveyors who evaluate the documents requested and decide if the hospital meets the standards to be accredited. This process does not, in my view, provide proof that a high level of quality of care exists in a hospital who meets all of the prepared criteria of the accrediting organization, since it does not address the specific level of performance of a specific hospital. The standards of the surveying organization could not possibly apply to all the hospitals that are surveyed. Some of the surveying organizations survey 5,000 or more hospitals. Thus, the same criteria cannot be uniformly applicable to all hospitals surveyed.

It is my studied opinion that each hospital should have its own evaluation personnel and process to identify quality issues and develop processes to correct the identified issues. The team, of a size that is appropriate for each hospital, should include a physician that has the ability and understanding of developing corrective activities that can make the quality improvement a reality that includes a method for a permanent correction of the identified problem(s). Because of identifying the quality deficiencies present in each specific hospital and developing corrective activities, the hospital could then legitimately improve their specifically identified quality issues. The patients, hospital staff, physicians, community, and more would soon become aware of the improved quality of care, and that would promote further improvements in quality. The improved quality of care would also lead to lower costs of care.

In fact, the United States ranks rather low among the most developed countries of the world—37th in the WHO's 2000 report (*http://www.who.int/whr/2000/en/whr00_en.pdf?ua=1*).

WHO looking at world health: *http://www.who.int/whr/2000/media_centre/press_release/en/* (Par 16):

> "WHO's assessment system was based on five indicators: overall level of population health; health inequalities (or disparities) within the population; overall level of health system responsiveness (a combination of patient satisfaction and how well the system acts); distribution of responsiveness within the population (how well people of varying economic status find that they are served by the health system); and the distribution of the health system's financial burden within the population (who pays the costs)."

Based on those criteria, the United States ranks high on responsiveness. We have many resources to provide when someone is ill. We rank low on fairness because of our payment methods—many people are not covered by insurance because they cannot afford it.

DALE System

Concerning the level of health, the World Health Organization (WHO) uses the DALE system. DALE stands for **disability-adjusted life expectancy**. If one is in full health and lives to be 95, that life is "fuller" than one who lives to 95 but does so bed-ridden in a nursing home, unable to recognize loved ones or unable to communicate.

If one visits the Insurance Guru website (*https://www.internationalinsurance.com/news/ranking-top-eleven-healthcare-systems-country.php*), which looks at eleven highly developed industrialized nations, the USA ranks at the bottom.

> The United States rated 24th under this system, or an average of 70.0 years of healthy life for babies born in 1999. The WHO also breaks down life expectancy by sex for each country. Under this system, U.S. female babies could expect 72.6 years of healthy life, versus just 67.5 years for male babies.

> 'The position of the United States is one of the major surprises of the new rating system," says Christopher Murray, M.D., Ph.D., Director of WHO's Global Programme on Evidence for Health Policy. "Basically, you die earlier and spend more time disabled if you're an American rather than a member of most other advanced countries.' (Murray, Christopher, WHO Issues New Healthy Life Expectancy Rankings, Pars 7 & 8)

We don't live the longest, we don't have the best infant mortality statistics, we don't have the highest ratings on overall health, and so on. Our outcomes are worse than many industrialized nations, and yet we pay the most per person than any country in the world. We are worse than Costa Rica and only a little better off than Slovenia and Cuba! The USA ranks last in health among the wealthiest 11 countries:

https://www.internationalinsurance.com/news/ranking-top-eleven-healthcare-systems-country.php (InsuranceGuru, January 12, 2018) and yet outstrips them all in expenditures. We spend 16% of our GDP on healthcare, while Japan spends only 8%. And all of Japan's outcome statistics are better than ours. Japan has the longest lifespan (of good life, not of sick life) in the world and the lowest infant mortality. T.R. Reid's book states that Japan's life expectancy (male and female combined) in 2006 was 81.25 years, while the same statistic for the United States was 77.85 years (2010, pp. 252–253).

So, we are not the best as measured by several criteria, but we DO spend the most and we do have many resources if only all our people could afford all the resources. This situation begs the question, where are there good healthcare models around the world?

Successful Healthcare Delivery Systems

T. R. Reid also narrated a video, written and produced by Jon Palfreeman for Frontline in 2008, that is quite interesting, describing healthcare around the world. The reader is highly encouraged to watch this video (*https://www.pbs.org/wgbh/frontline/film/sickaroundtheworld/0*).

The film highlights the healthcare practices of five industrialized nations: the UK, Germany, Switzerland, Japan, and Taiwan. All five countries highlighted had better healthcare with better outcomes than the United States (in terms of fairness, responsiveness, DALE longevity figures, and so on).

Japan

Japan had the best and healthiest longevity (refer above to the DALE system, in which while ranking the nations, WHO took into consideration not just how long people lived until death,

ASK DR. DEAN:

Question 2: Can you provide some further information on QUALITY CONTROL in MEDICINE, including some general concepts, history, and definitions?

GENERAL INTRODUCTION TO THE HISTORY and Development of Quality Control in Medicine

There is no doubt in anyone's mind that there are quality problems in hospitals (and in all other healthcare facilities). The definition and priority of what those problems are and how to improve them is a topic of concern to multiple constituencies and depends on their position and beliefs as well as what they have to gain, or lose, as a result of the solutions that are chosen and implemented. A significant allied issue is that the intricacies of this complex topic are monumental. The information presented in this chapter is not designed to offer an overall solution but to present an overview of an approach that may contribute to efforts to improve quality in a local facility.

The concept of healthcare quality improvement has been discussed, written about, legislated, taught, discarded, debated, endorsed, and embraced. Quality improvement initiatives began to be seriously addressed about 18 years ago in 2001 when the U.S. Center for Medicare and Medicaid Services and the Joint Commission developed and agreed upon the "core measures" that hospitals were incentivized to implement. The efforts of hospitals to achieve greater reimbursement based on those quality measures were followed by intense efforts to achieve higher and higher compliance rates. There were policies and education, along with comparisons between and among hospitals to determine how to improve those rates. As a result, scores improved, and everyone's goal was to be in the "top 10%" of hospital performance. Therefore, it became more difficult to get to that level.

The negative aspect was that other identifiable quality improvement issues were set aside.

As time has passed since the initiation of the core measures, a number of quality measures have been proposed and mandated by the federal government, insurance companies, and various "quality improvement organizations."

As a consequence of focusing attention on quality deficiencies in healthcare, it is now common for hospitals to have quality departments and directors of quality. A further result is that there are a variety of software, books, journal articles, and seminars relating to improvements in healthcare quality or performance improvement. However, a one-size-fits-all, or a simple easily implemented program that will solve the quality problems, is not likely to succeed. Instead, developing a process that takes into account the unique structure and functions of a healthcare entity and designing well-planned approaches to solve specifically identified problems with broad input and involvement is much more likely to be successful.

Definition(s) of Healthcare Quality

If one is going to attempt to improve healthcare quality, it is important to understand what healthcare quality is. There are multiple definitions promulgated by various organizations and individuals.

The Institute of Medicine (IOM) has been the earliest healthcare quality improvement motivator, beginning with its book *To Err is Human*. The IOM definition is "the degree to which health services for individuals and populations increase the likelihood of desired health outcomes and are consistent with current professional knowledge." That is certainly comprehensive and conveys the correct concept. They followed up that initial report with the following "aims" of a high-quality healthcare system with specific goals for healthcare as listed below:

- ■ *Safe—avoiding injuries to patients from the care that is supposed to help them.
- ■ *Effective—providing services based on scientific knowledge to all who could benefit and refraining from providing services to those not likely to benefit (avoiding underuse and overuse).
- ■ *Patient centered—providing care that is respectful of and responsive to individual patient preferences, needs, and values and ensuring that patient values guide all clinical decisions.
- ■ *Timely—reducing waits and sometimes harmful delays for both those who receive and those who give care.
- ■ *Efficient—avoiding waste, in particular waste of equipment, supplies, ideas, and energy.
- ■ *Equitable—providing care that does not vary in quality because of personal characteristics, such as gender, ethnicity, geographic location, and socioeconomic status.

Other organizations have definitions of healthcare quality that fit their particular niche in the overall scheme of healthcare.

There are two (or more) audiences to which an appropriate definition applies. Those two are the providers of healthcare services and the recipients. Varied and more academic definitions fit the providers and relate to evidence, technology, procedural competence, and meeting specifically accepted goals. Much simpler and practical definitions apply to the receivers. The providers need to be cognizant of both, while the receivers need to be confident that they will receive the care defined with their concerns included.

> **The IOM definition does include the providers of healthcare services, but the definition for the receivers deserves to be separate from the providers.**
> A definition for the receivers of care might be as follows:
>
> > "Care for me that respects me as an individual, that includes my participation in and understanding of decisions related to all illnesses and healthcare issues that I might face, and that includes consideration of my financial and educational level, as well as my goals for healthcare outcomes." This definition for the receivers of healthcare simply states what the IOM definition includes, but in simpler, more understandable words.
>
> Healthcare providers, especially in hospitals—physicians, nurses, technicians, administrators, and all the other support staff—can contribute to appropriate outcomes in keeping with the IOM definition of quality. *In order to do that, however, it is imperative to have a quality department that has the sole priority of monitoring and measuring the quality of the care provided*. With that information, processes, procedures, programs, and education can be developed and implemented that raise the level of care.
>
> Even in the highest quality institutions, there is always room for improvement, and the quality department's vigilance can provide that service.

but how well they were as they aged. Being a fully healthy person until death was the most desirable and counted the most for longevity). Japan also spent one half what the USA was spending—only 8% of its GDP. You might think that the Japanese use doctors less than we do, and that's why their expenditures are less. No! They go to the doctor three times more than we do! And they can go to specialists whenever they need to without a referral. They can often get same-day appointments. The Japanese incorporate technology when-ever innovations arise, much of which incorporates preven-tive medicine. They don't spend much time at their doctors' offices—about three minutes on the average, whereas, in the USA, the average is about seven minutes. Many of the visits are just to recheck blood pressure, or get a throat culture, for example. Those things can be taken care of by office person-nel with the briefest of visits.

The Japanese are thin compared to Americans, and this alone can help to contribute to their higher longevity using the DALE criteria, and opiods are not such a problem in Japan.

The Japanese government sets the uniform costs of every-thing every two years—it's not difficult to know what an MRI costs—it costs the same for everyone everywhere in the country. In the USA it is very difficult to know what services will cost. I once asked what an X-ray would cost that the doctor wanted me to get. The staff knew all about schedul-ing the test, but no one in the office could say how much it would cost. They couldn't even give an estimate … $100 or $1,000—they couldn't say. They said, "Don't worry, your insurance will pay for it." But I knew very well that someone would be paying—we all were paying the insurance compa-nies! Negotiation of prices is very important. If no one nego-tiates, then we patients need to figure out how to negotiate for ourselves. The video stated that in the USA, an MRI of the neck costs on the average about $1,200, while in Japan the cost was about $98. Japan may have to start paying more, however, as the film stated that most of the hospitals in Japan were running in the red.

United Kingdom

In the UK, the government owns the hospitals and all the doctors are government employees. No one pays premiums or deductibles. There are no medical bills. They simply go to the doctor when needed. The UK spends about 18% of its taxes on healthcare and that amounts to about 4.5% of the average incomes, according to Josh Chang, Felix Peysakhovich, Weimin Wang, and Jin Zhu. (The UK Healthcare System, 2015, *http:// assets.ce.columbia.edu/pdf/actu/actu-uk.pdf*). However, taxes are high in the UK for those earning the most. If one earns $234,484 or more, one pays 50% in taxes (*https://financeson-line.com/top-ten-countries-with-highest-tax-rates*). Yikes!

In times past, the United Kingdom was known for long waits for service in its public system, and there still is some waiting but it has gotten better. The UK introduced a few market concepts into its model. Patients can now choose their hospital rather than being assigned one. This simple change has introduced enough of a competitive edge so that hospitals must garner good customer relations or will go under. One other idea was that even though prices were set for primary care physicians' services, bonuses were assigned to those who kept their patients healthy. Payment to keep people healthy! Now there's an idea worth pursuing!! The UK, the film stated, has become a world leader in preventive medicine.

Germany

Germany's system, according to Reid, was initiated in 1883 by Chancellor Otto von Bismarck, who introduced the Sickness Insurance Law. That law became the "world's first national health care system" (Reid, 2010, p.66). Many of the elements in today's national programs were instituted then—individuals contributing by withholding, as well as employer contributions. From there, the German system has evolved. Basically, it is a social (but not really socialistic) system in which everyone in the country is covered, including non-citizen "guest workers." One salient quote from Bismarck is, "We cannot protect a man from all sickness and misfortune. But it is our obligation, as a society, to provide assistance when he encounters these difficulties ... A rich society must care for the poor" (Reid, 2010, pp. 73–74).

Germans can choose their own doctors and hospitals, and provided they have selected an insurance plan, it must pay; bills are not given to patients. The insurance plans or "sickness funds" are all privately run, and Germans can pick which- ever one they would like to use. The hospitals are mostly run by the government, but private hospitals are emerging. Because the funds are privately held and run, the system is not socialistic. The private funds (private but **not for profit**) compete for patients. Patients pay on average 15% of their pay, split between them and their employers. They don't pay for a separate insurance premium. Plans have **no shareholders** and do not have to pay dividends. Plans must accept anyone who applies (**no pre-existing conditions** clauses). If patients wish, and about the top 7% of earners do this, they may decide not to join a sickness fund and can pay for private (for- profit) insurance and go to private hospitals. They pay more if they opt for private insurance.

One important element is that the sickness funds **negoti- ate prices** with the medical practices and clinics and hospi- tals. The prices are higher than for many countries (11% of Germany's GDP). The United States is at 18%, so 11% sounds pretty good by comparison. One reason for the lower cost is that Germany eliminates administrative paperwork by use of a **smart card** for each participant, and in fact the administra- tive costs are about 1/3 of those of the United States. Consider that the treatments are in the directory, and if the treatment is in there, it cannot be turned down for payment—no need for some kind of decision process on the part of the insurers. In addition, and perhaps due to fewer administrative activities, patients are seen much quicker than they are in the USA. All public plans follow the same rules and payments.

PCPs are the gatekeepers to specialists, and the process is con- trolled by the big directory that is also negotiated. The directory

ASK DR. DEAN:

Question 3: Dr. Dean, we understand you spent 10 years developing a quality control unit in a major hospital— can you tell us about that and what you learned?
Quality Department in Hospital

Yes, I spent ten years of my medical career serving as a medical director of quality (my actual title was Medical Director of Clinical and Operational Performance Improvement). I learned quite a bit from this, as there were continually new issues that needed to be addressed.

The quality department in a hospital needs to be an independent department reporting to the chief medical officer. The medical director of quality should be the quality department director but needs another person, with a clinical background, IT experience, and personnel management expertise. The quality department assistant should be tasked with the administrative functions of the department to free the medical director of quality to observe, develop policy, appoint quality-related committees, prepare reports for the executive team, board of directors, medical staff, and other stakeholder audiences, plus develop solid relationships with all of the medical staff members. Another significant task of the medical director of quality is to participate with the medical staff secretary, particularly with regard to issues related to medical staff applicants and their qualifications. A not uncommon issue for the medical staff secretary pertains to odd issues that arise related to an applicant's past which the typical application for privileges may not cover. The secretary needs a physician that can help her address such problems that arise. Although this may fall under the purview of the chief medical officer, that person is often overwhelmed with other tasks such that some of the functions of that position do not get addressed in the desired time frame. In my view, selecting physicians to add to a medical staff is very much related to the quality of care in the hospital. Providing input to medical and surgical policy, related to the quality of care, is another important function of a medical director of quality. The medical director needs to be alert to additional duties that may be unique to the hospital where they are employed.

Issues Discovered

In the course of my ten years of effort as a medical director of quality, there were quite a number of issues that came to my attention. My way of functioning was to become aware of the primary reasons for the occurrence of any practice that was causing, or could cause, harm to a patient and working to correct or improve the faulty practice. A specific policy at my hospital was developed to address the traditional attitude of punishing a hospital employee when an adverse event occurred. The only thing punishment accomplishes is to hide events in the future. That does no good for future patients. We promulgated a policy of identifying/reporting quality-related problems and educating any involved person or persons so that the problem did not reoccur or was prevented if it was something that could create an adverse outcome.

Learning about poor quality issues was an initial and ongoing step in identifying where I needed to devote my efforts. The following is a list of some of the issues addressed and on which resolution or improvement occurred:

- Improvement in performance on "core measures"
- Appropriate hand hygiene (nationally is at 40%—very poor)
- Reduction in preventable mortality
- Identification of the main post-operative infections and development of prevention techniques

- Addressing other hospital-acquired infections, their causes, and prevention
- Reducing ventilator-acquired pneumonia cases
- Reducing urinary catheterizations and catheter-associated urinary tract infections
- Improving early sepsis identification and rapid initiation of treatment (especially in the ED)
- Formation of an antibiotic stewardship committee to address the inappropriate use of antibiotics
- A major program to improve the education of hospitalists, other medical staff, and nurses in the newer methods of diabetes treatment (including the use of basal-bolus insulin)
- Methods of reducing patient falls
- Improving the content of documentation generally (doctors, nurses, all other personnel) and legibility
- Improvement and understanding of ways to deal with urinary incontinence
- Education on the importance of teamwork
- Nurse well-being, the importance of effective communication
- Focus on other issues, including physician support and encouragement and appropriate physician behavior

The above are examples but not a comprehensive listing of the projects undertaken over time.

The quality department is the repository of data from the clinical departments. The analysis of that data is one of the main avenues for the identification of quality issues that need to be addressed. Those departments from which data needs to be gathered include the following list:

- *Nursing
- *Physicians (all disciplines)

- *Laboratory
- *Infection Control
- *Respiratory
- *Pharmacy
- *Coding (including documentation information)
- *Surgery
- *Anesthesiology
- *Emergency Department
- *Psychiatry
- *Social Services
- *Coordinated Care
- *Housekeeping
- *Admission and Discharge
- *Physical Therapy
- *Rehabilitation
- *Six Sigma (or other similar activities)

In addition to reviewing data, I was able to discover quality issues and promote quality performance by other more traditional methods. The value of electronic medical records systems cannot be denied, but personal interactions with physicians, nurses, and other personnel of various types should not be overlooked.

Following is a listing of job duties I undertook on a routine basis:

- *Facilitation of the bimonthly board quality committee meetings that involved the following:
  - Informing the members about quality issues/concerns/problems/programs/successes

- Prepared the agenda
  - Reviewed the agenda with the Chairman prior to meetings

- Prepared and delivered information about quality topics relevant to the hospital
- Prepared the board quality committee's report to the full hospital board of directors

■ *Facilitation of a clinical advisory/peer review committee's quarterly meeting
- This multidisciplinary physician committee's role was to provide input about their quality concerns and the needs of the physicians relative to their practice in the hospital
- Prepared the agenda for meetings and invited speakers on topics relevant to the members' concerns
- Reviewed and edited minutes of meetings
- Prepared presentations as needed of peer review issues as they arose

■ *Appointed and led quality teams to address quality issues that arose based on data reviewed, internal chart reviews (based on information received), or internal research

■ *Managed the peer review process by identifying and responding to suspected physician quality of care concerns, reported to me by any of the various departments or individuals, following the medical staff's peer review policy

■ *Performed special projects, such as 2X2 mortality reviews, catheter-associated UTI review, and others as needed and prepared reports of the reviews for appropriate bodies

■ *Met with medical staff physicians as-needed concerning quality or behavioral issues or to discuss their performance or failure to address identified documentation or other requirements, such as the use of order sets, legibility, required quality measures, etc.

■ *Oriented new physicians and mid-levels to acquaint them with our specific quality measures, standard orders, unsafe abbreviations, expectations, etc.

■ *Performed a daily review of mortalities and evaluated the need, if any, of cases needing an in-depth review to determine if the mortality was potentially preventable

■ *Performed a daily review of the surgery schedule to identify whether a procedure that might represent a quality issue was being addressed surgically or a surgeon had scheduled a procedure for which he/she was not credentialed that was prohibited by policy. (Example: Tonsillectomy was not to be performed on a child under age 3 but must be referred to a facility that has pediatric ICU.)

■ *Attended the meetings of the medical care evaluation committee

■ *Attended all clinical department quarterly meetings and reported on quality issues, if needed

■ *Attended council meetings (General Surgery, Vascular Surgery, Cardiology, Emergency Care, Hospitalist) and provided quality perspective related to their specialty

■ *Helped develop and participated in a diabetes task force formed to address the seriously inadequate treatment of hospitalized diabetes patients that were admitted either because of their diabetes or because of diabetes co-morbidity

■ *Attended monthly operations council meetings

■ *Attended the monthly hospital board of directors meetings

■ *Attended the medical executive committee meetings and reported on quality initiatives, peer review cases, and activities and responded to questions from members

■ *Served as medical director for the following:
  - Employee Health Department
  - Quality Department
  - Coordinated Care Department
  - Diabetes Foot Clinic, and served as the supervising physician for the four nurse practitioners who worked in that clinic

■ *Miscellaneous activities as follows:
  - Chaired utilization review committee
  - Responded to problem calls from any department, unit, nurse, or physician to help resolve any issues that arose
  - Assisted with medical record deficiency process (such as calling physicians or policy questions)
  - Was available to treat employee patients as needed
  - Consulted on coding issues and coding specialist queries as needed
  - Along with the hospital's risk manager, I met with patients and/or family to discuss adverse outcomes that occurred while a person was hospitalized to help answer questions about the care provided and explain what occurred

I list all of the above to illustrate the wide-ranging involvement of a physician who takes on the role of medical director of performance improvement (quality). That is not to say that every hospital would require, or even encourage, the doctor in that position to assume responsibility for all of those duties. The point I am making is to demonstrate that a full-time physician in that position needs to keep his/her ears open, cultivate positive relationships with hospital staff, medical staff, administration staff, and all others in order to be cognizant of as many of the quality issues as possible. Then steps can be taken to work collaboratively to find solutions to improve what needs attention.

Additional recommendations for a medical director of quality are to participate in quality organizations, such as the Institute of Healthcare Improvement (IHI) and the American Board of Quality Assurance and Utilization Review Physicians. There are a number of other such organizations, and the importance of participation is to broaden one's knowledge and learn new ways of improvement and about new tools. Being aware of and reading about quality issued from other quality organizations is likewise valuable. Those organizations certainly include CDC, SHEA, and IDSA, among others.

One dictum I have repeated often that is at least a partial answer to the increased healthcare costs is "the highest quality of medical care produces the lowest cost."

says what procedures and treatments the system will pay for. For years there were also no copays, and prices for any surgical procedure are next to nothing. Reid (2010) explained that he could have had a shoulder replacement for a total cost of $30 for him. Starting in 2006, to help pay for the rising costs, patients were told they had to pay one copay per quarter when seeing the doctor. That amounted to about $13 per quarter. Oh my!

Medical school is free for physicians, so they do not have huge bills after graduation. In addition, malpractice insurance is very inexpensive ($1,400 per year for a family doctor was given as one example by Reid (p. 78)). Still, doctors are not paid well compared to US standards. In fact, the controls are so very tight that physicians are having to use creativity to make additional profits by offering weight loss, Botox injections, and other things that are not in the directory and for which they can charge independently of the standard practice.

These "business" practices are likely a result of the fairly recent reforms that set a limit of paying for 700 patients per quarter. When the physician sees more than 700, there are no further payments. The system is not utopian.

Taiwan

One of the most successful countries in terms of populace satisfaction was Taiwan. Taiwan studied successful models from around the world and incorporated only the things that seemed to work. Taiwan had a system that was basically the pay out of pocket model. Insurance programs were for those who were in the military, other governmental employees, and big companies. Most of the people had no plan at all. Interestingly, the turnaround was instituted by the conservative Nationalists. Taiwan's Democrats were calling for a healthcare system for all and the Nationalists were adamant about keeping what they had, but suddenly the conservatives changed their minds and went for a single-payer National Healthcare System in 1971–1975 (Lu and Chiang, 2011, p. 88). The incumbent president, Lee Teng-hui, was reelected in 1976. In the years that followed, Taiwan concentrated on improving the quality of its healthcare. The National Health Insurance (NHI) program was rolled out in March of 1995 (Lu and Chiang, 2011, p. 96). Up to that time, the system had only covered about 57% of the populace. After 1995, it was to cover all citizens. "The government planned for its new NHI system to achieve three essential objectives: providing equal access to healthcare for all citizens, controlling total health spending within a reasonable level, and promoting efficient use of healthcare resources" (Lu and Chiang, 2011, pp. 96–97).

To develop its single-payer system, Taiwan looked to other countries such as Canada, the United Kingdom, and Germany to find the best elements for Taiwan. The resulting program costs about 6% of GDP. Participants can choose their own doctors, and it covers "prevention, primary care, and hospitalization ... and additionally traditional Chinese medicine, traditional herbal medicine, dental, vision, acupuncture, and long-term care" (Anne Underwood, par./Question 8, *https://prescriptions.blogs. nytimes.com/2009/11/03/health-care-abroad-taiwan/*).

They also adopted the smart card technology, again helping to reduce administration costs. Patients carry the card with them, and when they go to the doctor, they pull out the card that has all their information on it.

Commonalities of the Successful Models

- All imposed some sort of limits. For example, insurance companies had to accept everyone (without regard to pre-existing conditions), and companies were not allowed to make a profit on basic care.
- Everyone was mandated to buy insurance, and the government paid for the poor. One twist was for Germany, in which the basic coverage was for all (public insurance), but the wealthy could, instead, opt to purchase their own private insurance instead of accepting the public insurance.
- Doctors and hospitals had to accept one standard set of prices for services, and those prices were negotiated. Negotiation was very important and needed to keep prices down. Negotiation is one thing that the United States lacks. Here, prices are not transparent and rise at rates beyond inflationary factors. Most people would rather be alive and bankrupt than dead and save money, and so most will accept expensive life-saving alternatives. Bankruptcies due to medical costs are frequent in the USA.

A model that was not explored above, is the direct care, free market system, which is described in Chapter 7.

One argument in favor of a free market system is that doctors who don't care or who make misdiagnoses, etc., would soon be out of business. In systems where medical personnel are paid regardless of outcome such as Medicare, then they don't have to care as much. Patients MUST be in the loop.

Four Main Healthcare Models Used Around the World

Here is the summary of these four ways (From Reid, 2010 and this website: *https://www.amazon.com/Healing-America-Global-Better-Cheaper/dp/0143118218/*):

1. **The BISMARCK MODEL**: Found in Germany, Japan, Belgium, Switzerland, and to a degree in Latin America. Both providers and payers are private entities. But unlike US health insurance, they are basically charities that cover everyone and there is not a profit. The hospitals and doctors are private businesses—privately owned. Tight regulation of services and fees gives much of the cost-control "clout."

2. **The BEVERIDGE MODEL**: In the British medical system, this is financed/provided by the government through tax payments. No medical bills; medical treatment is a public service, like the fire department or the public library. Hospitals and clinics are owned by the government; some doctors are government employees, but there are also private doctors who get their fees paid by the government. LOW COSTS PER CAPITA. Government controls what doctors can *do* and also what they can *charge*. In addition to the UK, it is also in Italy, Spain, and most of Scandinavia. Hong Kong still has its own version of this BEVERIDGE system. (This model is probably what Americans have in mind when they think of "socialized medicine.") The two purest examples of this BEVERIDGE model are found in Cuba and the US Department of Veterans Affairs.

3. **The NATIONAL HEALTH INSURANCE MODEL**: Has elements of both the BISMARCK and the BEVERIDGE systems: providers are private, but the payer is a government-run insurance program that citizen pay into. No need for marketing, no expensive underwriting offices, and no profit. *A single payer covering everyone*—thus they have the *power* to negotiate for *lower prices*. The best example, maybe only one, is Canada.

4. **The OUT-OF-POCKET MODEL**: Only about 40 of the world's countries, industrialized nations, have an established healthcare system. Most nations are too *poor* and too *disorganized* to provide mass care. This rule is simple and brutal: ***the rich get medical care, the poor stay sick or die***. Areas that have this include rural regions of Africa, India, China, and South America (hundreds of millions of people go all their lives without *ever* seeing a doctor.) All of this is PAID OUT OF POCKET. Out of pocket payments also account for 91% of total healthcare spending in Cambodia, 85% in India, and 73% in Egypt. (In contrast, the figure in the UK is 3% and in the USA is 17%.)

For the USA: we have elements of ALL FOUR OF THESE MODELS in our American "CONVOLUTED NATIONAL HEALTHCARE APPARATUS."

- For US Working people under 65—we are "Germany or Japan": Bismarck Model fashion
- For US Native Americans, military personnel, and veterans—we are "British or Cuban"
- For US people over 65—we are Canada
- For the 45 million uninsured Americans—we are Cambodia (or Burkina Faso, or rural India)

AND yet the USA is like no other country ... because it maintains separate systems for separate classes of people, and relies heavily on for-profit private insurance plans to pay the bills. With its **fragmented array of providers and payers and overlapping systems**, the US healthcare system does NOT fit into any of the four recognized models.

AMERICA IS RESISTANT TO CHANGE ... the VESTED INTERESTS are doing well in Healthcare now!!!

- Insurance companies
- Hospital chains
- Pharma companies

BUT these three "vested interests" have also **blocked** any significant re-engineering of the American Healthcare system ...

What can be done? Chapter 7 will provide several solutions ...

References

"2016 Annual Report: Comparison with Other Nations." (2016, October). America's Health Rankings. https://www.americashealthrankings.org/learn/reports/2016-annual-report/comparison-with-other-nations.

Carroll, A.E., and Frakt, A. (2017, September 18). "The best health care system in the world: which one would you pick?" *New York Times*. https://www.nytimes.com/interactive/2017/09/18/upshot/best-health-care-system-country-bracket.html.

Dicker, R. (2017, January 11). "Obamacare isn't one of the Top 10 public health care systems in the world." *U.S. News*. https://www.usnews.com/news/best-countries/articles/2017-01-11/10-countries-with-the-most-well-developed-public-health-care-systems-ranked-by-perception.

Du, L. and Lu, W. (2016, September 16). "U.S. health-care system ranks as one of the least-efficient." *Bloomberg*. https://www.

bloomberg.com/news/articles/2016-09-29/u-s-health-care-system-ranks-as-one-of-the-least-efficient.

Fox, M. (2016, November 16). "United States comes in last again on health, compared to other nations." *NBC News.* https://www.nbcnews.com/health/health-care/united-states-comes-last-again-health-compared-other-countries-n684851.

"Health Care System Performance Rankings." (n.d.). Commonwealth Fund Reports. https://www.commonwealthfund.org/chart/2017/health-care-system-performance-rankings.

Lu, R. J., and Chiang, T. (2011). "Evolution of Taiwan's health care system." *Health Economics, Policy, and Law,* 6(1), 85–107. doi:10.1017/S1744133109990351

Oliver, D. (n.d.). "Health Buzz: The U.S. has the worst health care System on this list." *U.S. News.* https://health.usnews.com/wellness/health-buzz/articles/2017-07-17/report-us-has-the-worst-health-care-system-compared-to-these-countries.

Palfreman, J. (Producer). "Sick around the world." (2008, April 15). *Frontline.* https://www.pbs.org/wgbh/frontline/film/sickaroundtheworld/.

Potyraj, J. (2016, February 11). "The quality of US health-care compared with the world." https://www.ajmc.com/contributor/julie-potyraj/2016/02/the-quality-of-us-healthcare-compared-with-the-world.

Reid, T.R. (2010). *The Healing of America: A Global Quest for Better, Cheaper, and Fairer Healthcare.* London, UK: Penguin Books Ltd.

Sawyer, B., and Gonzales, S. (2017, May 22). "How does the quality of the U.S. healthcare system compare to other countries." Peterson-Kaiser Health System Tracker. https://www.healthsystemtracker.org/chart-collection/quality-u-s-healthcare-system-compare-countries/#item-start.

Schneider, E.C., Sarnak, D.O., Squires, D., Shah, A., and Doty, M.M. (2016). *"Mirror, Mirror 2017: International Comparison Reflects Flaws and Opportunities for Better U.S. Health Care."* Commonwealth Fund Reports. https://interactives.commonwealthfund.org/2017/july/mirror-mirror/; (Source: OECD Health Data 2016).

Senthilingam, M. (2017, March 17). "How health care works around the world." *CNN.* https://www.cnn.com/2017/03/17/health/health-care-global-uk-national-health-system-eprise/index.html.

"The World Health Report 2000—Health Systems: Improving Performance." (n.d.). World Health Organization. http://www. who.int/whr/2000/en/.

"World Health Organization's Ranking of the World's Health Systems." (n.d.). *The Patient Factor.* http://thepatientfactor.com/canadian-health-care-information/world-health-organizations-ranking-of-the-worlds-health-systems/. (Accessed August 2018).

Chapter 4

Current and Future Trends: Rectifying the Crisis–Chaos of the Past Few Decades Through Medical and Healthcare Research That Uses Quality Control, Predictive Analytics, and Decisioning That Is More Powerful Than Previous Methods in Leading to Accuracy and Correct Actions

What is needed in healthcare is innovation, revised methods, and even a disruption in the way things have been done in medicine. We patients tend to assume that the practice of medicine is based on sound research, that patients are at the center of that practice, that the most expedient/efficacious methodologies using quality controls are used, and that our doctors know how to individually treat us when we are ill. However, those assumptions are not always true. In fact, as well-meaning as our health professionals are, often those assumptions are not met.

Not all innovation leads to the kind of disruption that synthesizes disparate points of view into a dynamic evolution of sparkles and light. In addition, as in Figure 4.1, new methods, such as predictive analytics that allow predictions tailored to the individual, can cause disruption, particularly among those who cannot adapt to the new ideas. Politics can get in the way. People have done things in the same way for all their lives. Some of them are at the pinnacle of their profession, and to change … well, it is sometimes seemingly better to just rewrap one's old ideas and call them new, rather than to adapt and adopt truly new ways of doing things. However, when

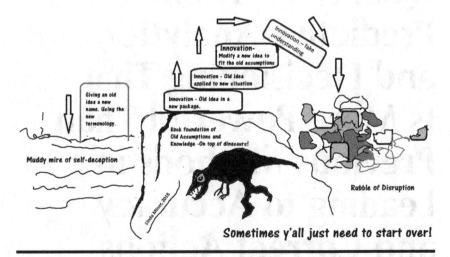

Figure 4.1 Innovation that leads to—disruption rubble. (Figure by Linda Miner.)

new ideas come from elsewhere and one cannot revise, adapt, or mold, then disruption can, and perhaps should, happen. Please see Figure 4.1.

An interesting site that talks about innovation and disruption is *http://blackbird.marketing/influencer-marketing-innovative-disruption-rebranding/*.

New ideas potentially pose more of a threat of disruption for those stuck in the past than for the early adopters in terms of idea development. Figure 4.2 shows the potential for new ideas—they can be built upon and made even more useful when adopted.

Who might be considered early adopters in medicine? Certainly not Dr. Bliss, who disregarded the concept of tiny biological agents of infection—germs—and basically killed the 20th President of the United States. Only if an idea sees the light of day can that idea be potent. Threatened power is not pretty. Medical institutions are quite powerful, and power does not like to lose power. Nonetheless, as in all life situations, disruption is sometimes necessary.

Why do we think disruption may be warranted in medicine? When medical errors are the **third largest cause of death in the United States**, when medical insurance is too

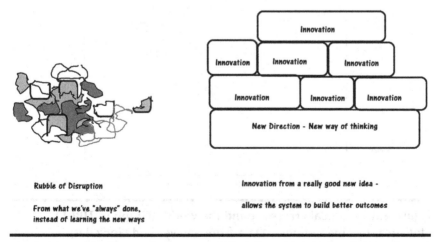

Rubble of Disruption

From what we've "always" done, instead of learning the new ways

Innovation from a really good new idea -

allows the system to build better outcomes

Figure 4.2 Ideally, new ideas provide a firm foundation for productive innovation. (Figure by Linda Miner.)

expensive for many, and where medical bankruptcies occur, it seems we need to radically change our current practices.

Bradley Sawyer and Selena Gonzales in 2017 provided a graph of percentages of medical errors for medical care, medication, and lab errors of the United States compared to other countries, and ours are higher in absolute terms (*https:// www.healthsystemtracker.org/chart-collection/quality-u-s-healthcare-system-compare-countries/#item-start*). In many other countries, there are no medical bankruptcies—none. In many other countries, all citizens are covered for healthcare (Figure 4.3).

The mean of the "errors" for these otherwise comparable countries is 16.55 with a standard deviation of 5.077. Now if we look at a box and whisker plot of the nine countries, as in Figure 4.4, we see that all the values fall in the same general area within two standard deviations. However, the percentages

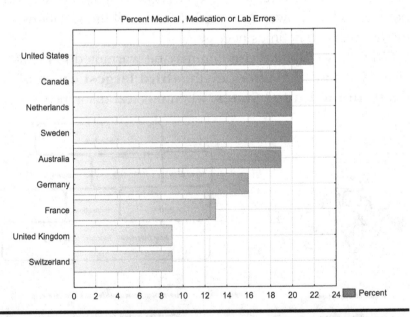

Figure 4.3 Medical errors around the world. (Graph in TIBCO-Statistica, by Linda Miner—Data from Sawyer and Gonzales, 2017 graph: *https://www.healthsystemtracker.org/chart-collection/quality-u-s-healthcare-system-compare-countries/#item-start*.)

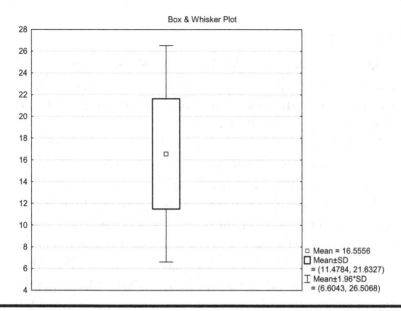

Box & Whisker Plot

□ Mean = 16.5556
□ Mean±SD
= (11.4784, 21.6327)
I Mean±1.96*SD
= (6.6043, 26.5068)

Figure 4.4   Box and whisker plot of the simple percents from nine countries, showing the countries all could be considered from the same population with likely no statistical difference between. However, the denominators for the raw data from which the numbers were calculated, were huge. The data were per 100,000. So then, the small differences in total percentages are, indeed, significantly different. (Figure by Linda Miner, using TIBCO-Statistica and based on Sawyer and Gonzales, 2017.)

were based per 100,000, and thus the differences were all likely significant.

The point is that the United States ranked as the highest in terms of medical-related errors and was worse off when it came to medical errors than all the other countries shown in Figure 4.3 with universal healthcare.

Medical Research Articles Are Likely Flawed

The next fact might be somewhat frightening … Medical research articles are retracted from reputable journals more than those of many disciplines. If retracted, the journal is

ASK DR. DEAN:

Question 1: What changes have you observed in medical practice, especially with costs in terms of both money and time, over the years since you opened your first solo practice in the early 1970s?

When I observe the changes in medical practice over the past 47 years, it is enough to stir one's thoughts and wonder, how could that have happened?

I have thought about my experience over that time, and even though that is a long time, the changes have occurred quicker than I could have imagined. When I began my family practice in Stone Mountain, Georgia, in 1971, my office visit fee was $8! Now the same visit charge is $70–235, depending on the length of the visit and seriousness. I would see ten to 20 patients per day, four-and-a-half days per week. I was on call seven days per week and made hospital rounds daily, again seven days per week. When I was on call, I received a "beep" on my pager. If I was away from home or the office, I had to be sure I had a pocket of quarters and could find a pay phone on a corner to respond to the call and to call the caller. Over the time I did obstetric deliveries, the first five years of practice, I delivered 300 babies. My charge for a delivery, which included pre- and post-delivery care, hospital delivery, and any additional needed office visits was $300! How many deliveries did I do for which I was not paid in full? NONE. I was proud of that. At one time I had a second office in the country, and the office visit charge was $6! I worked at each office five days per week (half days at each) and a half day at my primary office on Saturday. There were other medical-related activities in which I participated. After being in practice for seven years with no partner or other available doctor, I had the entire load on my own. Then three new doctors arrived, and we shared weekend call, which helped a great deal. You might think I was suffering burnout! Actually, no, I did not burn out. After being in that practice for 17 years, I had an opportunity to change, which I accepted. I became a public health director for the North Georgia District. That included a ten-county district in northwest Georgia, and I was CEO for public health, mental health, mental retardation, and substance abuse programs in all ten counties. After four years of public health service, I moved back into family practice in a small town near Rome, Georgia. I worked there in practice with another family physician for six years. My next work was at Floyd Medical Center covering vacation/time off physicians for the Floyd Family Practice group, and then as a consultant to improve physician documentation to reduce a large amount of money that was not being realized due to inadequate physician documentation. My next position was as the medical director for quality, a position I held for ten years, after which I retired from Floyd Medical Center in 2011. All of this took place over my 45 years of active medical practice.

What do I understand now about the level of physician medical activity as a result of my varied career?

There are several areas of physician service that are very different. The list that includes my understanding of the changes is the following:

1. Increased charges for office visits
2. Reduced time of physician/patient contact
3. A suspicion that a correct diagnosis for many conditions requires more time and attention than is typically provided
4. The patient–physician body of understanding each other is lost and creates a gap in the relationship
5. In the past, patients had a "family doctor" who provided ongoing care over time, and now patients tend to go to a doctor who is available

In spite of the outstanding and helpful technology, which is extremely important and very helpful, to lose the bonding of patients and physicians and the recollection of its benefits is of questionable value. It is difficult for me to comprehend now, at this time in my life, how technology can replace the importance of that relationship.

supposed to state in the next issue that the article has been retracted and should not have been published. Having many retractions occurring in medical journals has not always been the case. Medical retractions are increasing. Naik (2011) reported that the retractions increased five-fold from 2001–2005 to 2006–2010: from 87 to 436. During that same interval other journals had the numbers of retractions declining, and in fact, *The Astrophysical Journal* had **none** during 2006–2010 (Winters-Miner et al., 2015). The pressure to publish to receive grants has never been more intense, especially at universities and medical schools where advancement and tenure depend upon publications and the acquisition of grant funding. At times, the salaries of the medical researchers as well as the schools' accreditations, depend on publications and acquisition of grants.

As a result, not all articles submitted are good ones. Stated in Winters-Miner et al. (2015), when medical articles were reviewed by statisticians from a variety of medical journals, most of the articles were flawed in one way or another, rendering their conclusions suspect. In one study, 85% of the articles reviewed were flawed (p. 24)! That is a shocker! In addition, some of the retracted articles were found to have data that were **fabricated**. One can only imagine that a researcher fabricating data was desperate to publish and he or she fudged the numbers! There are other times in which those who are conducting the research are being paid by the makers of the device, medication, or procedure. In other words, unconscious bias could be introduced to the research.

(Most reputable journals today require the researchers to say whether they have received those types of remuneration. However, a way around that rule sometimes is that the entity providing the funds gives the funds to the university that the researcher works for, and the researcher can legally say he or she did not receive any funds from a company related to the research but is paid by the university.)

Hernandez and Greenwald, in a Wall Street Journal article (2018 August) titled "IBM has a Watson Moment—Big Blue promised its AI platform would be a big step forward in treating cancer. But after pouring billions into the project, the diagnosis is gloomy—Can Watson Cure Cancer" (*https://www. wsj.com/articles/ibm-bet-billions-that-watson-could-improve-cancer-treatment-it-hasnt-worked-1533961147?*) stated that IBM Watson's impact on cancer care has not positively impacted cancer patients and their treatment. If you recall, IBM Watson is the supercomputer that won *Jeopardy!* against humans in 2011. IBM Watson has an immense capacity for "crunching" mega amounts of text and other data to answer questions and make predictions. By programming in all known articles in some field, such as psychology, engineering, or medicine, the machine would be able to discover unseen patterns and make accurate predictions based on those articles. What could go wrong?

Why Did Watson Lose in Medicine?

Why did Watson win at *Jeopardy!* and lose in medicine? There are no doubt many reasons. For one, the questions that are asked in *Jeopardy!* are at the bottom of the cognitive levels—they simply ask for the facts—names, dates, places, and so on. These are at the factual level and do not require much synthesis in thought. Predictive analytics attempt to match patterns and determine fit. If we wish to match a patient to a treatment or drug to see what works best for that individual, it is incumbent that we know the salient patterns of the patient and that we know all the patterns of anyone who has been treated by the method or drug. Most of the research that has been done and is in medical journals deals with patterns of populations or groups and not individuals, such as is noted in Chapter 1. Further, if most of the research is flawed, then those who feed the articles to Watson would be inputting flawed information into the machine. It would be impossible for the machine to make accurate analytic algorithms that could accurately predict when using flawed information.

If a treatment's effectiveness for individuals is unknown in the literature, how can medical folk proceed? With experience, doctors develop intuition about effectiveness for individuals. Our brains are also amazingly good at crunching data and experience. In fact, the learning algorithms of data mining work, ideally, the way the human brain works. So, what happens to that brain when it is given gold standards based on the published literature? What if those gold standards have been developed from flawed studies, or from studies that predict to groups and not individuals? Physicians listen to experienced colleagues, listen to their own experience, and basically try whatever is thought to work.

Genomics present such promise, but the research is just not there yet to be able to accurately predict in most cases. We hope the research will be well done and come quickly. When that great promise comes true, then Watson and those of us that work with predictive algorithms will be in our prime! Until then, we are all at the mercy of what little we know, even if we really don't fully understand what we think we know for sure.

Disruption—Research Is Needed at the Individual Level Rather Than the Group Level

One thing is certain. Research needs to be at the individual level. I (Linda) recently worked on a study concerning disseminated intravascular coagulation (DIC) with a team at Loma Linda Hospitals (Chandnani et al., 2018). We had over 11,000 individual records of children with DIC symptoms, which include uncontrolled bleeding due to infections and various traumas. We had our data in individual rows in our data set, so we were at the individual level. We received the data from that which was collected by the hospitals' IT, and the data recorded were thought to be accurate. There was no bias in terms of our wanting some outcome. We only wanted to find out if we could accurately predict who was at greatest risk of dying by determining what variables were most predictive of death and which for survival. We knew which patients had died and which had lived. Unfortunately, the data were not complete, and we had to work with the fact that we did not have all the data for each child. We did our best by using techniques to impute values based on nearest neighbors, plus eliminating records with a lot of missing data, and, in the end, we believed that we had a good prediction—at least we had a prediction model that we could then work with in the future, to test and to further increase the model's accuracy. Our prediction using only three lab tests, when tested on new cases (holdout data), was as accurate as those from the past that had used eight or more lab tests. Using fewer tests could speed up the time for increased treatment.

We mention the above study because such a study of individuals is in the vein of what we need in the future, but even so, it is very difficult to complete research in our current medical environment. Data are very hard to get—it becomes quite expensive to construct a study, and most of the time we must use data that are available in records, which are sometimes missing and possibly inaccurate at times.

Disruption—Make the Data Available

Research data is something to really think about. Who owns the data? We need privacy standards (HIPAA), but such laws mean that data is very difficult to come by. Patients should

ASK DR. DEAN:

Question 2: What can doctors do to improve the doctor/ patient relationship?

The relationship between patients and doctors is a critically important issue, especially given the changes that have occurred in medical practice in the last ten years. The issue has several aspects at present, due to the difficulty of doctors to figure out how best to conduct their practice in ways that address their medical school debt, which may be staggering, managing their personal financial needs for them and their families, and addressing their schedule in a rational manner. In the past, those issues were more often just the way things were at the time. In past times, a family practice physician, after finishing training, would open an office (usually rented), purchase equipment (on borrowed funds), hire a staff (receptionist and aide), put up a sign, and wait for patients to show up. Advertising was not legal, so one had to figure out how best to become known by doing public activities. Working part-time in an emergency room, for example, would help provide some income until the practice became supporting. The most significant issue was the amount of time required to conduct office hours, work extra hours for income, make hospital rounds every day (including weekends and holidays), respond to hospital calls about inpatients and patients presenting to the emergency room (day and night), and manage office staff and personnel. It is hard to imagine that I actually did all that on a routine basis. The new physicians learned about this kind of schedule and did not believe it was healthy, desirable, or necessary. That then led to the more recent system of physician's work scheduling.

I recount the above to point out that the availability of physicians now is different, and the change has been a gradual shift. It is understandable, if less than desirable for patient care, especially in regards to the patient/physician relationship. For the best level of care, there is a specific need, for a primary care physician in particular, to get to know the patient and the patient to get to know the physician. Over time, the relationship can develop in a way that can only occur by means of repeated contact related to the physical and emotional problems that patients suffer. This type of relationship, in addition to all the technology available, leads to more accurate diagnoses. An accurate diagnosis is required in order to know what treatment to provide. Absent the doctor/patient relationship as described leads to negative outcomes more likely than without the described relationship. Nowadays patients are less likely to be treated by the same doctor when healthcare is needed.

What can doctors do to improve the doctor/patient relationship? It appears to me that it is unlikely that the relationship is being fostered today (or occurring in a well-developed manner)—this is a part of some of the fairly recent changes in medical care. Perhaps it will, over time, when the importance of that relationship is again valued ...

(See the OAK STREET HEALTHCARE SYSTEM in Chapter 4, and also in Chapter 7, where the patient and the patient-medical provider is put on the throne as the "center of healthcare"—so it is happening again in various places.)

own their own data and should only give it over if they choose to do so.

Think about these agencies that are collecting data as they sell a service to individuals—23AndMe, AncestryDNA. They now have genetic information from many individuals. What can they do with the data and what not? Have you contributed yours? Do you know what they can do with your genome information?

What happens to research when cases select or do not select to be in the research? In other words, some people may choose to give over their data and others not. How could that choice skew the research? Could there be a genetic difference between those that give up their data and those that do not? Would we then be able to develop the most accurate prediction models? Should there be a huge repository of information that researchers could draw from? How could that work? Could data be available through our medical portals? How could privacy be guaranteed?

Data needs to be available to researchers who know how to conduct predictive analytic studies that predict to the individual. Perhaps patients themselves could disrupt the system by demanding that their data be available for researchers to use.

Disruption—Interoperability

Good Predictive Data Analytics requires good data, and good data can only be available when there is true interoperability of data among medical healthcare facilities. The lack of good interoperability is the "break in the stepping stones" to accurate predictions for the individual using predictive data analytics, and it must be addressed soon. Recently, as the authors finished writing this book, we were seeing signs of real concern on interoperability coming from big corporations like Amazon, Google, IBM, and Microsoft expressing a goal of removing any barriers to interoperability in healthcare data (Sullivan, T. August 13, 2018; Amazon, Google, IBM, Microsoft, Oracle and Salesforce Pledge to Remove Interoperability Barriers; *https:// www.healthcareitnews.com/news/amazon-google-ibm-microsoft-oracle-and-salesforce-pledge-remove-interoperability-barriers?*).

Disruption—Need for Quality Control

In Chapter 1 we talked about past and not-so-past medical horrors. We said that today's procedures might be tomorrow's horrors. We always need to think, what could go wrong?

In August 2018, the Patient Safety Network (PSNET) published "Wrong-Site, Wrong Procedure, and Wrong-Patient Surgery (*https://psnet.ahrq.gov/primers/primer/18/wrong-site-wrong-procedure-and-wrong-patient-surgery*). It is rare in the United States that such wrongs occur in surgery. Indeed, the Agency for Healthcare Research and Quality (AHRQ) has reported that wrong side, wrong site, wrong procedure, and wrong patient errors (WSPEs) occurred at a rate of only one in 112,000 surgeries (Kwaan et al., 2006). Of course, for those in which the error happened, it would have been devastating. But the odds are in your favor in this study.

However, another study said that the number of surgical errors is much higher—about a half a percent of surgeries (Gardner, 2010, *http://www.cnn.com/2010/HEALTH/10/18/health.surgery.mixups.common/index.html*). Here is an example of Gardner's research, which also included mistakes outside the surgery suite:

> Over a period of 6.5 years, doctors in Colorado alone operated on the wrong patient at least 25 times and on the wrong part of the body in another 107 patients, according to the study, which appears in the Archives of Surgery (par 2).

Removing the wrong ovary, taking the wrong child to an operating room, mixing up samples, removing the prostate of the wrong patient—even having a mix-up on what was meant by the patient signing the affected limb—thinking the patient signed the good side rather than the one to be operated on.

> Overall, one-third of the mistakes led to long-term negative consequences for the patient. One patient even died of lung complications after an internist inserted a chest tube in the wrong side of his body (par 11) (Figure 4.5).

Okay, now what does the mark mean?

Figure 4.5   Cartoon by Linda Miner of effort at surgery on the correct side.

Quality Control

If used anywhere in our society's institutions, excellent quality control should be exercised for medical treatments. We do not want mistakes or to spend unnecessary time dealing with our illnesses.

Quality control measures were traditionally found in business. Companies wanted to reduce errors, to reduce time in production, and to bring quality products to their customers in a timely fashion. Techniques were developed using statistical process control techniques in what was called a six-sigma environment (Pyzdek, 2003). W. Edward Deming introduced the models into business at the end of World War II, mainly to the Japanese, and they were later adopted by American companies, known as Total Quality Management (TQM)

ASK DR. DEAN:

Question 3: How can the doctor and other medical providers help with patients' weight control?

It is very important for physicians, especially family practitioners, to provide help to patients who are overweight. A significant percent of family practice patients (female and male) have weight issues, and it is very typical for the physicians to ignore or very briefly toss out a comment about how to address it. For a patient to mention their concern about their weight signifies, in most cases, that they are concerned about what to do to reduce their weight. It is common, given all the television, magazine, newspaper ads, etc. about diets, exercise facilities, weight loss clinics, and other programs for patients to have confusion about what they should do to deal with the weight issue they have. In my opinion, physicians should either take the time to address the issue or schedule an appointment or refer them to a known effective and appropriate program. Given the significant effect of excessive weight and the physician's patient-care-related responsibility, it is incumbent upon them to provide an honest effective effort to address their concern. Also, to brush off such an issue, by a brief comment in the hallway, is inappropriate and uncaring. The physician should have information about a program that they can provide (personally or by a trained staff person) or be prepared to recommend. Weight issues are a common public health problem that is not well understood by the average person, and a physician's honest input on an improvement method carries "weight."

(Winters-Miner et al., 2015). These techniques found their way into medicine in the 1980s and really got going in the 1990s. To constantly improve, reduce risks, and increase positive outcomes, various techniques are used. When errors occur, instead of concentrating on punishment, analysis of the error and error prevention are stressed.

Root Cause Analysis

Systems analysis studies in medicine help to identify problems that can produce errors. It was hoped that by **not** concentrating on punishment for errors, errors would be more freely admitted and that the errors could be analyzed. Root cause analyses would be performed (Winters-Miner et al., 2015, p. 146):

- Do all reasoning from solid evidence.
- Determine what influenced the consequences, i.e., determine the necessary and sufficient influences that explain the nature and the magnitude of the consequences.
- Establish tightly linked chains of influence.
- At every level of analysis, determine the necessary and sufficient influences.
- Whenever feasible, drill down to root causes.
- There are always multiple root causes.

Basic to medical root cause analysis (RCA) is revealing the underlying, perhaps unseen, causes of the errors. As such, RCA does not focus on the individuals involved as responsible, but rather, on systemic problems. Interviewing those involved in the error is crucial, as is collecting all data and facts surrounding the error (PSNet, August 2018, *https://psnet.ahrq.gov/ primers/primer/10*). Then, a multidisciplinary team analyzes the data and sequences of the error to come up with a solution to prevent further similar errors.

Root cause analyses have identified communication problems as the most consistent cause to emerge regarding medical errors— think back to the confusion of knowing which side is signed, the good side or the bad side. The solution prescribed was using a timeout period before any invasive procedure and using checklists. Instead of diving into the task, wait and review all details. A timeout was originally only for surgeries but now is being applied to any procedure that is invasive. Of course, errors still can and do occur, but root cause analysis is one technique to reduce errors.

Root cause analyses can help bring about fundamental changes in the system—a disruption model, but at times the entire system must be disrupted to overcome root problems. An example of a disruptive kind of change resulting from analysis of the system is the Virginia Mason Hospital in Seattle, which used continuous improvement methods found in car manufacturing plants to improve on the experience of their patients (Cat Vasko, 2012: *https://www.radiologybusiness.com/topics/quality/waste-not-want-not-inside-virginia-mason-production-system*). The hospital staff looked for ways they could reduce the time it took patients to get information, obtain scheduling, and obtain their results. Their goal was to eliminate waste and costs and improve the patients' welfare. Using value stream mapping, the imaging process for back pain was changed, for example:

> We realized that the way we had been handling back pain was this: The patient would see the primary-care provider, who would order an MRI exam, and then they would send the patient to a physical therapist. Maybe a month down the road, the physical therapy might be started," Glenn says. "We realized that the patient needed to be started on physical therapy right away, and then—if there's still an issue after six weeks—to get an MRI study (Par. 3).

Use of quality control, when used correctly, reduces waste, increases good outcomes, and puts the patient in the center of care.

We Need to Think—It's Not All Up to Quality Control

Even though the medical community is working hard to reduce errors and to keep their patients healthy, we, the patients, have a responsibility too. We are responsible for ourselves. We need to think and do what we can to stay healthy. There are times when we are so very ill that we simply must put ourselves into the hands of our medical professionals and trust that they have our best interests in mind. However, for our routine medical care and elective procedures, we need to become part of the decisions and use our good brains.

We need to acknowledge that medicine has made great strides through history. Much has been learned due to scientific research and through quality assurance/control. Physicians are, for the most part, intelligent, compassionate, and knowledgeable. As are nurses, technicians, and allied health professionals. We, as the book authors, are not picking on the medical community. However, we would like to influence the **system** so that they may more effectively help people. In addition, we are not assuming that all patients are victims, or on the other hand that they are all motivated to help themselves. All can contribute to both good and bad outcomes.

Medicine has made great strides. From bloodletting, unsterile conditions, and magical thinking to scientific discoveries, designer medications, and machines—medicine can be amazing in its ability to overcome disease and life challenges whether genetic, accidental, or environmental.

However, medicine is not perfect. Research can be flawed, doctors may misplace their mental focus because of unconscious dislike of the patient producing wrong diagnoses, data may contain unseen biases or be too global, as when predicting to the average. Communication may not be ideal, greed can cloud the mind. Yes, medical workers may desire power and be overly ambitious, which are conditions that may also influence medical care.

In addition, our country has **not figured out a good way or ways of paying for our healthcare** that work for everyone's best health. Finally, we patients do not always take care of ourselves even when we know better. Yet, we expect our doctors to be gods and fix us when we break ourselves. Sometimes the doctors confuse themselves with gods. All medical people and patients are people, and as such, all are liable to make mistakes. And if they trust all medical research, that trust is often misplaced—as was discussed, medical research is inaccurate in up to 85% of the articles published. Even with fervent dedication, if a medical professional has trusted research that was actually flawed, what good does the dedication do?

Disruption—Need to Reduce our High Rate of Medical Errors

Surely the emphasis on quality control and root cause analysis will reduce medical errors. More needs to be done, however, if errors, indeed, are the third largest cause of death in the United States. Here are more examples of present-day errors, including some that were sent when asked of friends on Facebook. Their names and places have been omitted or changed for their privacy.

Patient Tales of Errors

We'll start with a funny modern-day error (not even of the United States): In the last episode (8) of Season 7 of *Doc Martin*, Dr. Ellingham made an emergency call to the farm home of Annie Winton, who lied that she had an emergency leg problem. In fact, Annie wanted a second opinion for her husband, Nicholas, diagnosed with malignant cancer in his neck. The false emergency call angered the doctor, as he had patients waiting in his office. The doctor was aware of his patient's diagnosis from a specialist and told the couple to simply follow the course of treatment given by the oncologist. But Annie had become so frustrated by her husband's worsening condition that she held Doc Martin by gunpoint until he more thoroughly considered Nicholas' diagnosis

ASK DR. DEAN:

Question 4: Does controlling weight in chronic disease help?

My response to this question is "yes," it does help, due to the consequences of maintaining an excess weight that is higher than normal. Those consequences include the following:

Diabetes (type 2)
High blood pressure
Heart disease and stroke
Sleep problems
Osteoarthritis
Liver disease
Kidney disease

All of those are chronic illnesses that require a lot of medical attention as well as being expensive, uncomfortable, and causing a shorter life than would be the case if you were at normal weight.

Body mass index (weight in relation to your height and a score of that information that indicates a category):

Normal weight: Body Mass Index (BMI) 18.5–24.9
Overweight: Body Mass Index (BMI) 25–29.9
Higher weight: Body Mass Index (BMI) 30 or higher

himself. In the end, through all the comedic twists and turns of the program, the doctor ended up saving Nicholas' life when he realized Nicholas' labs lacked a definitive diagnosis. As it turned out in the episode, the poor man, rather than having throat cancer, had a thyroid cyst, which by the end of the program started filling with blood, choking him—ultimately the condition would have caused an earlier death than the cancer might have. Nicholas and Annie were unknowingly partly at fault, because Nicholas had not returned to get a confirmatory lab test. Plowing through the many pages of the report, Doc Martin noted that the first scan was "equivocal," when the oncologist had pronounced the diagnosis of probable cancer. Where was the follow-up, and why did the oncologist provide a plan for treatment on an equivocal scan, one wonders?

Medical errors can happen just as in this story. Both doctors AND patients can be at fault.

■ Bone marrow transplant example:

From Brawley and Goldberg's (2011, pp. 32–36) book is the story of "Helen," who had a bone marrow transplant. Helen was diagnosed with aggressive breast cancer, which might not have succumbed to hormonal therapies. Helen chose a mastectomy rather than a lumpectomy. Her doctor prescribed, and she submitted to, a very strong chemo that would destroy her bone marrow. The oncologist took some of her bone marrow ahead of time to save for reimplantation after the procedure (autologous bone marrow transplantation). The oncologist assured Helen that her insurance would pay for most of the cost of the procedure and that she'd be hospitalized only for a few days, plus some side effects. Helen agreed, and the procedure was done.

Helen's side effects were very severe—gum and mouth, heart rhythm problems, problems with electrolytes, respiratory problems. At one point she was put on a ventilator and had to spend five months in the hospital. Later she found out about a medical trial to determine whether the procedure would prolong the lives of breast cancer victims. This happened when she read a news story on the trial, and that the procedure was found not to work! When she asked her doctor, he told her that everyone was doing the procedure. She remembered him to be quite certain of the benefits. She then wondered if the procedure was done because it was expensive. "Was it possible that she had nearly died to help her doctor and various Atlanta medical institutions accumulate wealth?" (p. 34). The doctor said, "This was what everybody was doing at the time" (p. 34). Brawley said their thinking was that "more would automatically be better."

Here are the costs that Brawley and Goldberg provided: "Each transplant procedure cost at least $150,000 when it became commercially available. Later the price was knocked down to about $60,000, roughly the price of a luxury car. Complicated cases such as Helen's were worth $1 million or more in medical services. Is it unreasonable to think that at times, money can motivate treatment?

Facebook Contributions to Discussion of Current Medical Errors

We are certain the reader can also add to the tales of woe related to medical mistakes. The following are some stories from friends on Facebook. The question was whether anyone had had any particularly good or bad medical experiences—these are the ones that related to medical errors.

Friend 1: (A story of a good [and a little bad] medical experience): When my son was 13, he got the flu (it was two weeks before Christmas). When I took him to the doctor, his BP was 185/105 (or something crazy like this). They took it several times—both arms and legs—always the same high result. They scheduled him for an EKG ... results were normal. So, they said, "it's probably just due to the flu—we will wait it out." Ummmm. No. NO ONE should have BP that high—especially not a healthy 13-year-old boy. I contacted another pediatrician and spoke to his nurse. She immediately got him on the phone, and he asked several questions and had me come in that afternoon (it was Thursday—one week before Christmas). By the time I got to the office, he had consulted several doctors and had multiple tests scheduled for that day and Friday (mind you—we had NEVER seen him before this visit). The following Monday, he called me and told me they would be admitting my son at a hospital in another city and asked me to leave immediately. He was in kidney failure—his bladder was not working, and his kidneys were slowly shutting down—thus the high BP. Children's nephrology is a specialty, and the only doctors specializing in it in a three-state area were at this hospital. We were at the hospital for a week and through Christmas. My son had to go through many tests and medical procedures—and now has regulators (pacemakers) attached to his sacral nerve (sacral nerve stimulation) so that his bladder will function properly. This doctor, whom we had never seen before—but knew without a doubt high BP in a 13-year-old was a sign of something more serious—saved my son's life. It is likely that my son will eventually have to have a kidney transplant, but for now he is a healthy 20-year-old … all thanks to a wonderful doctor.

Friend 2: I was told I had a large tear in a tendon—surgery was my only option. I had the surgery … they made three large incisions, found no tear, and in addition, they improperly closed one and I had to go to wound care.

Friend 3: I knew an old minister who was suffering from severe pain in his abdomen. He grew weaker and sicker. Exploratory surgery revealed a large crusted tumor. When the surgeon pinched the tumor with "tweezers," he discovered a green thread. The tumor was a green surgical towel left in the old minister's abdomen from a previous surgery. He framed the towel.

Friend 4: (who works in a hospital in HR): In our high-reliability class, we ask this question and have trainees stand up if they or family members have experienced one or more of several scenarios of medical errors. It's shocking how many people stand in every class. Usually more than 50%.

Friend 5: Yes, I had ehrlichiosis, which can be deadly, a disease caused by a tick bite, while working on my MBA. I went to the ER twice within 36 hours and was sent home both times being told that I was having an allergic reaction, even

ASK DR. DEAN:

Question 5: Should a patient take statins for reducing or preventing heart attacks and strokes?

One of the very common, worrisome issues about health relates to prescribed medicines and their potential effects. Cardiologists (and other medical specialists) have been pre-scribing statins for high cholesterol on blood tests. Due to the amount of publicity about taking or not taking statins, the issue becomes one of common concern. The question then becomes: what should I do and what is best for me with regard to this medicine?

Statins are prescribed for patients who have an elevated cholesterol level on a blood test. The normal cholesterol is said to be no higher than 200, and if it is higher, then you should be taking a statin drug prescribed by your physician. The reason this is said to be the appropriate step is because it has been said that high cholesterol levels can lead to heart attack or stroke because of the negative effect of cho-lesterol on your arteries. The high cholesterol is described as being related to fat consumption in one's diet and other features such as what you inherit.

There is heated debate between esteemed cardiologists concerning the taking of statins to reduce heart attacks and strokes. There is no agreement, and both sides have rationales for their recommendation to take or avoid taking statins.

Unlike most medical issues, the effectivity and safety of which are typically universally accepted by all physicians, this one is very controversial, especially among cardiology specialists. The issue is weighing the potential benefits of taking a statin when a person has an elevated cholesterol level or has had a first heart attack versus the potential of side effects of statin (which are significant in terms of occurrence rate and seriousness). If a person is cared for by a physician on one or the other side of the conflict, then it will either be prescribed or not, depending on their opinion.

It is difficult to know what the best decision about this issue is. In my opinion, it is advisable not to take a statin. There are several reasons for my opinion. I have a concern about the number of prescribed medicines nowadays. Anyone taking more than four medicines is taking on an increased risk of medicine side effects. Obviously, there are situations where limiting the taking of more than four is not appropriate for some folks.

A connection between high cholesterol and heart disease and stroke has been disproven.

Taking a statin is more like I recently heard from another physician—"Taking cholesterol out of the body may be like bloodletting was many years ago."

So, having cholesterol in your system is important for the function of many body tissues, and reducing it does not make sense. An appropriate treatment for health conditions such as heart disease and others is to follow a healthy lifestyle that includes proper nutrition and fitness.

ADDENDUM from author Dr. Gary Miner: During the past two years at my annual physical, for which the purpose is primarily to "see him once a year so he can renew my prescriptions," my family doctor has "sat me down and given me a lecture": This LECTURE both years has been identical—"Do NOT take statins!!!" Then (to cover himself legally), he hands me a prescription for a statin (for all of my bloodwork, higher CHO is the only thing that falls outside the "normal range"). So this has led me to begin studying about statins. There has been much written in the medical literature in the past few years indicating that the original studies, decades ago, that showed a correlation between CHO and HEART disease may have been analyzed without the availability of the latest predictive analytic technology, and thus their conclusions are faulty. Of course, the pharmaceutical industry has made "zillions" producing statins, and we still see today advertisements on television, during the evening prime news hours, about new injectable medicines to control high CHO that state that high CHO causes heart disease. Yet recent research shows otherwise. I, as a patient, am still studying this, but after taking statins for a year and not liking some of the side effects, am now NOT taking statins for a year; after this year I will re-evaluate.

REFERENCES on LACK OF VALUE of STATINS for ELDERLY:

1. *https://www.mdedge.com/ecardiologynews/article/138907/preventive-care/statins-no-benefit-primary-prevention-elderly*
2. Han et al. (2017, May 22). *JAMA Intern Med*. doi: 10.1001/jamainternmed.2017.1442

though my white blood cells showed I had a massive infection somewhere within my body. My primary doctor had called the ER ahead of us going the second time to request a certain test be run (like the blood test). This made the ER doctor mad, and she came in the room and said, "You want tests you're going to get tests. EKG, chest X-rays, and tons of other random tests." At one point she had me catheterized for no reason. I will never forget the nurse just kept saying how sorry she was and knew this didn't have to be done. She was also the one that told us about the blood test results. After all the tests were done, the doctor came back in and said, "See, I told you nothing was wrong!" and sent me home. When we asked about why my blood count was so high, she said those tests won't be back for days. A day later my head had swollen in size and I couldn't walk from the pain. My primary doctor, bless his heart, went ahead and met with us and got me the correct diagnosis and medication. When the bills from the ER started rolling in, I wrote a letter to the hospital's board of directors and my primary doctor made a phone call on my behalf as well. The ER doctor did not lose her job, but she did have to send me an apology for how I was treated, and the bills were written off. A few months later we went to visit someone at the ER and there were huge signs up stating symptoms to look for after tick bites.

Friend 6: A VA surgeon went to remove a cancerous polyp from my colon after a private doctor diagnosed me with colon cancer from a colonoscopy. The VA "surgeon"—I use that term loosely, because he was terrible, but instead of a small 3-4" incision below my navel, he cut me from groin to lower chest, saying he had to do this to find the thing to remove it. He said the guy that did the colonoscopy didn't pinpoint where it was, so he had to perform exploratory and essentially gutted me. I found out later from my private primary physician AND the doctor who PERFORMED the colonoscopy that the VA surgeon was lying. He was totally inept. I SAW the documentation pinpointing exactly where the polyp was. I've thought MANY, MANY times of suing this jerk. I've been told the VA surgeons and doctors are held to much lower qualifications than private physicians. Yes, I'm sure there are good ones—another of my VA doctors is one of the finest anywhere. But this surgeon guy needs to be barred. THEN ... he kept giving me a BP med that was causing a horrible cough that I had for eight weeks. I would have daily coughing fits resulting in the dry heaves for hours at a time. Finally, a nurse at the emergency center that I went to THREE TIMES ... discovered the side effect of this BP med was a severe cough. I stopped the med; the cough went away. There are many other things he did to me during this eight-week period that I won't go into further here, but it was the most inept, awful, unqualified, unprofessional surgeon I've ever had in my life. Moral of the story??? NEVER, NEVER, let the VA in (town) perform surgery on me EVER, EVER again. I have a LONG scar down the front of me now forever that constantly reminds me of this jerk who isn't qualified to play the GAME "Operation," much less work on a real person.

Gone are the days where we just put our lives in their hands and follow their [medical professionals'] every word. Now ... I research every medicine any doctor provides and all the care they suggest for me. I will never just take their word for anything ... ever again.

Friend 7: A warning from a posting from a physician friend, former head of a large health insurance plan:

> "In my particular position, I've seen a lot of problems with physician behavior. But be careful ... I've heard of just as many horror stories with demanding patients who had no clue. Not enough space here to go into them all ... on either side."

It is important to remember that errors can originate from either patients or doctors. Communication is extremely important when it comes to working with one's doctor. And communication errors can also come from either the patient side or the medical side. Considering that errors can occur, what should we do? Please refer back to Ask Dr. Dean question 2, p. 94 for developing a good relationship with your physician.

And for another area, we should try not to be unduly swayed by television commercials of medications and procedures and run to our doctors asking for them. Doing so could end up in a self-initiated error. (See next section.)

Disruption—We need better ways to test new treatments, medications, and devices; how might some pharmaceutical and devices clinical trials be "out sick"?

Drug companies spend fortunes on developing new medications using clinical trials. They take tremendous risks in the development of such, and progress in the treatment of

ASK DR. DEAN:

Question 6: What are the difficulties with interoperability among different medical clinics, providers, and hospitals?
One of the difficulties with interoperability, as I see it now, is related to the HIPAA requirements. With HIPAA it is a chore to transfer medical information from one clinic, hospital, etc., to another. In addition, transferring that information is time-consuming and not at the top of the list of things to do. If an interoperability system could reduce the time and make medical information more easily and quickly transferred, that would be better for patients. Or, if the interoperability system involved the patient having their own medical record information that they could share with whomever they wanted, obviously the task could be done easily.

ailments often comes through their research efforts. What could be problematic?

Because the costs for developing medicines are so expensive, pharmaceutical companies really want to recoup their expenses and make a profit. If a medication is good for one condition and logically it might be good for another condition, it is conceivable that the medication might be used for conditions that were not directly connected to the drug trial.

■ Example: Use of three red blood building medications was approved by the FDA after a drug trial of patients on dialysis, for use in patients with kidney disease (Peter Whoriskey, 2012, *https://www.washingtonpost.com/business/economy/anemia-drug-made-billions-but-at-what-cost/2012/07/19/gJQAX5yqwW_story.html*).

The drugs increased red blood cells and lowered the signs of anemia. The makers also noted there were few harmful side effects. The drugs were approved in 1989 and 2001. The drugs did provide benefits to patients who were severely anemic and seemed to restore those patients' vitality. The drugs allowed those patients to have fewer transfusions, eliminating some of the infection risks they would otherwise face.

Then it was thought that if lower doses made patients feel better, higher doses would make the patients feel even better. *(This claim had to be withdrawn 13 years later because the FDA did not believe the makers met the statistical standard for proof.)* Then came a long period in which results were lost, misfiled, and so on. The companies claimed the drugs were also good for cancer patients, but when they tried conducting a trial on patients with small-cell lung cancer, the company was unable to recruit the 400 patients they needed for results and got only about half that. Medicare researchers going over the data noted the patients taking the drugs appeared more likely to die, and the maker finally had to agree.

Giving the drug was quite lucrative for physicians, and the more of a dose they gave, the more they earned (the greater the "spread"). If patients' hematocrit levels were only slightly low, doctors administered the drug. People died. People had strokes. Patients "feeling better" could not be verified with statistics. The drug companies said the deaths were not statistically significant. The FDA analyzed data and finally stated that there WAS a statistically significant difference and set guidelines for use of the product (*https://www.fda.gov/Drugs/ DrugSafety/ucm259639.htm*). Doctors ignored the guidelines and prescribed what they wanted to prescribe. Then Medicare said it would not pay for the increases over the guidelines. One maker spent $2.4 million dollars on lobbyists and went to congressional hearings. Eventually, Medicare changed the recommendations to 20% higher, meaning an increase of $2,000 for each dose.

Dialysis clinics were receiving up to 25% of their revenues from the drugs, and so they were obviously in favor of the higher levels. One of the largest chains of dialysis even promised its chief medical officer "a $200,000 bonus if the rules for the drugs' use being considered by regulators were dropped or delayed. He was to receive an additional $100,000 if the then-new legislation, known as the Medicare Modernization Act, didn't cut into the company's revenue" (*https://www.washingtonpost.com/business/economy/anemia-drug-made-billions-but-at-what-cost/2012/07/19/gJQAX5y-qwW_story.html?noredirect=on&utm_term=.e76beb71cc68*).

Patients were recruited to give testimonials, which they did.

The lobbyists were winning until research studies started being produced which said the medications were dangerous—one published in the New England Journal of Medicine in 2006 said that kidney patients who received higher doses were hospitalized more often and were at higher risk for strokes and death (*https://www.medpagetoday.com/nephrology/generalnephrology/4540*).

Additional research kept coming that the medication was associated with higher deaths and increased tumor growth in cancer patients.

So, let us again consider what could go wrong with drug trials?

Again, drug companies spend fortunes on developing new medications using clinical trials. They take tremendous risks in the development of such, and progress in the treatment of ailments often comes through their research efforts. What could be problematic?

Jerry Seinfeld and Jimmy Fallon at one point discussed commercials in *Comedians in Cars Getting Coffee*. They talked about how commercials seemed to show lots of happy people, thus making the viewer want to buy the product. They then turned to advertisements for drugs, also seemingly highlighting happy people. Seinfeld quipped that we watch commercials for drugs that are interrupted with law firm ads suing for drugs that commercials convinced us to take last year.

Netflix, *Comedians in Cars Getting Coffee*, Season 1, Episode 2.

Do you ever pay attention to the possible side effects of medications advertised on television?

And yes, it is true that some of the medications advertised just a couple of years ago are now involved in class action lawsuits due to unanticipated side effects. We must keep in mind that all medications and devices have what are called "adverse events" during their trials. Most are not even caused by the products but occurred during the time the product was being used. Companies must list them regardless. Some are causative. Causative versus non is not easy to differentiate in a trial. ***However, if we could use predictive analytics to determine who might get what, those side effects might be averted in practice.***

We must remember that companies are quite anxious to bring out their products and start making a profit from them. On the other hand, those companies do not want to be sued a year after the medication is introduced due to some missed adverse side effect. Clinical trials are regulated by the government as a means of testing the products/procedures/medications/devices before bringing them to the public, and tests are costly to the drug company (estimated to average $2.6 billion per drug). How could this method go wrong? Brian Krans in a 2006 article, "What's Wrong with Our Prescription Drug Trials," uses a blood thinner as an example (*https://www.healthline.com/health-news/whats-wrong-with-drug-trials#2*). And it should be noted that the original study that was referenced in the Krans article no longer can be found. The problem was brought up and was responded to by the company. Krans mentioned one concern—that of the potential problem of company employees participating while being authors on the study. Krans said the study would be 22 times less likely to contain negative statements about the product (par 5, in the section called, "Study Sponsors Influence Outcomes").

■ Example: (Company) was attempting to see if blood thinning agent 1 was as effective as the older medication (Medication 2) in keeping blood from clotting unduly (a blood thinner). A potential problem with the 2011 study was that four years after the drug trial was completed, the FDA issued a recall-correction for the instrument that had measured the international normalized ratio (INR) in the study. (INR is a standard measure of coagulation of blood.) In the drug trial, the numbers for the drug were thought to be possibly lower than they should be, which might have influenced the outcome of the drug trial. In the end, this concern turned out to be unfounded, but for a time, the potential problem was quite worrisome for the company.

Because of the identification of the possible problem, the **study authors** conducted a post-hoc analysis of the data, completed by "two physicians" who were blind as to which patients came from which drug. Adverse events were examined and found to be equally spread between the two conditions. The study authors concluded:

> These results are consistent with the overall trial findings and indicate that possible malfunction of the point-of-care device used for INR measurement in the ROCKET AF trial that potentially led to lower INR values than would be obtained by laboratory testing did not have any significant clinical effect on the primary efficacy and safety outcomes in the trial (par 7, *https://www.nejm.org/doi/full/10.1056/NEJMc1515842?query=recirc_curatedRelated_article*).

This study was defended, but think about this. It was four years after the study was completed that the potential problem was found and revealed. Clinical trials are extremely expensive, and the company has a vested interest in the results. The Federal Drug Administration works to keep the trials balanced and fair. But sometimes damage is done before all the adverse conditions that result can show themselves. The adverse conditions can also happen later and not appear during the drug trial, after the drugs or devices have been released.

■ Example: Here is another example of possible side effects—a drug for metastatic breast cancer advertised in 2018 for treating hormone-receptor-positive cancer, intended to delay the disease progression. Now, any medication can have adverse side effects, and the company must list them all due to possible litigation if they don't. But drug companies push drugs out at a rapid pace to start earnings rolling in, and only when drugs are new and the patents give the company exclusivity in sales can pharmas really charge the most to recoup their expenses and make a profit. (However, it should be known that even generics in 2018 were becoming much more expensive.) In summary there could be unknown side effects for which patients might sue the company in the following years when those new side effects become apparent.

For the breast cancer drug, the company gave as many of the adverse effects as they knew—in low, hushed tones over the upbeat music, while the viewer sees a very healthy actress moving through a happy life—the medication can cause low white blood counts, which can cause serious infections that lead to death!! (So, taking this drug can lead to your death!) The patient must warn her doctor if she has fever, chills, signs of infection, or liver or kidney problems. Side effects can include low red blood cells, low platelet counts, infections, tiredness, nausea, sore mouth, abnormalities in liver blood tests, diarrhea, hair thinning or loss, vomiting, rash, and loss of appetite (from a commercial, 3-9-18).

In 2017, the FDA approved more new medications than in years past—46 medications were approved, including a pill that can track time taken and the information sent to the doctor. That medication was intended for depression, schizophrenia, and bipolar disorder (*http://fortune.com/2018/01/02/new-drug-approvals/*). The medication sounds amazing when compliance is a concern for those diseases. How wonderful that the pill could inform the doctor about compliance. One wonders, what is the mechanism? How long was that mechanism used in the human body before release?

How do we know if new medications are tested long enough to know everything about how bodies might react in the long term? Are we simply guinea pigs for pharmaceutical companies as they work to push out medications at a breakneck speed?

■ Example: Drug A, meant to lower blood sugar levels for people with Type 2 diabetes.

In March of 2013, the FDA approved it for treatment of Type 2 Diabetes. It was the first SGLT2 inhibitor to be approved in the U.S.

https://drugclaim.com/invokana-history

In true Seinfeld fashion, about a year later patients started complaining about ketoacidosis complications and amputations of limbs. Websites began to advertise for patients to sue the drug company for not informing them of the dangers of Drug A. By 2015 websites began to emerge offering lawsuits to patients who suffered severe adverse events for any of that class of drugs. Here is one of those: *https://www.youtube.com/watch?v=vp0oM0bU5-o*. In the comment section, the firm provided a figure that the reader can look up that gives the name of an agency.

ASK DR. DEAN:

Question 7: What are the time wasters of EMR systems?
Medical records that are in the EMR (electronic medical records) system were developed without appropriate physician input and are much more time-consuming than the previous medical record systems that were mostly handwritten or dictated/typed. Admittedly, that was a faulty system, specifically if handwritten or if another physician or clinic needed a copy of the information. Frequently it was unreadable. So, that ended up being a time waster to get medical information from one place to another, not including the difficulty in interpretation of a non-revealing medical record. In general, transferring medical record information has been a time waster, just due to the hassle of the process.

Karen McDivitt, PhD, started a website for patients who have experienced ill effects from various drugs (*https://drug-claim.com/*). She also co-founded the McDivitt law firm.

One realizes that such websites may have multiple goals, informing patients but also attracting potential clients as the law firms sue drug companies.

Money can be made both by developers bringing out new medication and then by law firms suing companies after further problems with the medications develop. How do we know what to take and what to think? All medications have adverse events, and all those known at the end of the clinical trials are mentioned in the medication inserts. How do we know, as patients, if the medication is safe for us to take?

■ Device Example: One such example is a contraceptive device. The FDA in 2016 issued a "black box" warning on the implantable device in order to encourage more discussion between doctors and women who are considering the device (*https://www. healthline.com/health-news/fda-warning-essure-contraceptive-device#1*), due to women having device migration problems, resultant hysterectomies, pain, perforation of organs, and so on (Sara Joan Swann, 2016, *https://www.healthline.com/health-news/ fda-warning-essure-contraceptive-device#1*).

Physicians continue to implant the device because it is thought that the incidences of problems are low.

Patients should find out everything they can before procedures, particularly elective procedures. Weigh the potential risks and benefits. Talk to the doctor—find out whatever you can about the devices, how long they have been used, what are the possible problems, what do patients who have had it say. Be a part of the decision and don't simply accept everything said without thought. Doing so is not always easy when one is in extreme pain or quite ill, but it is incumbent upon us to try whenever possible.

Again, Predictive Analytics Are Needed

Quality Control and double-blind research designs can greatly help to ensure safety. **But if there were good predictive analytic studies, doctors might be able to predict ahead of time which patients would be okay with the device and which might have problems.**

Predictive analytics research can help even more. Part of the problem when considering adverse events is that medications and devices are devised for groups of people, while individuals are using them. Predictive analytics would help with medication problems because in predictive analytics, medication efficacy is predicted for **the individual**. Many lawsuits could be avoided if medications were only given to those that could most benefit from them—adverse events could be avoided.

Using Predictive Analytics would be helpful in considering:

- Pros and cons of statins (see Ask Dr. Dean Question 5, pp. 108–110)
- Eliminating segments of the population in clinical trials research and then ending up prescribing to them after the medications come out
- Screenings—do they cause more problems than they solve? (We should all know by now that PSA tests should not simply be used as definitive.) The reader is encouraged to read Brawley and Goldberg's (2011) book in which the horrors of one man with a slightly high PSA screening are told. Predictive analytics could help differentiate which patients need treatment and which do not.
- Also, in Brawley and Goldberg (2011) is the tale of Bezwoda—who made up data on bone marrow transplant research (p. 39). Refer to Helen's story above, in which the doctor replied that everyone did it. Again, see the section on maximizing revenues (p. 25).

Could Greed Ever Play Into Medicine?

Predictive analytics could help stop the practice of prescribing medicines to everyone, regardless of how much pharmaceutical companies would like to make a profit from everyone. At one point, doctors were thinking that everyone should be on a statin as a prophylactic—it would not harm anyone and would provide protection. Where might they have gotten such an idea?

Is It Time for Medical Procedures Costs to Be Negotiated and Standardized?

It is time for predictive analytics to be used in that process so that we know which procedures and medications would be good for which patients. Until we know those things, it becomes difficult to accurately standardize procedures and then assign costs. Such is coming, however.

Think: What Could Go Wrong?

Yes, until enough data are available (through interoperability), thus allowing predictive data analytics to develop more accurate individual predictions, we need to think and explore and question as patients. Think, what could go wrong? What could happen to me? Am I willing to live with that adverse event if it should happen to me?

Think about the following, some of which are older and some are being advertised on television at the time of this writing in 2018. What could go wrong?

■ With freezing your fat cells?
■ With using a plastic cup and metal head in a replacement hip or with using the newest knee prosthetic? (At the time of this writing, metal on metal had already been found to be problematic, and so the cup was replaced by plastic ...)
■ With sewing medical mesh over a herniated intestine?
■ With taking a blood pressure medication?
■ With using a device in one's artery intended to catch blood clots before they reach a vital organ, such as the brain or a lung?
■ With putting a stent into one's heart?
■ With getting dental implants?
■ With taking medication to lower A1C rather than losing weight and switching to a better diet?
■ With taking statins?

All the above are easily found on the Internet, and we encourage you to look them up. Particularly before starting a regimen or having an operation, one should look up everything one can find and consider all the known side effects. If the procedure or medication is so new not to have any information, then should you really be trying it? For surgeries, find out how many such operations your surgeon has completed, in what time frame, and how many problems there were. Ask around and find out if your doctor is recommended by others you trust. What kind of anesthesia will be used? Are there side effects for using that anesthesia? For your age group?

Need for More Research and Innovation

Innovation in research from the United States has declined since 2004 (University of Rochester Medical Center (URMC), 2015: *https://www.urmc.rochester.edu/news/story/4233/u.s.-slipping-as-global-leader-in-medical-research.aspx*). Pharmaceutical companies increasingly wish to invest in the late stages of clinical trials (phase III studies) rather than in early stages, because there is an easier path to launching the drugs and a faster payoff. Many fewer dollars are spent on health services, which could potentially help many, and more money is being spent on rare diseases where there are fewer governmental regulations to bringing such medications to market.

Basically, research goes where the money is, whether private or public.

> If current trends continue, the U.S. will be overtaken by China as the global leader in medical R&D in the next ten years. China has already surpassed the U.S. in terms of the size of its science and technology workforce and global share of patents for medical technologies, and is closing the gap in published biomedical research articles (URMC, 2015, par 8).

Of course, it does not help us if China steals our developing technologies:

To get an idea of how much forced technology transfer costs the US, some experts say to look at the costs associated with the theft of trade secrets. Total theft of US trade secrets accounts for anywhere from $180 billion to $540 billion per year, according to the Commission on the Theft of American Intellectual Property—as "the world's principal IP infringer," China accounts for most of that theft (CNN Money, 2018, par 11, *https://money.cnn.com/2018/03/23/technology/china-us-trump-tariffs-ip-theft/index.html*).

Technology theft notwithstanding, it seems there is a tradeoff going on when it comes to innovation. We need regulations for new drug and new devices research so that patients stay safe. Regulations slow down the process and are costlier. Private companies are most anxious to obtain patents and start production. Who can blame them? But due to regulations innovations of those companies are reduced.

Disruption—Change How We Define the Funding Model

Government funding tends to go to **the historically supported elite veteran research groups** (Robert Klein, 2012, *https://www.ncbi.nlm.nih.gov/pmc/articles/PMC3727685/*, par 11). The established research groups have track records, and research that is recognized putting the researcher in a better position to get new funding. Nothing is inherently wrong with that. Experienced people tend to be more knowledgeable. However, it is harder for newer researchers to find stable funding. Klein proposed that the traditional funding cycles be rethought. From timed cycles to focusing on a problem area—in his case, stem cell research. The time period would be longer in his plan because the funding would be thought of as "an

ASK DR. DEAN:

Question 8: What is the importance of a patient's lifestyle?

One of the health issues of concern to physicians, especially primary care physicians and other specialists, is a person's lifestyle and how it relates to general health. It is a difficult problem to deal with, both for the physician as well as the patient.

A medical definition of lifestyle disease is a health problem that is related to the way a person lives. One's life choices affect their health. So, if you smoke, drink alcohol inappropriately, have eating habits that are unhealthy, and are not physically active, the likelihood of developing a lifestyle illness is increased. One related problem to consider is that such illnesses develop very slowly over time, then suddenly the effect of the lifestyle behavior occurs, and curing the problem is difficult to correct or impossible. Therefore, living a healthy lifestyle and avoiding the behavioral lifestyle that causes those illnesses is very important.

A problem that is related to the lifestyle issue is how you deal with your eating habits and consequently your weight. It is very common to have difficulty deciding what is an appropriate diet that is desirable, tasty, and satisfying, but does not lead to weight gain or difficulty losing weight. The advertising of weight loss programs, weight loss clinics, and an unbelievable array of diets is very confusing. How can you make an appropriate decision when there are so many possibilities, and how do you know which would be a help for you? The best way to make that choice of a healthy diet (not for weight loss specifically) is to ask your physician or a dietitian to recommend a source for appropriate diet information.

intellectual capital resource" and separating those funds from operating costs. Klein asks:

> Is medical research an operating cost of the country or society, or is it the 'intellectual capital infrastructure' for the health care system?

Klein, 2012, p. 3

Perhaps we do need to fundamentally rethink funding methods—particularly those from our government. Reframing what we want and how we define our goals can lead to disruption and better ways of operating.

Disruption—Change How We Conduct Medical Research

When I (Linda) was an evaluator for grant proposals at a funding organization, as our group reviewed proposals I continually stressed that what was needed were proposals that focused on individual outcomes, rather than group outcomes, not even small-group outcomes (in which the "small" group was defined as 500 or more individuals). The group became a bit agitated, and in frustration, one person from a prestigious university angrily stated, "But I can't DO that! I can't predict to the individual!"

Given the anger of that utterance, I realized that the people selected to evaluate grants (I was the exception to that) were at the top of their game. These were the major players at well-known institutions who had come up the ladder by hard work and many publications. They also were steeped in the old ways of conducting research and were trying to make their old population algorithms work for smaller and smaller groups without losing validity. I knew they couldn't do it because the models were flawed and dependent on populations, and not because they lacked will, or intelligence, or any other needed element—except for destroying their "tried and true" methods and seeking a different paradigm—and learning new ways. Their entire lives and careers were based on the old paradigms. One could see that it could be difficult to shift grant monies to the newer techniques, slowing the transition to predictive analytics.

The New Paradigm: Predictive Analytics

Predictive Analytics Can Be Used for all Aspects of the "Healthcare Delivery System".

The new paradigm means for all aspects of healthcare delivery system processes used by providers, patients, and payers, including from the business operation of the hospital to the diagnosis of the patient to the discharge and follow up of a patient. Our 2015 book presented 26 tutorials showing how predictive analytics can be used from diagnosing a disease to predicting the number of hospital beds needed, etc. We will not go into more examples of the use of predictive analytics in this book but refer the reader to this 2015 book to find examples of predictive analytics making more accurate methods in provider diagnosis and treatment, payer processes, and patient needs (see Winters-Miner et al., 2015).

Concerns about the US healthcare system expressed over the past 15-plus years:

Others have written about our "broken healthcare system" over the past 10 to 15 years, but even with all this concern, nothing has really been fixed; instead, a complete disruption and re-engineering of our current system must occur.

Here is one example from 2009 expressing the need for a **disruptive solution** for healthcare; numerous additional examples can be found in the **Enrichment Bibliography** at the end of this book, which lists numerous books written by various people on the need for change in the US system.

The Innovator's Prescription: A Disruptive Solution for Health Care (Christensen et al., 1st Edition, 2009)

Clayton M. Christensen is a Harvard Business School professor whose earlier bestselling book, *The Innovator's Dilemma*, revolutionized the business world. In this book (Christensen et. al., 2009) on how to disrupt healthcare for better delivery, he and his co-authors present ideas that can bring about better solutions, as follows:

- ■ "Precision medicine" needs to be embraced as it reduces costs and can provide personalized care
- ■ Disruptive business models improve quality, accessibility, and affordability by changing the way hospitals and doctors work
- ■ Patient networks enable better treatment of chronic diseases
- ■ Employers can change the roles they play in healthcare to compete effectively in providing better and more cost-effective care
- ■ Insurance and regulatory reforms could stimulate disruption in healthcare

Advent of Predictive Analytics—Definitions and Examples:

What are predictive analytics in medicine? The term predictive analytics is becoming more prevalent. When we wrote the book *Practical predictive analytics and decisioning systems for medicine* (Winters-Miner et al., 2015), there were few people talking about the topic. Today, we see the term being used for many fields, from education to business and to medicine. But what does it mean? As mentioned in Chapter 1, predictive analytics analyzes data for individuals rather than for groups of people. There is a place for traditional p value statistics. It might be good to know if medication A works better or worse, overall, than medication B. But predictive analytics strives to answer the question: which medication is best for you—the individual! You don't want to have to use trial and error to know if something will work for you. Predictive algorithms are developed and are tested for accuracy. An algorithm is simply a mathematical combination of the research elements to spit out the outcome: will work for this person or will not work. Or, in the case of the DIC study, this child was at risk for death or not. Without accurate prediction algorithms, trial and error is what your doctor is left with. When my doctor said I needed to take a medication to reduce my blood pressure, we had to try several before finding one that worked. Wouldn't it be better to know which one would work to begin with?

In the field of predictive analytics, much confusion comes from the varying meaning of the word "algorithm." The following provides the definitions that we are using to add precision to the field of predictive analytics.

Definitions

■ **Algorithm**: For the field of mathematics in general, the term algorithm means a process for solving problems. Algorithms are the steps that one follows for completing a solution. Much like a recipe for making cookies, the algorithm specifies what to do first, second, and so on. These steps can easily be programmed into a computer, and mathematical solutions can be found in a standardized way.

■ **Predictive Analytic Algorithms**: These algorithms are specific to machine learning, which has been developed and implemented in predictive analytic problems. These became widely available to researchers from about the year 2000 onward, and the use of which are what we call "modern data analysis" compared to the "P-value traditional statistics" of the 1900s. Algorithms such as classification and regression trees (CRT), neural networks analysis (NNA), boosted trees, MARS splines, and so on are specific for making predictions to individuals. The predictive algorithms may be used separately or in a hybrid fashion.

■ **Solution Algorithms**: Solution algorithms are developed and are tested for accuracy. Without accurate solution algorithms, trial and error is what your doctor is left with. When a researcher uses predictive algorithms, sometimes the best model will be a "hybrid model" that first uses a combination of more than one predictive analytic algorithm; the final "solution algorithm" is generally written out in code, such as PMML or C++ and others. This solution code is a solution algorithm and can be used to deploy to unknown cases. In the DIC study (p. 92) we used the predictive algorithm, boosted trees, and then generated a PMML code of our solution algorithm to be used later for testing accuracy and for making modifications in the future to hone the code for even more accuracy. The reader needs to be aware when reading studies and listening to researchers in the PA field that many predictive algorithms have already been generated. They basically are often referring to their own research, in which they are trying to develop a solution algorithm in one of the coded methods, which makes use of one or more of the already developed predictive algorithms.

Example No 1: Fighting Hospital-Acquired Infections with Predictive Analytics

This example comes out of work done at MGH (Massachusetts General Hospital) and the University of Michigan. The solution algorithm developed predicts a patient's risk of getting a hospital infection (*Clostridium difficile* (C-diff), a potentially deadly healthcare-related infection) better than the doctors can spot the warning signs.

C-diff causes diarrhea, intestinal distress, and in some cases, life-threatening inflammation in a patient's colon. The predictive analytic models developed predicted the infection an average of five days sooner than doctors could, which could mean the difference between life or death (*https://futurism. com/ai-fights-hospital-acquired-infections/*).

Example No 2: Algorithm for Pneumonia

A Stanford team developed a solution algorithm to diagnose pneumonia from X-rays. The researchers, machine learning experts, called their solution algorithm CheXNet, which "is a 121-layer convolutional neural network trained on ChestX-ray14" (Rajpurkar et al., 2017, *https://arxiv.org/ abs/1711.05225*, par 1). CheXNet was more accurate than radiologists in predicting pneumonia in individual patients.

Example No 3: Medical Team uses "Deep Learning" to Help Overworked Diagnosticians

This example comes from a Tel Aviv University lab engineering practical solutions to meet the demands of radiologists who are overburdened in the number of scans they need to read due in one part to a shortage of radiologists. The department of biomedical engineering in the TAU Faculty of Engineering has developed computer-assisted tools for the routine diagnosis of X-rays, CTs, and MRIs. In other words, they are using "deep learning" (deep learning involves a neural network's type of processing—e.g. a machine learning modern PA method) to provide more accurate diagnoses (*https://phys.org/news/2016-04-team-deepoverburdened- diagnosticians.html#nRlv; and https://phys.org/news/2016- 04-team-deep-overburdened-diagnosticians.html#jCp*).

Example No 4: A Predictive Analytic Algorithm Diagnoses Heart Arrhythmias at the Same Level as a Cardiologist

This example comes out of Stanford University (Kubota, 2017). A new machine learning solution algorithm can sift through hours of heart rhythm data generated by some wearable monitors to find sometimes life-threatening irregular heartbeats, called arrhythmias. It performs better than trained cardiologists. And it is able to sort through data from remote locations where people don't have access to cardiologists. People suspected to have an arrhythmia will usually get an electrocardiogram (ECG) in a doctor's office. But if an in-office ECG doesn't reveal the problem, the doctor can have a person wear a portable ECG monitor that continuously sends signals that are recorded in the doctor's office. It would take a doctor or technician many hours to search through hundreds of hours of recorded data to find a heart rhythm abnormality—but the deep learning algorithm can do this in a fraction of a second (*https://techxplore.com/news/2017-07-algorithmheart-arrhythmias-cardiologist-level-accuracy.html#nRlv*).

Example No 5: Computers Learning to find Australian Cancers and Broken Bones that People Miss

A new predictive algorithm, which is an offshoot from CNN (convolutional neural networks) (Shang et al., 2016), was used in Australia to diagnose conditions that doctors missed (Science in Public, 2015, *https://medicalxpress.com/news/2015-10-aus-tralian-cancers-broken-bones-people.html#nRlv*). The Silicon Valley company Enlitic, "founded by Melbourne serial entrepreneur Jeremy Howard" (par 3), uses the deep learning systems to develop solution algorithms for predicting such conditions as missed cancers and broken bones from X-rays, CTs, MRIs, and other medical images. As with all learning systems, "The more data and computing time it gets, the more it learns and the more accurate it becomes" (par 9). This system could help radiologists and even those that are in remote areas, as long as the images can be electronically shared. Algorithms such as this one can find faint patterns in huge amounts of data and help to take the guesswork out of diagnoses.

Example No 6: Predictive Analytics Help Identify the Early Stages of a Stroke.

Survivability requires fast diagnosis and treatment in the case of stroke. Through the information embedded in genes

and made available with Microarray analysis, a data model
has been constructed that can efficiently classify whether
a patient is currently undergoing a stroke. In this model
or solution algorithm, the scientists made use of k-nearest
neighbors (KNN) and principal component analysis (PCA)
to isolate a small number of genes whose combined expression levels could indicate a stroke was in progress. A good
predictive solution model can help classify a patient's
condition as "stroke" or "no stroke," with radiological imaging as the gold-standard test, providing case labels for
training and evaluation in making the model. A technique
proposed by O'Connell et al. (2016) measures the levels of
expression of ten specific genes to determine if a stroke
could be happening (*https://www.elderresearch.com/blog/
analytics-identifies-early-stages-of-strokes*).

**Example No 7: Success at University of Iowa
Hospitals in Preventing Surgical Site Infection
by Use of Real-Time Predictive Analytic Model
In the Surgical Suite during Surgery**

The University of Iowa Hospitals and Clinics has experienced a 74% drop in infections due to a predictive modeling program focused on surgical sites. John Cromwell,
M.D., a clinical associate professor of surgery at the
University of Iowa, is the leader of this project. His team
used a combination of processes, technology, and human
factors in order to leverage live surgical data that was
needed to inform decisions regarding the model—and
does this in real time, right in the operating room, before
closure of the surgical wound. After feeding critical last-
minute real-time data from the operating room into the
model, a decision is instantly output by the predictive
analytic model, which allows the surgeon to decide which
method of wound closure is most appropriate for this
unique individual patient. Surgical site infections are probably the most costly complication of surgery and the leading source of readmission for patients to the hospital, thus
reducing this both saves money and importantly greatly
reduces the risk of complications for the patient.

REFERENCES for John Cromwell, M.D., University of Iowa Real Time Predictive Analytic Diagnosis Model

- Chapter 24 by John Cromwell in 2015. *PRACTICAL PREDICTIVE ANALYTICS and DECISIONING SYSTEMS FOR MEDICINE: Informatics Accuracy and Cost-Effectiveness for Healthcare Administration and Delivery Including Medical Research.* Boston, MA: ELSEVIER/ ACADEMIC PRESS.
- Tutorial D by John Cromwell in 2015. *PRACTICAL PREDICTIVE ANALYTICS and DECISIONING SYSTEMS FOR MEDICINE: Informatics Accuracy and Cost-Effectiveness for Healthcare Administration and Delivery Including Medical Research.* Boston, MA: ELSEVIER/ ACADEMIC PRESS.
- Winters-Miner et al. (2015). PRACTICAL *PREDICTIVE ANALYTICS and DECISIONING SYSTEMS FOR MEDICINE: Informatics Accuracy and Cost-Effectiveness for Healthcare Administration and Delivery Including Medical Research.* Boston, MA: ELSEVIER/ACADEMIC PRESS.
- *https://iowamedical.org/iowa/Iowa_Public/Public_Affairs/ Spotlights/2016/John_Cromwell_MD_Reviews_Success_of_ Predictive_Analytics_at_University_of_Iowa.aspx.*
- Millard, M., 2016: *https://www.healthcareitnews.com/news/ university-iowa-slashes-surgical-site-infections-74-through- predictive-analytics*

Example No 8: Eye Disease Diagnoses as Accurate with AI (Artificial Intelligence = Predictive Analytic Algorithms) as with Doctors

A study by **Moorfields Eye Hospital** in London and the Google company **DeepMind** found that a machine could learn to read complex eye scans and detect more than 50 eye conditions. A team at DeepMind based in London created a solution algorithm, to enable a computer to analyze optical coherence tomography (OCT), a high resolution 3-D scan of the back of the eye. Thousands of scans were used to train the machine how to read the scans. Then the computer was asked to give a diagnosis in the cases of 1,000 patients whose clinical outcomes were already known. The same scans were shown to eight clinicians—four leading ophthalmologists and four optometrists. Each was asked to make one of four referrals: urgent, semi-urgent, routine, and observation only. The predictive analytic algorithm performed as well as two of the world's leading retina specialists, with an error rate of only 5.5%. But more importantly, the solution algorithm did not miss a single urgent case (DeFauw et al. (2018, August 13; "Clinically applicable deep learning for diagnosis and referral in retinal disease." *Nature Medicine. www.nature.com/articles/s41591-018-0107-6; 2018: https://www.bbc.com/news/health-44924948.*).

The above was also reported in the following places in mid-August 2018:

- *https://phys.org/news/2018-08-artificial-intelligence-equal-experts-eye.html*
- De Fauw et al. (2018). "Clinically applicable deep learning for diagnosis and referral in retinal disease" *Nature Medicine.* DOI: 10.1038/s41591-018-0107-6
- *https://phys.org/journals/nature-medicine/*
- *https://www.forbes.com/sites/samshead/2018/08/13/ google-deepminds-ai-can-detect-50-eye-disease-conditions-and-save-sight/#7b4fabaf27f3* (DeepMind, a Google-owned artificial intelligence company, has developed an AI system that can accurately identify 50 different types of eye condition as accurately as a doctor)
- *https://www.upi.com/Health_News/2018/08/14/ Research-Artificial-intelligence-quickly-accurately-detects-eye-diseases/1941534254224/*
- *https://www.theverge.com/2018/8/13/17670156/ deepmind-ai-eye-disease-doctor-moorfields*

ASK DR. DEAN:

Question 9: What benefits have you experienced after 40years of family medical practice?

Experience is important! Over the course of my career I was exposed to many different issues in medicine (including delivering babies, which I did 300 times). I am a family medicine physician, which means that my practice accepts patients who have any medical problem. If I am able to diagnose the problem, then treatment is provided. If the problem cannot be diagnosed by me or additional examination or a procedure is needed, then it is my responsibility to make a referral to another physician in an appropriate specialty. Based on my experience as described, over time I was able to diagnose and treat most patients who presented to my practice. The variety of cases and the relationship that was developed with individual patients was the most rewarding aspect of that work.

BAD STATISTICS—GOLD STANDARDS— MODERN PREDICTIVE ANALYTICS

Bad Statistics

Most doctors and associated medical researchers did not learn how to use 20th century Fischerian (p-value type) traditional statistics correctly. Thus a good percentage (up to 70–95%, depending on the journal) of medical research papers either present incorrect statistics or interpret the statistics incorrectly (see Nisbet, Miner, and Yale, 2018, Chapter 20 for a list of references/documentation; also Winters-Miner et al., 2015).

Gold Standards

As previously stated, **gold standards** or **standards of care** are used by doctors, as at present, these are the best solutions that they have had for healthcare delivery. However, the gold standards have been based on potentially flawed research and actually may have little or no scientific proof ...

The gold standards have usually been based on evidence-based medicine and at best are developed from research to the mean instead of the individual. Only reliance on two things will correct these **misuses and misunderstandings** of what EBM should be about and lead to "Real EBM":

1. Adding genomics—genetic differences in individual people (which means, among other things, individual differences in response to medications and treatments), and
2. Ruthlessly well-done predictive analytics, where the individual (and not the "mean" or "group" of a human population ...) is provided, by the doctor, as an accuracy of results for just the patient—as an individual for how that person will react to any drug/medication or treatment, and thus the patient can decide prior to receiving the drug, treatment, surgery, etc. whether the probability of it being effective for them is "worth it."
    What this means is that:
    a. the medical delivery field has to do an about-face in how they think about and how they act in providing treatments for the individual patient, and
    b. medical research has to do an about-face, which means **firing their misuse of p value/multiple p tests research** and embracing fully predictive analytics methods where the individual is the focus (instead of the mean of the human population, which is currently still the case even though the modern PA methods have been available to medical research since about the year 2000, nearly 20 years ago!!!!).

In the future, many more studies will be done to find good predictive algorithms for treatments, medications, outcomes, surgery procedures, and so on. If researchers have access to accurate data, this dream can become a reality.

Source for Data: Portals and Wearable/Handheld Devices

Medical practices are increasingly using portals. Patients are going online to review notes from their recent visit, to obtain lab results, and to communicate with their healthcare personnel. Patients are increasingly using wearable devices that track exercise, heart rhythms, blood pressure, and even if the person is dizzy and potentially falling. Recently there is a device that can track one's heart rhythm. All these numbers can be sent to the person's portal for the healthcare personnel to review. The numbers from wearable devices are what is known as **hard data**. If researchers had access to portal data, more predictive analytic studies could be conducted.

Doctors can also use web-based apps to help them in their practices (Reisenwitz, 2018: *https://blog.capterra.com/top-7-medical-apps-for-doctors/*). These apps can help them with calculations and with up-to-date information concerning diagnoses and treatments, as well as drug information and interactions.

There are also television apps that allow doctors and patients to have a visit online. Telemedicine apps are becoming more popular all the time (Katz, 2018), with many healthcare clinics using virtual medicine such as Kaiser Permanente, the Cleveland Clinic, Intermountain Healthcare, Dignity Health, and Avera Health (p. 60). Virtual care allows for home care in which the patient can stay at home, saving time, especially if the patient is far from a clinic, and saving transportation for doctors who wish to make home visits. In addition, conditions can be treated earlier and chronic conditions can be monitored more easily and efficiently, with first-class care anywhere (p. 59).

Data Solution—The Need for Interoperability with Data Among Healthcare Delivery Facilities

Patients could give permission for researchers to use their data to help with predictive analytic projects—this would greatly help getting sufficient data and a sufficient number of different variables to allow making **predictive analytic** models that predict at high rates of accuracy, e.g. in the 90+ percentage range.

Patients should absolutely consider allowing researchers access to portal data. The parameters of such access need to be specified and agreed upon so that patient confidentiality is preserved. Those parameters should also include open access to all qualified research projects so that data are not hoarded by a single entity. Patients should own their data and not researchers.

CORE COMPONENTS Needed for SUCCESSFUL HEALTHCARE SOLUTIONS

Here are some of the core things needed for new healthcare models—core adjustments that must be made in order to be effective both in reducing costs and providing superior patient experiences:

- ■ Use of new smart technologies
- ■ Targeted therapeutics
- ■ Smart diagnostics

- Advanced predictive analytics/informatics … this is needed at each phase/each component of healthcare delivery, from making diagnoses accurate, to keeping the right amount and right kind of supplies in stock in the medical delivery locations, to making billing and reimbursement transparent
- All phases of healthcare deliverable "understandable"—straightforward—simple for the patient's understanding …
- Digital (includes cell phone diagnoses from anywhere …)

This will redefine healthcare as:

- Less reactive
- Less dependent on traditional facilities
- Less dependent on acute interventions
- Instead, dependent on proactive management of health
- More people remaining healthier for longer periods of time (of their lives)
- Thus more people will have FEWER HOSPITAL STAYS and almost NO READMISSIONS
- Healthcare will move to PRECISION MEDICINE

CHANGE IS COMING: Patients First—Patients at the Center of Their Healthcare—The Patient as CEO

The idea of PATIENTS FIRST—patients being at the center of healthcare delivery, or the patient as CEO of their care—is a concept we have held for some time. It involves servanthood of the payers and providers to the patient, and in many aspects was the way healthcare was delivered prior to the 1960s in the USA, back when doctors even made house calls.

But this changed drastically as corporations needed to find ways to attract workers when there were worker shortages after WWII and the Korean War of the early 1950s. This is when corporations started providing ***healthcare benefits*** to their employees. Employers providing healthcare benefits was seemingly innocent at first, but this change has been the arrow that has thrust the USA into its current position of runaway healthcare costs, runaway **double digit** inflation on pharmaceuticals, medical education costs that take a doctor a lifetime to pay off, and all the other things that have made US healthcare one of the worst among the industrialized nations.

Change is coming, however. Even at 2018's HIMSS (the big healthcare conference held each March), keynote talks were given on the importance of making the "patient first." To do this, things like "interoperability" and "having all data in one place" were emphasized. These things are essential to make better and more accurate PREDICTIVE ANALYTIC models, and thus place the emphasis on the "individual" (and not "group") patient for any one diagnosis. (Reference: "Seema Verma rolls out new CMS interoperability initiatives at HIMSS18: *https://www.healthcareitnews.com/news/seema-verma-rolls-out-new-cms-interoperability-initiatives-himss18?.*)

Interoperability is essential for any of the five "healthcare solutions" we present in the last chapter, Chapter 7. This is very important and cannot be overemphasized!

What is needed in interoperability is an overall architecture that can umbrella any of the current, diverse EMR systems. Currently the systems cannot communicate with one another, and an overall architecture could alleviate that fault, allowing for better and more accurate communications between institutions and medical personnel—and is the reason that in othe countries, patients can carry their own smart card which can be read at any healthcare facility. Please see the article by Tom Sullivan on September 19, 2018, in *Healthcare IT News*, "Interoperability needs an architecture in addition to APIs", HIMSS CTIO Steve Wretling says: *https://www.healthcareitnews. com/news/interoperability-needs-architecture-addition-apis-himss-ctio-steve-wretling-says?mkt_tok=eyJpIjoiTURjeU9XVm-*

lNbUZtTldZeCIsInQiOiI3a0xXNWVTOXM4NG9TT2lyZ-DR6QTlxQTU5Q1p4NDhQRHp1S04xM2l1cUtSa2RHW GgwNmlsV1BhMlhzTWFDUDVsZDFBY2ZUOE5VRXlGO-XpzZiszaU5NeUFPZlhHZnVjZnA1ZFZXZlZUZ2haeW1UZzM 0eUZGR2hSNkZKaDU2YU1nayJ9.

References

Brawley, O.W. and Goldberg, P. (2011). *How We Do Harm.* New York: St. Martin's Press.

Chandnani, H., Goldstein, M., Khichi, M., Miner, L.A., and Tinsley, C. (2018). Prediction Model for Mortality in Patients with Disseminated Intravascular Coagulopathy Based on Pediatric ICU Admission: Three Factors Identified. *9th World Congress on Pediatric Intensive and Critical Care 2018*, Singapore. PICC8-0680. Oral Presentation.

Christensen, C.M., Grossman, J.H. and Hwang, J. (2009). *The Innovator's Prescription: A Disruptive Solution for Health Care.* 1st Edition. New York: McGraw-Hill Education.

Christensen, C.M., Grossman, J.H. and Hwang, J., *The Innovator's Prescription: A Disruptive Solution for Health Care* 1st Edition; New York: McGraw-Hill Education, 2009; reprinted as paperback 2016.

Cromwell, J. (2015). Chapter 24 (p. 1040) in *Practical Predictive Analytics and Decisioning Systems for Medicine: Informatics Accuracy and Cost-Effectiveness for Healthcare Administration and Delivery Including Medical Research.* Boston, MA: Elsevier/Academic Press.

Cromwell, J. (2015). "Tutorial D." in *Practical Predictive Analytics and Decision Systems for Medicine: Informatics Accuracy and Cost-Effectiveness for Healthcare Administration and Delivery Including Medical Research.* Boston, MA: Elsevier/Academic Press.

Han, B., et al. (2017). "Effect of statin treatment vs usual care on primary cardiovascular prevention among older adults – The ALLHAT-LLT (Antihypertensive and Lipid-Lowering Treatment to Prevent Heart Attack Trial–Lipid-Lowering Trial) Randomized Clinical Trial." *JAMA Intern Med.* Doi: 10.1001/jamainternmed.2017.1442

Hernandez, D. and Greenwald, T. (2018, August 11). "Can Watson cure cancer?" *The Wall Street Journal.*

Katz, D.L. (2018, February/March). "Is this the future of medicine?" *The AARP Magazine.*

Klein, R. (2012).A new paradigm for funding medical research. *Stem Cells Translational Medicine* 1: 3–5.

Kwaan, M.R., Studdert, D.M., Zinner, M.J. and Gawande, A.A. (2006). "Incidence, patterns, and prevention of wrong-site surgery." *Archives of Surgery*, 141: 353–358. https://psnet.ahrq.gov/resources/resource/3621.

Moon, M.A. (2017, May 24). Statins – No Benefit As Primary Prevention In Elderly 2917." *E-Cardiology News.* https://www.mdedge.com/ecardiologynews/article/138907/preventive-care/statins-no-benefit-primary-prevention-elderly.

Naik, G. (2011, August 10). "Mistakes in scientific studies surge." *Wall Street Journal Eastern Edition*: A1–A12.

O'Connell, G., Petrone, A., Treadway, M., Tennant, C., Lucke-Wold, N., Chantler, P., and Barr, T. (2016). "Machine-learning approach identifies a pattern of gene expression in peripheral blood that can accurately detect ischaemic stroke." *Genomic Medicine*, 1(16038). Doi:10.1038/npjgenmed.2016.38. Retrieved from: https://www.nature.com/articles/npjgenmed201638.

Pyzdek, T. (2003). *The Six Sigma Handbook.* New York: McGraw-Hill.

Shang, W., Sohn, K., Almeida, D., and Lee, H. (2016). Understanding and Improving Convolutional Neural Networks via Concatenated Rectified Linear Units. *Proceedings of the 33rd International Conference on Machine Learning.* New York, NY, USA, JMLR: 48.

Sullivan, T. (2018). "Amazon, Google, IBM, Microsoft, Oracle and Salesforce Pledge to Remove Interoperability Barriers." https://www.healthcareitnews.com/news/amazon-google-ibm-microsoft-oracle-and-salesforce-pledge-remove-interoperability-barriers?

Winters-Miner, L.A., Bolding, P.S., Hilbe, J.M., Goldstein, M., Hill T., Nisbet, R., Walton, N., and Miner, G.D. (2015). *Practical Predictive Analytics and Decisioning Systems for Medicine.* Boston, MA: Elsevier/Academic Press.

Chapter 5

The "Right" Paradigms for Maintaining One's Best Health

It is time for us to "go to the doctor" differently. We have "patiently" sat back and waited for the doctor to do something to make us well. Now, I'm not talking about confrontation, disrespect, or rudeness. Rather, I'm talking about assuming more responsibility for our own health, particularly when something goes wrong. I'm talking about more partnering with the medical community rather than assuming they will know everything there is to know about our condition. And I'm talking about finding ways to prevent illness so that we don't need to "go to the doctor." In other words, I'm talking about patient-directed medical care (Chapter 14 of Winters-Miner et al., 2015).

Maintaining one's best health is in the person's best interest, naturally. There are ways in which we can do just that. We must be both involved and empowered to do so. We are the ones who, ultimately, direct our own medical path. We call this patient-directed medicine. Patient direction involves our communication skills, becoming consumers of medicine, considering how we pay for our medical care, and how we

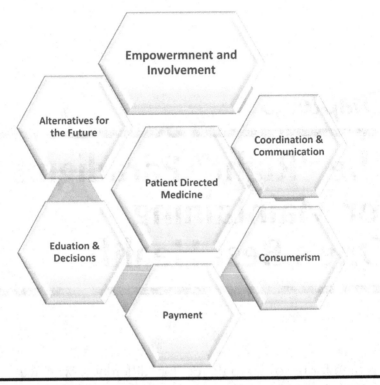

Figure 5.1 The empowered patient. (Winters-Miner et al. [2015, p. 206].)

educate ourselves, which impacts all the other areas. In addition, we need to become aware of future trends with also might affect each of the areas of empowerment (Figure 5.1).

We must depart from old attitudes about medical care. In the past, we visited the doctor with our ailment and expected our healthcare professionals to "fix us." They knew; we didn't. Illness "happened to us," and was beyond our immediate control, or at least so we thought.

The new paradigm is self-direction. Certainly, events may simply happen to us; for example, accidents or perhaps our genetic endowment may cause us to become vulnerable to maladies. However, many conditions are preventable and in our own control (Please see the CDC's The Power of Prevention article found at: *https://www.cdc.gov/chronicdisease/ pdf/2009-Power-of-Prevention.pdf*). In the cited CDC article, we find that 75% of healthcare costs are for chronic conditions: heart disease and stroke, cancer, diabetes, arthritis, obesity, respiratory diseases, and poor oral health (our teeth!!). These conditions are highly related. More weight makes for strain on our joints, and osteoarthritis can result. Type 2 Diabetes implies obesity and respiratory diseases (asthma), heart disease, and even cancer—all are related. Poor oral health can affect our hearts. Respiratory diseases, such as sleep apnea, might make us sleep with our mouths open, and that can be a cause of tooth decay. Tooth decay may lead to an infection that goes to our hearts. Smoking, if we either smoke or live with someone who smokes, can lead to lung cancer, COPD, and respiratory diseases. Addictions, such as in our current opioid crises, lead to ill-health, and often, death.

In other words, our own behaviors contribute to our well-being or lack thereof. Trust me, people who smoke wish they were not addicted to cigarettes. People who are fat think about their girth each day, wishing they had enough "will power" to eat less and exercise more. I am not trying to lay on the guilt! But honestly, we control a lot of our health, and if we could eliminate bad behaviors, our health would improve, and we could avoid medical care, thus saving money! Cha-ching!!

In more detail, the following are common threats to our health. Some we can control and some we cannot. However, we can control some aspects of nearly all of them, mentioned in the solutions for each section.

Directing Our Health: Threats to Our Health—And Some Solutions

There are quite a lot of things that threaten our health. The following lists just some of them. None of us makes it out of here alive—we all die of something. That something is partly in our control and partly not. We should try to change what we can to increase our longevity and our quality of life while here. (Please note, I, Linda, am not a physician, so you should consider any of my homespun advice just that. I am not dispensing medical advice—consult your doctor for your medical treatment. However, I endeavor to base my comments on research—except the vinegar part. Regardless, do not consider any of the below to be medical advice.)

Age

Aging is something we cannot help if we continue to live. Age is associated with death. The older we are, the more likely it is that we will die. Age is one of those variables that is both a blessing and a curse.

> Solution: In our youth society, we often try to make ourselves look younger. Instead, we should be doing things that help our bodies **be** younger—such as keeping our weight at a reasonable level (not necessarily thin, however—people who have a little fat on them tend to do better in old age than people who are very thin). We can exercise (but again, not too much—we only have so many steps that we can climb until our joints give out—though moderate exercise is good for them). We need to keep as many of our own joints as possible. Prosthetic joints bring problems of their own, over time. So, we should eat moderately, exercise moderately, laugh a lot, and make time for friends and family. If we are old, get a pet. (Not a hoard of pets, just a pet.) Pets help us live longer, especially if we need to walk them.

High Cost of Medications

I wanted to renew a prescription, and the medication that just a few months ago cost about $50 now costs $250! Unless something happens, we'll all go broke trying to get our medications that help us live longer.

> Solution: What is the answer? Don't need medications. Perhaps I can find another way to overcome the symptoms that I'm having so I won't need the medication. I think I've found an alternative, but I needed to Google many things to get there. We need to be smart. We are not victims. (In fact, I did find an alternate route—works better and for pennies rather than hundreds of dollars!) However, many people must have a certain medication to live and if they cannot afford the medication, it is a very real and dangerous problem that we as a society **must** address!

Lack of Exercise; Easy Chairs; Sitting at Work

In our society, unless we have a job such as construction work, landscaping, or some other physical job, many of us are in an office sitting most of the day. Regardless of our job, often when we get home, we want to rest. We do have things to do at home, such as cleaning, washing, and so on, but, in the United States we mostly tend towards sedentary lifestyles. (See Figure 5.2.)

Oh, how Gary and I love sitting in our lounger chairs—push the button and let it cradle our tired, aching bodies, lie back and watch TV. What is wrong with that picture? Follow this link and you'll find that up to 80% of us tend to be sedentary (*https://stateofobesity.org/physical-inactivity/*). A sedentary lifestyle is unhealthy. Asthma gets worse, for example. And the worse the asthma, the more the person wants to rest. Learn about asthma, a very common illness, here: *https://www.ncbi.nlm.nih.gov/pubmedhealth/PMH0072704/.* There are so very many illnesses and

Okay, Mr. Wilson, which is it to be - six pack abs from diet and exercise, or six packs with fries and six feet under?

Figure 5.2   Speaking the truth. (Cartoon by Linda Miner.)

conditions that are either caused by or exacerbated by lack of exercise. Go to this NIH article to see them (*https://www. ncbi.nlm.nih.gov/pmc/articles/PMC4241367/*)—some of those diseases are depression, heart disease, insulin resistance, obesity, various cancers, arthritis (both rheumatoid and oste-oid), type 2 diabetes, fatty liver disease, and on and on. We help to create our own problems!

> Solution: If I am sedentary, I need to start exercis-ing—I need a dog to walk!! I must make myself get up and move—there's always housework and yard work. I can stand up to grade papers or write books. I have a great place to do that in the kitchen (coun-ters and island), and I am standing now as I write and can see Gary working in his garden. I can go

Figure 5.3   Vicious Circle.

online and find physical therapy exercises that will relieve my aches and pains. I need to get going. Am I alone here?

We need moderate amounts of exercise to keep our muscles functioning well. Exercise is also important for our brain functioning. If we spend all our time at a desk at work and then come home and sit in an easy chair because we are (quite naturally) tired, we will soon become run down and need more prescriptions (which will cost us a bunch of money and require us to work more)!! This process becomes a **Vicious Circle**! (Figure 5.3).

Overeating—Especially Sugar and White Flour

If you are like me, you love anything with sugar in it. I do believe it's addictive. Those in the food industry count on it being addictive—they add it to just about everything. There are things that make us sick, and sugar is one of those things. Sugar and foods that turn to sugar (glucose) in our bodies are harmful if overeaten. The body turns many foods into sugar (for a good explanation of carbohydrates and which are most and least harmful, see this Q&A site (*http://goaskalice.columbia.edu/answered-questions/confused-about-carbs-whats-good-carbohydrate-choice*)), and then the body must deal with all that glucose. The body turns the sugar into fat cells; sugar increases in the blood; the body has a hard time with all the sugar; diabetes can develop. Sugar doesn't cause diabetes, but it does not help—sugar can make us fatter and less sensitive to insulin. Our bodies have trouble managing too much sugar. Eating a lot of sugar will eventually make us get prescriptions, and we all know that prescriptions cost a bundle of money. Moral of this tale: Don't eat sugar or carbohydrates!! It's a **Vicious Circle**!

> Solution: First try to figure out how much sugar we eat. Then try to cut back on it. I once went without sugar for a year and a half. Only the first week was the truly hard time. But sugar called me back, and like the addict I am, I'm eating sugar again! Author, take your own advice!! I tell you what—I'll try the above and report back by the time we finish this book to let you know what happens. (The book is nearly finished, and I'm still addicted to sugar—but have cut way back on it, so that is good. Little steps!)

Physician Burnout

Something we don't always consider as a threat to our health. We go to doctors when we burn out and feel depressed. What if our doctor feels burned out and depressed? Burnout among physicians has increased in the past ten years or so—and with little wonder. Dike Drummond, M.D., listed a number of reasons, from the stress, working with sick people all day, working too hard, working too many hours, paperwork, documentation regulations, and changing organizational structures (*https://www.thehappymd.com/blog/bid/295048/physician-burn-out-why-its-not-a-fair-fight*). Getting paid is a struggle, with all the insurance companies, when the patients are oblivious and worse, when the patients "receive their care with no personal investment on their part." Politics makes for uncertainty, there is a fear of lawsuits, and after a time, the job becomes routine with its concomitant boredom.

One major threat to our health is that our doctors may take early retirements—if burnout afflicts our doctor, then perhaps this person who has known us for many years decides to give up his or her position due to burnout. The reader is encouraged to read the Canadian article by Dewa et al. (2014, *http//:www.biomedcentral.com/1472-6963/14/254*). In Canada at that time, family physicians accounted for 58.8% of the burnout costs among physicians. It is likely to be higher in the United States, due to all the uncertainties in governmental regulations. Patients really count on their primary care physicians, and when we find someone we can readily communicate with, losing that person for any reason can be detrimental to our health.

> Solution: We need to do something about our health-care system for the sake of the physicians and allied health workers as much as for the patients. The situation will not change much until we figure out a decent payment system or systems. Certainly, we want our physicians to use excellent science and to be efficient. But should they have to spend hours at night when they get home to do the governmental required paperwork?

> Solution: Are we patients making our doctors' lives miserable? Do we demand antibiotics even when our doctors say we don't need them (see superbug section)? Do we not take responsibility for doing what we can to stay healthy and then demand that they fix us? Do we use good or bad communication skills

in visiting with our doctors? Are we grateful for what they do? Do we treat the staff with respect, while at the same time realize that we do have a say in our own treatment? Respect ourselves; respect others.

Super Germs

If truth be told, people do like to get prescriptions from their healthcare workers. The prescription helps us feel validated in having visited our clinics. If we feel terrible, surely a pill should be able to help us. We have a sore throat, hacking cough, feel tired, and drag ourselves to the doctor. Our temperature is 99 degrees, for goodness sake. Surely, we need an antibiotic! If we get a prescription for an antibiotic, then we feel validated somehow—the doctor has agreed we are ill. We ARE sick! If the doctor says that the symptoms most likely are a virus that is going around and that we don't really have a fever and there is not a need for an antibiotic, then we must go home to fight the virus on our own (too late for Tamiflu) and feel even more miserable. No help on the way!

Or worse, we can feel we have overexaggerated our symptoms—which could lead to our becoming the **difficult patient**. We encourage the reader to watch Elaine from the show *Seinfeld* as she finds out her doctor labeled her a "difficult patient" in her medical record. One may laugh—but becoming a "difficult–patient" is not that difficult, particularly for women! Here is a link: *https://www.youtube.com/watch?v=7KXUVDUN2NM.*

Solution: In the above scenario in which no antibiotic is forthcoming from the physician, the doctor has likely done us a favor. Superbugs are making their way into our population. These bugs will not respond to the antibiotics we now have. Using antibiotics unnecessarily is helping to usher them in. We should not press our doctors to give us antibiotics.Solution: Besides reducing overuse of known antibiotics, the use of bacteriophage cocktails is gaining interest (Abedon, Kuhl, Blasdel, and Kutter, 2011; Ozkan, et al, 2016; Pallavali, et al, 2017). Disgusting to think about, bacteriophages, are harvested from sewage. As there are over 10 to the power of 32, or 10 with 32 zeros following, different bacteriophages, they must be researched and targeted for specific bacteria strains. The bacteriophages must be paired with the specific bacterium that they kill in order to work. If matching occurs, the phages eat up the bacteria without hurting healthy tissues. Phages can even be used with antibiotics. Obviously, much research is needed in this area, and would be a great predictive analytic project, perhaps by using the rule builder in the weight of evidence module in TIBCO-Statistica Software.

World Wide Transportation (Spread of Epidemics)

We all must remember the West African Ebola outbreak of 2014. It was the largest of its kind, and it came to the United States, among other nations, infecting 11 people here, with two deaths. As of this writing in 2018, Ebola has reemerged in the Democratic Republic of the Congo and seems to be increasing. Hemorrhagic illnesses are some of the most frightening that can occur. We seem not to be able to eradicate Ebola, and until researchers develop vaccines, the best defense is not to be exposed.

We live in an ever-contracting world with our transportation systems. One index (first infected person) can infect a plane full of people, who then can infect a myriad of others as

ASK DR. DEAN:

NOTE: Please see APPENDIX for "DR. DEAN'S HOME HEALTH KIT" description, which can supplement some of the specific information for ailments that are described below in this chapter's "Ask Dr. Dean."

Question 1: What is the VALUE of having a "FAMILY DOCTOR"?

A common pattern of medical care for many people in the past was to have a "family doctor" for most healthcare issues. In such an arrangement, there was a commitment of each to the other—the patient to the doctor and the doctor to the patient. Currently, in 2019, most patients do not really have a "family doctor," as was the case for many people even as recently as five years ago and certainly not like 10 years ago and decades in the past. Why is that true now?

There are several current ideas about personal medical care that have contributed to this change:

1. Whereas in the past patients had access to "their doctor" at least five or six days per week and a back-up doctor the other two days (except when their doctor was on "weekend call"), presently their doctor's office closes (in most cases) on Friday at noon, and the doctor is not available again until Monday. If one calls a doctor's office on Friday afternoon, until Monday morning the recorded message refers you to the emergency room of a hospital or to an urgent care. This may inhibit the patient from further pursuing their concern, delaying it until the next Monday workday. Or, if they do call the "alternative emergency/urgent care" facility, this alone can tend to disrupt an otherwise interdependent doctor/patient relationship where the doctor and patient understand each other and benefit greatly from that relationship.

2. The number of doctors who have a private practice has been progressively decreasing over the last several years. Instead, these doctors are taking on salaried practices in hospitals, clinics, and other practice facilities. Some of the reasons for this include college/medical school/residency debt; the cost of setting up a practice, which includes hiring and paying staff, technology acquisition, and the cost of programs and upkeep. These costs, plus the schooling debt, are extremely expensive, and rarely are new physicians able to shoulder those costs, as the expense may take decades to repay. This is especially true for those wanting to do primary family care practice in more rural areas and/or mission work in inner cities or third-world countries.

3. One solution to the costs (for the physician) and the changes in the format of practice settings referred to above is for a new physician to become employed by a hospital, clinic, or other entity involved in patient care. In a survey by the American Medical Association in 2012 (the most recent), 40% of physicians owned their practice and 58% were employed, with 3% serving as independent contractors. The number of doctors in private practice (owning the practice) as of 2014 was 31%. Obviously, the number of independent doctors is getting smaller and smaller.

4. The division of responsibilities for patient care includes office diagnosis/treatment, hospital care, emergency care, and also after-hours care, which is handled by different doctors and probably a variety of doctors depending on the time of day and other factors, rather than a patient's "chosen family doctor." This is a further splintering of medical care from how it was delivered in times past. This is a major disruptor, causing the current "chaos" in healthcare delivery, making it

such that an older person may need to "hire a service" to help them maneuver around all the in's and out's (barriers) to getting the care they need.

5. Another cause of the change in patient–doctor relationship is that the workload that previously was "normal" for a doctor is now divided among several people and even more than one "medical organization." To allow doctors to live a more "normal life" (e.g., have evening and weekends free for their families, etc.), over the years there were some halfway solutions developed, which included having several doctors share after-hours call. Even then, it was typical for many doctors to work long laborious hours each day, with some reprieve when the doctor was not the one "on-call" for an evening or weekend. Vacation time was unusual. Additionally, there were many extra hours, not for managing patient care, but for required meetings such as medical staff meetings, continuing medical education meetings to maintain medical competence and licensure, and others. Then there were after-hours patient care and calls (including calls and issues in the middle of the night from patients, emergency rooms, or hospital patient issues). These issues needed resolution not only for the mental and physical health of the physicians, but also for a way to "EFFECTIVELY" meet the healthcare needs of patients. There was no obvious solution; this need for constant awareness and attentiveness on the doctor's part is not humanly possible. The younger generations of doctors have not been willing to work these kinds of schedules. So this unwillingness on the part of doctors to play the role of the "old family doctor" has been a contributing factor to the chaotic/broken/uncommitted relationship problem between doctors and patients.

they land and disperse. If intentionally done, exposing a plane would become an act of terrorism.

Solution: There will always be epidemics—viruses and bacteria find ways to mutate. Whether those pathogens develop into pandemics depends greatly on agencies that screen people when they board and disembark from transportation modes. When there are epidemics, one can decide not to travel and can stay away from places in which large numbers of people frequent. We all hope that scientists are working hard for cures for the various hemorrhagic diseases and other infectious agents. The black plague is still a possible disease, but modern medicine can now control the plague, as opposed to, say, bloodletting and cupping during the Middle Ages. Truly, the more densely we populate the earth, the greater the risk of pandemics. If we were to try to control our population proliferation, there would be more space between people and less chance of germ transmission.

Salad Bars and Church Buffets

Speaking of contagion, food bars at restaurants and institutional get-togethers are a major way in which we humans spread diseases. We share serving utensils with everyone who has selected the foods we select. Glass used at restaurants provides a barrier to the germs we breathe and sneeze out over the food, but sometimes we have to kind of duck under the glass to reach the foods the restaurant places toward the back. Of course, at sit-down restaurants, we grab the germy arms of the chair to scoot up and often reuse menus that are laden with germs and pick up salt shakers others have used earlier in the evening. Then we pick up our roll with our fingers and eat the germs that have been thus transported to said roll. Further, if we later visit our doctor with our virus running wild, we transport our germs to the arms of the chair we sit in during our wait, thus transmitting the virus to the next person who sits there; a person who also will not get a prescription for an antibiotic, and who also has made a useless trip to the doctor. Germs are very smart.

> Solution: Be like my Great Aunt Mary, who would never go to a restaurant. She could outcook any of them and saved a ton of money. She was Scottish. Be like one of our children and carry hand sanitizer, lavishly used at each meal eaten out. Suffer through illnesses until your immune system is so strong that nothing gets through to you, a habit another of our children practices. Most of the time, we worry too much about germs. Our bodies were designed to fight their own battles when it comes to germs. Unless absolutely swamped by some horrible virulent assault, our bodies can create their own antibodies. We need to keep our bodies healthy by eating the right kinds of foods and using the right vitamins and minerals to aid our bodies, like zinc when exposed to a cold. Whenever I get a sore throat from someone with a cold, I spray my throat with vinegar— which really stings—but then the sore throat goes away, and I generally stay healthy from common pathogens. (My family equates me with Michael Constantine, the character who used Windex for every ill in My Big Fat Greek Wedding.)

Stress

Stress is a real killer. Emily Deans, M.D., explained how stress leads to heart disease and other disorders in her 2012 *Psychology Today* article (*https://www.psychologytoday.com/us/blog/evolutionary-psychiatry/201211/stress-the-killer-disease*). According to Deans, stress induces production of cytokines, which then overexcite our immune systems and which are linked to all manner of problems, such as depression, PTSD, cardiovascular disease, and various kinds of inflammation—to death itself. We all know stress doesn't feel good. The problem is that our society is laden with stress. The political climate at the time of this writing, with Donald Trump as our president, is certainly stressful, causing social media to be stressful as friends battle it out. Our work can be stressful. Anyone in jobs dealing with the public, illnesses, military, policing, firefighting, practicing law in a courtroom, teaching school—you name it—can experience stress. We go home and cannot sleep. We become stressed and sleep-deprived (see next topic).

Solution: In the Bible (Phil. 4:8, NIV), it says, "whatever is true, whatever is noble, whatever is right, whatever is pure, whatever is lovely, whatever is admirable—if anything is excellent or praiseworthy—think about these things." Such good advice. Thinking pleasant thoughts tends to reduce stress. But there are stresses that simply overwhelm us, and thinking good thoughts isn't enough. I tend to anxiety if I get too busy with too many demands. Financial problems can really send me over the fence! You need to find your own triggers and try to alleviate them if you can. For example, when financial issues were about to overwhelm me, we sold a property so that I wouldn't have to pay the utilities any longer. That helped a lot, and my stress level went back down.

One can visit a mental health professional (a shrink, if you will), and there is absolutely nothing wrong with doing that.

ASK DR. DEAN:

Question 2: What is the cost of educating a medical doctor today?
Looking at some colleagues I am familiar with, I discovered the following:

- Private college + private medical school—$412,100
- Public college + public medical school—$246,500

ASK DR. DEAN:

Question 3: How can I as a parent handle earache ("ear infection") in my children? Should I always call the doctor immediately? And what about earache in adults?

Earache is a common symptom that occurs more frequently in children but occurs in people of all ages. In my office, it was very common for mothers to bring their child to me with the statement that, "my child has an ear infection." The mother typically brought the child to me and expected that I would prescribe an antibiotic to treat the "infection" that she "knew" was present. After I had asked what the child's problem was and heard that "ear infection" was the reply, my next question was, "what has the temperature been," followed by, "how long has the earache been present?" It was also important to ask about other symptoms of the ears, nose, and throat. The history questions were followed by an examination of the eyes, ears, nose, and throat as well as checking the neck for enlarged and tender lymph nodes. The temperature was also checked. (Fever is defined as a temperature of 100.4 degrees or more.)

After the history and physical examination are completed, my main concern is to make as accurate a diagnosis as possible by analyzing the information I have collected by the history and examination, including what I already know about the child's overall health status from prior visits. Then I often recall the phrase I learned in medical school, "treatment is easy; it is the diagnosis that is hard." So, the most important job for me is to make a diagnosis based on the information I have gathered, independent of the mother's diagnosis.

If the diagnosis is indeed "ear infection," then I must decide on the appropriate treatment. Antibiotic treatment has long been the standard for middle ear infections. This was presumed to be necessary to prevent long-term hearing loss, spread of infection to nearby areas, and avoid rupture of the ear drum, as examples of some reasons for the treatment of these infections with an antibiotic.

Treatment of middle ear infection has changed over time. Just because a child has an earache, and even if there is evidence of infection, the appropriate treatment depends on such things as age of the patient (young children 6 months to 2 years are the most at risk of more serious problems), level of fever (a temperature of more than 102 degrees is more important), whether the infection involves one ear or both, whether there are more symptoms than just earache, and whether ear infections have occurred several times over a period of one year.

Sometimes the history and examination cannot confirm an accurate diagnosis. In that case, it is very important for the physician to treat the symptom or symptoms that are present and perform an examination at a later time so that an accurate diagnosis can be made and the correct treatment can be provided. Treating with an antibiotic without an accurate diagnosis is not the appropriate way to deal with an earache. Currently, there is an important medical fact that physicians must keep in mind. There is an overuse of antibiotics when an infection is suspected but there is nothing to prove that one is present. The overuse of antibiotics is one of the main causes of having fewer effective antibiotics due to the infection germs becoming resistant to the antibiotics being used when they were not needed and not helpful in curing infections. As a result, we may get to a time in the not-too-distant future when there will be no antibiotics to treat certain infections. That would lead to serious complications of what we now think of as easily treatable infections.

The practitioner may help you with progressive relaxation or with meditation.

Insomnia and Sleep Deprivation

Are you having trouble sleeping? Do you find it difficult to fall asleep or find it difficult to stay asleep, or both? According to the Centers for Disease Control (CDC), from a report in 2016, over 1/3 of adults in the United States do not get the recommended hours of sleep (*https://www.cdc.gov/media/ releases/2016/p0215-enough-sleep.html*). Many untoward conditions are associated with lack of sleep, such as obesity, high blood pressure, and diabetes—so insomnia joins the other related maladies—more within control if one had the resolve. Heart disease and stroke are also associated with insomnia. It's not always easy to determine which causes which. Do we not sleep because we cannot breathe because we are obese? Or is obesity increased when we cannot sleep? The research suggests it might be both ways. In fact, the relationship is another vicious circle. We're tired during the day and eat more both to become energized and to help improve our mood. Increasing food intake makes us fatter and makes it harder to breathe. We snore, and our breathing stops when our epiglottis falls, shutting off our airway. Then lack of oxygen wakes us up. Vicious indeed!

> Solution: Obviously, if we are having trouble sleeping, we have a problem, and so more sleep is in order. How to do that? My doctor once told me that the "poor man's CPAP" was to sew two tennis balls in the back of one's tee shirt. Doing so would keep the person from rolling on his or her back. Sleeping on one's stomach keeps the epiglottis in place and reduces snoring and stopping of breath. Another "hack" is to elevate the head of one's bed. Putting a triangle-shaped pillow under one's mattress

is one way to do that. Here is one design that one can find on Amazon (and I'm not getting a kick-back! The thing just works!!). CPAP can also help: *https://smile.amazon.com/gp/product/B006YZSM46/ ref=oh_aui_search_detailpage?ie=UTF8&psc=1.*

Sleep medicine can be a temporary solution, but one should not use a medication more than a few nights. The brain easily becomes tolerant to the medication when tachyphylaxis occurs. If the medication provides more neurotransmitters, then the brain will stop producing those neurotransmitters. A good article on the science of neurotransmitters and sleep, particularly the neurotransmitter dopamine, can be read online in the Scientific American, written by Scicurious (2012): *https:// blogs.scientificamerican.com/scicurious-brain/ sleep-deprived-mind-your-dopamine/.*

One way to trick the brain is to not use the same kind of sleep inducement each night. Use acetaminophen PM one night and then the next, try peanut butter on a cracker. Skip nights so that you use the acetaminophen PM only once a week at most. Something like that. Melatonin seems to be one medication in which tolerance is uncommon. One can ingest a small amount of melatonin about an hour before retiring to help induce sleep. Melatonin tends to work for about seven hours.

Good sleep hygiene, rather than sleep aids, is highly important and used ever night. It helps to ban the use of one's computer or television in the bedroom, reduce the amount of blue light going into the brain before sleep, go to bed at the same time each night, avoid napping in the daytime, and do relaxing things before bed such as taking a warm bath.

ASK DR. DEAN:

Question 4: How should a parent/family handle FEVER in their children or themselves?
Sub-Question "A": What is important about body temperature and fever?

The reason that a temperature lower than 98.6 degrees, or a little higher than that, is considered to be "normal," is that there are things that can cause a little lower or higher temperature than 98.6 degrees that are not considered abnormal. For example, if a person has had food or liquids just before the temperature is taken, that might affect the reading. Exercise is another example of something that may affect temperature. Some people just normally have a temperature different than the so-called "normal." The level of 98.6 is an average of many, many people who were not sick whose temperature was checked. Some of those people had a temperature a little lower than the average, and some a little higher. The average of all was 98.6.

There needed to be an agreed upon level of temperature to make a decision about what would be abnormal. The agreement of the medical experts who made a decision was that fever would be defined as 100.4 or more. A temperature above the agreed upon 100.4 level would therefore be more likely to represent an important symptom, rather than due to some random cause that was not important in making a diagnosis. In fact, a temperature of 100.4 degrees or more is necessary to know that fever is present, no matter what is "normal" for you or your child. So, if you have the symptoms of a cold or other illness and your temperature is 100.3 degrees or less, you do not have "fever," since the medical definition of fever is 100.4 degrees or more.

Sub-Question "B": Should I be worried about a very high fever?

There are certain situations in which a very high fever for a long period of time could let you know that a doctor should evaluate you and establish a diagnosis. What is a "very high fever" and how long a period of time is important? My first comment about that is that the fever itself is not the problem. The *cause* of the fever must be determined, so that the proper care and treatment can be given. If you look on the Internet, you will find a large number of different opinions about fever and what is a dangerous temperature and what you should do. My advice depends on the situation that is present. A "very high temperature" that indicates a serious problem is different for a very young baby (1 to about 6 months of age) compared to a child (6 months to about 6 years), an older child (7 years to about 18 years), and an adult. There are other situations in which a doctor's evaluation must be done sooner. Those other situations are beyond the goals of this book.

Sub-Question "C": Do you mean that there is nothing I should do about fever?

There are several things to do with a person (child or adult) who has a fever. Number one is to check the temperature several times a day. Doing that allows you to understand how the person is doing overall and when or if a doctor's evaluation is needed. Besides that, when a person has a fever, sweating typically occurs, more than would normally occur, and causes loss of body fluid. That fluid needs to be replaced. The normal amount of fluid one should drink to keep up with normal loss depends on factors like whether they are male or female (males should drink more), how much they sweat, and what size they are. The old recommendation that you should drink eight glasses per day is the minimum. If you have a fever, you need the eight glasses plus the amount of fluid you lose. You can't measure the amount of fluid you lose with fever, but it is important that you drink more than eight glasses of fluid when you have fever, vomiting, or diarrhea. If you do not drink enough, you have the possibility of becoming dehydrated. It is usual to feel tired or to lack energy when you are sick, but if you become dehydrated, those feelings might be caused, at least partly, by the dehydration.

In addition to drinking more, if you have aching or pain, it is okay to take over-the-counter medicines to reduce those feelings. Acetaminophen (generic name) or ibuprofen (generic name) are appropriate to help.

In summary, regarding fever and how you can deal with it properly, the following will tell you the principles for dealing with fever:

1. Fever is not a disease or illness by itself. It is a symptom. The cause of the fever is the important thing to deal with, especially if the fever is persistent, long-lasting (hours or days), and associated with symptoms other than fever that make the patient unable to function normally.
2. It is not necessary to treat a fever, with a few exceptions.
3. If a fever (temperature 100.4 degrees or higher) remains higher than "normal" for several hours, especially if there are other symptoms that are not normal, then you should have a doctor perform an evaluation to make a diagnosis that establishes the reason for the fever. Then the treatment that is ordered will help improve the cause of the fever and the patient can recover.
4. Concern about fever, especially in children, has a long history that even now affects people's actions

when it occurs. As a result, many people see their doctor when fever is present, for example, when they believe they have an infection that they think needs to be treated with an antibiotic. The origin of some of that concern, again, especially in children, was because the medical opinion in the past was that fever, especially a temperature higher than 102, was a cause of seizures. Years ago, if a child had a fever and developed a seizure, that child would be treated for seizures. They would be treated for at least a year or more, and parents were cautioned to always give their child medicine to reduce the fever and avoid another seizure. More recent research has proven that there is *not* a connection between "high" fever and seizure disorder. A long-lasting fever is capable of causing a seizure, but in general, treating fever is not necessary and may not be a good idea, since fever is one of the body's defense methods to help the body fight off infection by making the body a poor environment for the growth of viruses and bacteria and by causing the patient to remain at rest. Those methods of action, along with checking the temperature often to understand how the illness is doing, are better ways of dealing with a sick patient at home.

Some authors believe that the pattern that some develop of sleeping for a stretch and then waking for a time before returning to sleep is a throwback to our ancestors that would engage in the "two sleep" pattern (*http://slumberwise.com/science/your-ancestors-didnt-sleep-like-you/*), and that it really doesn't matter when the seven to eight hours of sleep occur, as long as one gets the sleep time. If one cannot sleep in the middle of the night, it might be good to get up, read a book, pray or meditate, write letters, or get some work done. After a bit, one might then feel like sleeping more and can return to sleep. Obviously, this two sleeps method will not work if one goes to bed at midnight and has to get up for work at 6 AM. One needs to go to bed early enough to allow for eight hours of sleep. Attention to sleep, no matter what one's pattern, is important, and your health depends on your ability to sleep adequately.

Pharmaceutical Advertisements

Discussed in Chapter 4, advertising for procedures and medications is a recent event. The first ads started in 1983 and have increased in frequency ever since (*https://www.ncbi.nlm.nih.gov/pmc/articles/PMC2690298/*). We need to pay attention to the side effects in those ads. Although usually rare, they can happen.

> Solution: We need to be involved in our care, certainly, and perhaps some advertised medication or procedure is truly for us. But we need to exercise much care—talk with people, research it out, consult with our medical resources—physicians, pharmacists, and so on. Remember, the advertisements use actors paid to smile and look healthy. When we are in pain or ill, we do not feel like doing research. We would like someone to fix our problem. However, researching can keep us from additional problems. Is there another option tested longer with fewer side effects? Is the alternative we are considering more popular yet with worse side effects? Prosthetic surgeries come to mind. Many are the ads on television for getting knee replacements or hip replacements.

For quite a few years, surgeons favored metal-on-metal hip replacements, thinking they would be more durable. However, the research revealed that metal-on-metal had the worst failure rates. All-metal hip replacements had a 6% failure rate after only five years (*https://www.arthritis.org/living-with-arthritis/ treatments/joint-surgery/types/hip/hip-replacement-failure-rate.php*), particularly among younger women. Recently, I've noticed advertisements for obtaining full sets of implanted teeth. The commercials tout cosmetic benefits, with the wide smiles of actors confidently eating things such as corn on the cob. They look wonderful. When one looks up what could happen in the risks/adverse events section, there are always many frightening possibilities (and again, these events are rare with low percentages, and may not even be related to the medication). Companies are required to say everything that happened to the participants in the clinical trials. However, if you are the one to whom the event later happens, for you, the percent could might as well have been 100 percent. The Mayo Clinic mentioned these risks for implanted teeth (*https://www.mayoclinic. org/tests-procedures/dental-implant-surgery/about/ pac-20384622*):

- Infection at the implant site
- Injury or damage to surrounding structures, such as other teeth or blood vessels
- Nerve damage, which can cause pain, numbness, or tingling in your natural teeth, gums, lips, or chin
- Sinus problems, when dental implants placed in the upper jaw protrude into one of your sinus cavities

I am not suggesting that you not get your teeth fixed and never do anything that is advertised, but what I am saying is

ASK DR. DEAN:

Question 5: How do I know if I'm getting accurate blood pressure readings at the doctor's office? Or are the ones I take at home accurate? Why are accurate BP readings important?

One of the most common medical procedures in hospitals and medical offices is the measurement of a patient's blood pressure. An immensely important feature of that process is that it is performed in a standardized manner such that no matter where it is done, or who does it, the blood pressure measurement is a consistent and reliable number that the healthcare provider can rely on.

Over a long time period and based on my observation, the taking of blood pressure is undervalued. It is vitally important that this test is accurate, due to the possibility that the results affect medical diagnoses, treatments, and the patient's health status history.

The multiple things that should be either AVOIDED or of concern in each blood pressure test; these include the following:

- the arm the blood pressure cuff encircles should be supported at heart level
- talking with/listening to the medical associate during the taking of blood pressure
- blood pressure cuff applied over clothing
- legs of patient crossed
- need for toileting during the taking of blood pressure
- no resting before taking of blood pressure (five minutes recommended)
- incorrect cuff placement
- lack of back support
- rounding off a blood pressure reading to the nearest zero

- white coat effect
- smoking within 30 minutes of measurement
- cuff size inappropriate for arm size (either too small or too large)
- inadequate training of medical associate
- having consumed coffee or other stimulants

Anyone or more of the above factors can affect the measurement of the blood pressure, either higher or lower than the actual. An inaccurate measurement can lead to not prescribing a needed blood pressure medicine or not providing needed medicine for a falsely high measurement.

In addition to the aforementioned steps, improved and adequate training of medical associates and/or other staff who take and record blood pressures is required for the needed accurate blood pressure measurement.

Of note are a couple of items not universally recognized. Having one's blood pressure done on a machine at a store is typically inaccurate, as the above list of necessary steps are avoided in the use of that type of blood pressure measurement. There is a need for increased appreciation of the necessity of accurate blood pressure measurement.

that you should do your homework. Every medication and every procedure have possible negative side effects; things that could harm us. At least we could be aware of those.

Solution: Research efforts on medication efficacy should focus on **predictive analytics**. What this means is that solution algorithms developed need to accurately predict if **you** will have a good outcome or have one of the side effects before you take the medication or submit to the procedure. Developing the prediction models is not that difficult to do, but developing such models will require data which are not at present available (mainly due to HIPAA). And even if the data were available, researchers want to patent their solution algorithms so they can make money off them. Predictive analytics will have its own problems—how will we know when stated predictions are accurate? My husband Gary showed me a supposed "genomic predictive analytics" website. I looked, and it was evident that there was no research to back up their claims. And yet, this company was soliciting from a nursing facility to go in and collect DNA samples to make predictions on which medications would work for each patient.

Ideally, data would be available to researchers, they will then use good scientific processes in establishing predictive algorithms, and they will provide those algorithms for the good of humanity. Society should pay scientists for working toward those goals and not for hoarding patents on their processes. Ideals generally are not the reality—but let us work toward idealism!

HIGH FAT—LOW CARB Diets May Be "More In Tune" with GENETICS OF HUMANS—OBESITY and DIABETES

The low animal fat and higher carbohydrate diet that has been proclaimed by our federal government—the Department of Agriculture—since the 1950s may not have done for us what was thought. This diet, with all of the fast food chains that have sprung up across the USA since the 1950s using fats produced from plants and all kinds of "processed" additives, may be the primary cause of the obesity epidemic in the

USA today. Generally, 90% of diabetics have T2D, and 5–10% have Type 1 Diabetes (initially called childhood onset diabetes). Since 1960, the United States has seen a 700% increase in diabetes from 1% of the population to 8%. Thirty million Americans have diabetes, and another 84 million Americans have pre-diabetes.

- The United States has the largest population struggling with obesity in the world: 109 million adults.
- Obesity and diabetes are highly linked: taking insulin often leads to obesity. Obesity often leads to T2D.
- More than two in three adults (Americans) were considered to be clinically overweight or have obesity (33.7% of adult Americans are clinically obese). Only one in three American adults maintain a normal healthy weight (federal CDC data from 2015 reported in 2016). (REFERENCE: 2016; *http://www.who.int/diabetes/global-report/en/*; *http://www.diabetes.org/diabetes-basics/statistics/*)

Complications

Diabetes of all types can lead to complications in many parts of the body and can increase the overall risk of dying prematurely. Possible complications include heart attack, stroke, kidney failure, leg amputation, vision loss, and nerve damage. In pregnancy, poorly controlled diabetes increases the risk of fetal death and other complications.

Costs for Diabetes:

- $327 billion: Total costs of diagnosed diabetes in the United States in 2017
- $237 billion for direct medical costs
- $90 billion in reduced productivity (*www.diabetes.org/advocacy/news-events/cost-of-diabetes.html*) (Figure 5.4)

ASK DR. DEAN:

Question 6: What are YOUR concerns, as a practicing family doctor, about the future of healthcare, the ever-exploding costs of US healthcare, and how these costs should be covered?

I have a couple of concerns about the future of healthcare. The folks predicting and researching healthcare do not seem to be including my concerns about the relationship between patients and doctors and its role. Technology and other progress do not take relationships into account, and the relationship between patients and doctors is critically important in order to provide an improvement in illness and emotional factors. Also, since the technology is and will be expensive, there needs to be an emphasis on a method of paying for healthcare. I have been seeing some ridiculous charges for minor ER visits and surgeries. One was a lady who went to an emergency room due to a bee sting, spent 30 minutes in the ER, minimal treatment was needed, and the charge was $12,000!! There are many similar cases.

My solution is to have a universal medical insurance that would cover everyone for a specific list of diseases, surgeries, and other medical issues. The list would be developed by a group of physicians and other knowledge-able individuals and revised at appropriate time frames. Additional health insurance for certain health problems/issues/procedures would be available for purchase on an open market for those who wanted the additional coverage. Such a program would be handled by a single agency and would not need to include multiple govern-ment programs addressing healthcare costs and would apply to all citizens. The cost would be shared by every-one. Due to the gouging of the costs of healthcare, medi-cines, etc. that are currently exorbitant and continually rising without reason and due to the lack of concern by the pharmaceutical industry and other providers, there also needs to be some system to manage this problem. There does not seem to be any effort to really address this cost issue effectively.

RESPONSE from DR. GARY MINER: Your observations on the exploding costs are correct. How we can deal with these costs will be covered in Chapter 7 of this book, and your suggestion here may well be included in our list of "SOLUTIONS THAT WILL WORK."

AN OBSERVATION from DR. DEAN:
In addition to my concern about the "patient–doctor relationship" being eroded with the new incoming technology, there is another area that is overlooked in what I read about technology and changes/improvements in treatments. There is a large percent of people who do not comprehend anything about health, healthcare, treatment, the importance of it, and how to implement a healthy lifestyle. The technological and other medical and treatment advances likely will have limited effect on this significant group, especially related to the large percent of the population that are under-educated about health issues or cannot afford care or education efforts that might change their knowledge and lifestyle.

RESPONSE from Dr. Gary Miner:
What you express about a segment of the population not interested in understanding and taking charge of their own healthcare is a legitimate concern. However, this could be the topic of a separate book. We have to limit ourselves and focus on one thing in this book: HOW to MAINTAIN AND INCREASE QUALITY OF HEALTHCARE while at the

same time BRINGING THE COSTS down to levels that other industrialized nations have done, and in the future having costs only increase at the same level as the cost of inflation and increasing wages and salaries.

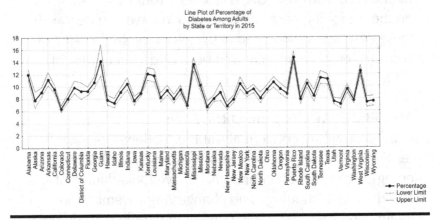

Figure 5.4   Percentage of adults with diabetes by the state in 2015. (Graph by Linda Miner using TIBCO-Statistica. Data from Diagnosed Diabetes, Age-Adjusted Percentage, Adults with Diabetes— https://gis.cdc.gov/grasp/diabetes/DiabetesAtlas.html.)

Looking at the graph in Figure 5.4, it is obvious that there is a great deal of diabetes in the United States. On average, in 2015, 9.36% of our adult population had a diagnosis of diabetes. No wonder diabetes costs so much! One in ten of us has it! Type 2 diabetes is an elective disease. We are choosing it when we choose our lifestyles. Please go back and look at the cartoon in Figure 5.2 once again. Drug companies must love that we are fat and out of shape. The sicker we are, the more they make! But, what kind of foods should we be eating? Exercise is crucial, but are we eating the right kinds of foods?

Bad Science and the Low-Fat Diet?

Americans in 1960 were healthy and had the finest food supply and medical care in the world. Why have we had the epidemic of diabetes and obesity? Many Americans ate butter, bacon, and eggs for breakfast in 1960. During the 1960s and 1970s, nutrition researchers convinced the American public and Federal Agencies that "fat" caused heart disease and that Americans should adopt a low-fat diet and replace fat with good carbohydrates (carbs) such as fruit, vegetables, whole grain bread, and oatmeal. However, the research studies were associative studies that showed a weak relationship between fat and heart disease; much of the comparative data was selected to support the researcher's objectives; data and countries that did not show relationships were dropped.

Recent reviews of the studies and supporting data have failed to show significant relationships between natural animal fat and fat such as that found in avocados and eggs and disease; many studies have shown positive impacts from healthy fats, including randomized clinical trials. We do not have randomized clinical trial studies that support the hypothesis that natural fats cause heart disease. We have many clinical studies that show a very low-carb, high-fat, moderate-protein diet can cause patients to lose weight rapidly and reverse diabetes.

Essentially, we have been on a big scientific experiment (without sound scientific research supporting the need to launch the low-fat focus): remove fat from the American diet. The result of eating more carbs is a 700% increase in diabetes and related conditions over the past 55 years.

Even the most recent 2015 federal nutrition guidelines recommend a high-carb and low-fat or non-fat diet: (*https://www. nal.usda.gov/fnic/dietary-guidelines*).

The American Federal Food Guidelines (low-fat, high-carb) have essentially been adopted by most English-speaking nations and many nations in Europe and elsewhere.

Professional diet-medical associations in Canada, Australia, South Africa, and the UK have fought against the concept of the low-carb-high-fat (LCHF) diet, taking actions against M.D. professionals and other medical providers who question the non-existent science behind the low-fat, high-carb American diet or recommend the high-fat diet for patients with T2D or to overcome obesity.

For example, in South Africa, the medical associations put Tim Noakes on trial to revoke his ability to practice as a M.D. Tim Noakes, M.D. and Ph.D., is a retired professor at the University of Cape Town: Tim was charged with recommending the LCHF diet that could harm patients. Tim is one of the leading scientists in South Africa and is known globally in the field of running and exercise physiology (he is the author of *Lore of Running*, the bible for long-distance runners, and the main researcher of "carb-loading" before long-distance racing). The South African Health Professions Council refused to take away Tim's ability to practice as a medical doctor in South Africa after a lengthy trial process (and very expensive legal bills for Tim) and review of the science behind the LCHF diet; the Medical Associations appealed the original verdict; Tim was cleared of all misconduct in the appeal decision in 2017. (REFERENCES: 2016 – *https://www.outsideonline.com/2140271/silencing-low-carb-rebel*; 2018—*https://www.diabetes.co.uk/news/2018/jun/low-carb-guru-professor-tim-noakes-again-found-not-guilty-of-misconduct-94449754.html*; 2018—*https://thenoakesfoundation.org/*; 2018—*http://foodmed.net/2018/02/noakes-virta-health-study-gold-diabetics-lchf/*.) (Good Reference: Noakes, T., and Sboros, M., 2018.)

For those readers interested in more details on the need for animal fats in our diets, these references provide that information plus a wealth of additional references, as these are some of the leading authors in the field of the low-carb-high-fat (LCHF) diet (with moderate protein). Many have reviewed or led the clinical research studies that have shown that a high-fat diet, if based on good natural fat, can lead to rapid weight loss and reversal of T2D for many patients. (REFERENCES: *https://renewbariatrics.com/obesity-rank-by-countries/*; Hyman, M.—Director of the Cleveland Clinic Center for Functional Medicine—2018. FOOD—WHAT THE HECK SHOULD I EAT?; New York: Simon & Schuster. Good overall Reference: Noakes, T., and Sboros, M., 2018; LORE OF NUTRITION—CHALLENGING DIETARY BELIEFS; South Africa: Penguin Random House of South Africa.)

> Note: Tim Noakes retired as professor of exercise and sports science at the University of Cape Town in 2014 and is now a professor emeritus at UCT. He is a lifelong athlete and is rated an A1-scientist by the National Research Foundation (NRF). He is also the co-founder of the Sports Science Institute of South Africa, along with rugby icon Morné du Plessis. In 2008, Tim was awarded the Order of Mapungubwe (Silver) by the president of South Africa for "excellent contribution to the field of sport and the science of physical exercise." In 2012, he received the Lifetime Achievement Award from the NRF for his contribution to sports science research. He is the author of several books, one of which, Lore of Running, is considered the global "bible" of running. Tim founded The Noakes Foundation in 2012 to promote unbiased nutritional research into the effects of low-carbohydrate, high-fat diets on all aspects of human health.

Three American Health Startup Firms that are attempting to manage T2D:

1. VitraHealth (*https://www.virtahealth.com/*)—diabetes and other chronic metabolic diseases

2. Noom (*https://www.noom.com/#/*)—programs for pre-hypertension, weight loss, and diabetes prevention
3. Pacific Health Portal (*http://www.pacificconferencing. com/about.html; https://www.linkedin.com/company/ pacific-health-software/*)—a free portal to be available February 2019 for education, training, coaching, and free university classes on nutrition, exercise, and health

These startups try to manage T2 diabetes by working with patients and patients-at-risk for T2 in various ways, including education and training, including telehealth methods with low-carb diets and exercise.

References

Abedon, S. T., Kuhl, S. J., Blasdel, B. G., & Kutter, E. M. (2011). Phage treatment of human infections. *Bacteriophage, 1*(2), 66–85. Retrieved from http://search.ebscohost.com/login.aspx?d irect=true&db=cmedm&AN=22334863&site=ehost-live

Noakes, T. and Sboros, M. (2018). *Lore of Nutrition: Challenging Conventional Dietary Beliefs.* South Africa: Penguin Random House.

Ozkan, I., Akturk, E., Yeshenkulov, N., Atmaca, S., Rahmanov, N., & Atabay, H. I. (2016). Lytic activity of various phage cocktails on multidrug-resistant bacteria. *Clinical & Investigative Medicine, 39*(6), S66–S70. Retrieved from http://search.ebscohost.com/ login.aspx?direct=true&db=hch&AN=120024695&site=ehost-live

Pallavali, R. R., Degati, V. L., Lomada, D., Reddy, M. C., & Durbaka, V. R. P. (2017). Isolation and in vitro evaluation of bacterio-phages against MDR-bacterial isolates from septic wound infec-tions. *PLoS ONE, 12*(7), 1–16. https://doi.org/10.1371/journal. pone.0179245

Winters-Miner, L.A., Bolding, P.S., Hilbe, J. M., Goldstein, M., Hill, T., Nisbet, R., Walton, N., Miner G. D. (2015). *Practical Predictive Analytics and Decisioning Systems for Medicine.* Boston, MA, Elsevier/Academic Press.

Note: Tim Noakes retired as professor of exercise and sports science at the University of Cape Town in 2014 and is now a professor emeritus at UCT. He is a lifelong athlete and is rated an A1-scientist by the National Research Foundation (NRF). He is also the co-founder of the Sports Science Institute of South Africa, along with rugby icon Morné du Plessis. In 2008, Tim was awarded the Order of Mapungubwe (Silver) by the president of South Africa for "excellent contribution to the field of sport and the science of physical exercise." In 2012, he received the Lifetime Achievement Award from the NRF for his contribution to sports science research. He is the author of several books, one of which, *Lore of Running*, is considered the global "bible" of running. Tim founded The Noakes Foundation in 2012 to promote unbiased nutritional research into the effects of low-carbohydrate, high-fat diets on all aspects of human health.

Chapter 6

Person Centered Medicine and Person-Directed Medical Care: Personalized Medicine

Defined in Winters-Miner et al. (2015) in Dr. Nephi Walton's Chapter 13, personalized medicine is basically the end-point for predictive analytics in medicine:

> Today, personalized medicine has a very broad definition that spans a number of medical fields: however, the succinct definition could be stated as "the tailoring of a treatment to an individual based on their unique characteristics."

Walton, N., in Winters-Miner et al., 2015, p. 177

Ideally, personalized medicine emerges from predictive analytics—from an accurate prediction based on a thorough knowledge of the **individual** patient: of the patient's genomic, psychological, and environmental make-up, which could then predict future problems as well as current recommendations for health. Personalized medicine would encompass preventive actions, specific medications, and specific treatments for that individual. It would be important to consider the patient's environment or milieu in making specific recommendations.

> How we respond to treatment is also affected by the things we do, what we have access to, and things we touch or eat. For example, certain medications are not as effective when taken with certain foods, or some people may have limited access to certain types of food.

Walton, N., in Winters-Miner et al., 2015, p. 179

As Walton stressed, traditional research tends to put people together who are quite different in terms of their genomes and in terms of their microbiome (the compilation of DNA from all sources, including the microorganisms that live within our bodies that are not actually part of our DNA). We need research into all of that and how all those things interact with our specific environments before we can most accurately predict the efficacy of treatment for any individual. Fortunately, that very research is being attempted. There is much to do, but the new research has begun. Until now, large heterogeneous groups have been used when studying the effectiveness of treatments and medications. This type of group analysis has been the backbone of **evidence-based medicine**, or **EBM**. Physicians had the feeling that they were practicing the best medicine possible due to their reliance on research and on the gold standards that arose from such research. However, as discussed earlier, this feeling was flawed for two reasons. First, as reported earlier, many research articles in the literature were flawed, so reliance on them might have been ill-advised. Second, unless individualized predictive analytics are used, one cannot begin to accurately predict to the individual from the mean of the group unless the patients' characteristics are close to the mean.

The future of medicine is two-fold:

- treatment of current illnesses of the individual
- preventing future illnesses

The physician cannot work without the input of the patient. This leads us to patient-directed medical care.

Examples of Personalized Medicine

Verma (2012) provided examples for breast, colon, lung, prostate, myeloid neoplasia, leukemia, and lymphoma cancers. In talking about lung cancer and specifically small-cell lung cancer, Verma stated a number of gene markers or specific identifiers were being used in research to find specific treatments. Even though the subjects in the research each had lung cancer, their genetic makeup was different. It would not be logical that the same therapeutic agent would work for all of them. Differences in types and responses to medications are being found based on differences in markers and identifiers. Verma also talked about new tools that are being used to help delineate the differences in individuals for research and recommendations. For example, in prostate cancer the comprehensive geriatric assessment is being used as a tool to help predict who will respond to which kind of treatment: hormonal, surgery, or radiation.

Again, research has started, but we are not there yet! And it is also important to realize that the predictor variables (measures of characteristics of individuals used to predict outcomes) do not have to be genomic, as in the case of the comprehensive geriatric assessment, which is basically a paper and pencil interview-type instrument to assess "medical conditions, mental health, functional capacity and social circumstances" of older persons (National Clinical Programme for

Older People, 2016, p. 2: *https://www.hse.ie/eng/services/pub lications/clinical-strategy-and-programmes/comprehensive-ger iatric-assessment-summary.pdf*). If the instrument accurately predicts a response to prostate treatment, then use it! If values on two medical tests can predict death or survival in DIC, then use them! If something predicts accurately to the individual, that is what we should do.

We in medical research need to be hunting for pre-dictor variables that can accurately predict outcomes for individuals rather than wasting time and resources on population health studies that use traditional p value statistics.

Patient-Directed Medical Care

■ Just as Angelina Jolie decided that she would not wait for breast cancer to strike her, some women are choosing mas-tectomies if they have breast cancer in their family and are found to have the BRCA1 or BRCA2 gene mutation.

■ Jabar is wearing a wristwatch that monitors his daily steps and his heart rate. His watch also tells him what foods would be good for him to eat that day.

■ Rachael recently purchased a $100 EKG device that allows her to send warnings of fibrillation to her doctor from home.

■ Sally, who has arthritis, wakes up with a very sore neck. While icing it down, she finds the exact muscle that is giving her problems by viewing an anatomy program on her Kindle. She then Googles to find a YouTube segment with a physical therapist who shows how to exercise that exact muscle to eliminate pain.

■ It seems to Wanda that she may have a urinary tract infection. She goes out and buys a test kit and determines she does indeed. She emails her doctor for advice, and the doctor prescribes, among all the antibiotics available, the one antibiotic that is appropriate for her, according to the predictive set of rules that her doctor has online.

■ Jim visits an online discussion group with other cancer victims to see how they are coping and to see what treatments have been successful with others. He then looks on EBCSOhost or another online library to find the latest research findings. He examines the literature to see if there is research using predictive analytics. He saves those articles to take to his doctor.

There is a revolution going on in medicine—patient-directed healthcare. New ground is being plowed and earth is being turned over. Patients are no longer waiting patiently for their doctors to tell them what to do. The role of the doctor is changing to that of a counselor and advisor. Patients are taking charge of their own medical decisions. The role of the patient is changing to **chief executive officer of healthcare (CEOH)**.

CEOH

Patient-directed medical care means that the patient takes responsibility for his or her own health and is an active participant in decisions related to his or her health treatment. Chapter 5 is basically patient-directed medicine in terms of taking care of oneself. We have a responsibility to ourselves, and we should not live badly and then expect others to fix us. (We authors know that's hard to do at times.) Patients can no longer be passive, waiting for the doctor to pronounce treatment upon them. We need to become proactive and knowledgeable to avoid errors and to help ensure good outcomes.

As stressed in Chapter 5, we are responsible for a large part of our good health. Of course, serious illness or trauma can befall us regardless of what we do—we likely will always need doctors and the medical profession no matter how effective Google gets. However, many of the threats to our good health are within our control. We need to eat well and exercise, for example. Do we do that? In this sense, we are truly the directors of our own medical care.

Being CEO of our healthcare also means we need to do what we can to check on healthcare costs and contain them by not simply accepting any price.

It is not always easy to determine the price of medical care. For some devices we can go to a source such as Amazon and see the prices of various electronic aids. Inputting the term "EKG monitors" yielded 20 pages of items, all priced and all with reviews that could be ascertained (Figures 6.1 and 6.2).

Truly, one can find just about any device on the Internet today. I tried for an MRI machine on Amazon but did not find any—might be a bit pricey for the normal Amazon searcher. However, there were some for sale when Googling the terms. Perhaps one could start his or her own MRI scanning in one's basement? (Just kidding—but corporations that provide medical care to their employees and their families

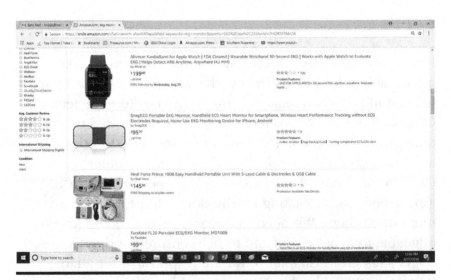

Figure 6.1   Amazon search for EKG monitors when Googling "EKG Monitors." There were many devices as well as their prices and where to find them.

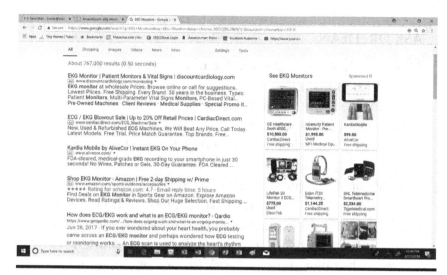

Figure 6.2   Googling EKG monitors

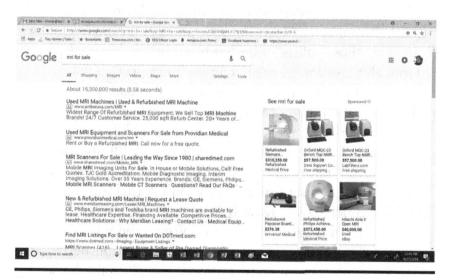

Figure 6.3   MRI machines for sale. Looks like a nice refurbished one for only $310,350. A bargain!

(see Chapter 7), surely could find devices on the Internet (Figure 6.3).

Getting information on costs from clinics is *not* always easy, but they truly should post the prices for various services for anyone to see when entering. Speaking of imaging, such as X-rays and MRIs, one service did post its prices at

ASK DR. DEAN:

Question 1: What is the VALUE of a family doctor–patient relationship?

The long-held idea of the importance of having a "family doctor" who knows you and who you know for years has drastically changed in the past several years. This is an idea that is, in my opinion, a poor one. Medical diagnosis and treatment is a complicated and serious field. There are several areas to be considered, which include appearance, symptoms, emotions, family relationships, thoughts, feelings, environment, ancestry, hobbies, type of work (or not working), etc. Family doctors provided care in their office, took care of you if you needed hospitalization, and some even made house calls. Now, hospital patients are managed by "hospitalists" who are hired by the hospital. How all these things relate can be an important feature of an illness. If you are seeing a physician for the first time, the range of information requested may very well depend on the presenting health problem. Then, over time, the information obtained covers all important relevant information. Tests that are ordered are not random but are performed based on information that the physician believes may be helpful to arrive at a correct diagnosis. Over time and shared information with the doctor, the doctor–patient relationship is established. The data, diagnoses, conversations, and all of the background information forms the basis of that relationship and also serves to help your physician manage your healthcare history and treatment. Often doctors become friends, and they may become the doctor for the entire family. That pattern has been in place for many years and has been proven to be an effective way to diagnose and treat folks.

Is that the way healthcare is done now? There are still some doctors who practice like that, but a significant number now are employed by a hospital, clinic, or other arrangement. By working in that type of setting, they have less work time, no night call, a salary, no overhead, and no weekend on call. The number of doctors who are employed has gradually increased. A change that has occurred for doctors who have remained in private practice is that their office hours are Monday to Thursday and a half day on Friday. Formerly, office hours were Monday through Friday and a half day on Saturday. When the office was closed, the doctor would be available by calling, and an answering service would contact the doctor and give the patient's name and number. That doctor would then call you and either manage your health issue by calling in a prescription, recommend you go to the hospital, or even come to the hospital and see you there.

The changes mentioned have additional features that are less desirable for medical healthcare. One feature that has a negative aspect is that the doctor–patient relationship is not the same. Patients are not as likely to have a doctor that treats them routinely. Folks go to different doctors depending on their own schedule; they go to whichever doctor is available when they are available or go to an urgent care, which is always available all day and late in the day or evening. Under these circumstances, the relationship feature of the family doctor is lost, unfortunately.

Why have doctors begun to be employed as mentioned? There are several reasons for that change. The most likely reason is that when a woman or man goes to medical school, the school tuition is very expensive, thus many of the students must rely on loans in order to remain in school. Medical school tuition and fees are as much as $76,202 or $34,595 for one year, depending on the chosen medical school, and the programs last for four years. Not all medical schools cost that much. There are some that are considerably lower priced, but the cost is still difficult to pay as you go. So, when a student doctor finishes medical school, can she or he begin to practice and start earning? No, not at all. After medical school, the next step is residency for three to five years more, depending on the medical field one chooses. During residency the doctors do earn some money, but the amount is not large, and the hours are long. By the time a doctor has finished all the required training, she or he is in the late 20s or early 30s or even older, depending on the specialty chosen.

If the doctor has decided on family medicine and to open their own solo practice, then, in addition to the education debt, there is the cost of renting office space and purchasing desks, chairs, and other office accouterments. Then a wide array of examination tables (one for each examination room), many instruments, tools, e-X-ray machine, laboratory equipment and chemicals, liquids, and an assortment of other items must be purchased, depending on the doctor's preferences and style of practice. The combination of educational costs and then equipping an office, plus hiring staff and all that goes with that and the amount of money needed to accomplish all of that, is staggering. Those costs contribute to why new doctors choose employment. Another option is to join a physician group practice. That way is less complicated in that a new doctor in an existing practice can practice independently based on her or his knowledge and training, rather than absorbing the cost of a one-doctor practice or as an employee that may have to practice according to the methods required by the employer.

The practice of family doctors in the past was admittedly stressful and involved many hours daily. The office was open five and one-half days per week. Additionally, there were after-hours calls seven days per week, trips to the emergency room to attend to a doctor's patients who needed medical attention of one type or another, and daily hospital rounds of the doctor's hospital patients. Then there were hospital staff meetings, committee meetings, and reading and studying to keep up with new medicines and medical treatments. A couple of additional things requiring a doctor's attention were family responsibilities and sleep.

Now when you understand some of the lifestyle doctors endured for many years, you can possibly recognize that younger doctors desire to have a different lifestyle. That has led to the references regarding office practice, on-call responsibilities, hospital requirements, etc., as noted. The younger doctors have decided on avoiding the stress and responsibilities of the newer lifestyle versus the former.

Now the doctor's office hours are four and one-half days per week. Family doctors do not make hospital rounds, since their hospital patients are cared for by a doctor hired by the hospital. Typically, the doctors are not available after office hours. The office telephone has an answering device that recommends that if you have a healthcare need that you go to urgent care or to the hospital emergency room for care. In the office there are some people who seek care from the same doctor whenever they need treatment for an illness, but often, when the doctor is not conveniently available, patients end up going to several doctors over time and do not have the same doctor–patient relationship described earlier.

If the changes I have described are unsatisfactory for the population and a more acceptable style of medical care is desired, what needs to be done? While I do not have the full answer, there are some ideas already being implemented that seem to be able to improve some things. For example, if the computer technology is changed so that each individual's health information is stored electronically and could be shared with any doctor, any hospital, any clinic, at any time, then all of your healthcare information would be available and would be consistent at all times. Previous laboratory tests and results, X-rays, and all other procedures would not have to be repeated no matter where you were located and needed to have that information. An additional benefit of this system would include your healthcare information so that many tests, X-rays, etc. would not have to be repeated and charged again, in the event that the information needed would already be available. There are other system changes that have been suggested, but it will be a considerable time before all needed changes can be evaluated and implemented.

There have been many people that complain about the cost of medical care and there is, at least, a partial answer to that. I am referring to what you can do for minor health problems at home. If you do that and the problem worsens, you can then seek a doctor's help.

the intake desk. Prices are not on the website, so perhaps it is not done now, but five years ago when I, Linda, needed an MRI of my shoulder, I walked in and found a price list posted clearly for patients to see. I had gone to various imaging facilities in the community asking the prices, and they ranged from about $3,000 down to the $600 or so that was charged at the facility I was visiting that day. They had only one location at that time, and the thought crossed my mind that perhaps it wasn't as good if they charged so little. But I saw that a physician was in charge that I'd known for years as an excellent physician and radiologist. So, I went there. **They speak the truth when it said they were patient-centered, even before the term was generally being used.** It was a top-notch facility, which provided a top-notch scan. At present, the facility has spread out to quite a few cities in the region.

The point is, we can help to keep prices down. If we have time to seek out alternatives, we should. We need to select good providers, those that we can relate to. We need to inform ourselves and become active participants in evaluating treatment plans when challenges come our way. We need to use good communication skills whenever we interact with our medical providers, and we need to keep an eye on our payments. Just because insurance pays, we still need to understand the charges and correct any mistakes, and it is incumbent upon us to seek good care for less whenever possible.

In consulting with our doctor advisor, good communication skills are vital. Communication depends on our assumptions. At times, our assumptions are not all correct. Look at the following assumptions that doctors and patients have often had. Which are correct and which are not? Our communications will depend on our assumptions, for good or bad.

Chief Executive Officer for Our Own Health: Communication and Collaboration

The best situation develops when both patient and physician believe that patients should participate in their own healthcare as much as possible. Listed are aspects of this topic below.

Patients need to feel empowered to help direct their own healthcare. Along with taking care of our bodies as best we can, it is crucial that we are able to communicate with our healthcare professionals. How we view them is very important for that communication and for our health. They are not gods; but they know a lot, and likely more than we do. So, a healthy view of one's healthcare professionals is to respect their expertise but not expect them to "fix" us automatically. We need to be involved! Remember Figure 2.4 in Chapter 2. In the old process, everything was directed by insurance and the providers. In the new process, everything should center on the patient, and the patient needs to be contributing to the direction of that personalized care. If you have a doctor that does not believe in the patient being involved in decisions and treatment and you do, then you might need a different doctor. Generally, positive interactions with one's physician tend to associate with more patient involvement in care. It's good to get along well with your doctor and to find healthcare professionals that get along with you.

Assumptions and Communication When Consulting with a Doctor

Both doctors and patients can make assumptions while communicating—old assumptions left over from the past. The most important aspect of the visit to a physician, for a patient, is the communication—what do I tell the doctor and what does the doctor hear? What does the doctor say, and has the doctor truly heard me? Have I truly heard the doctor? Here are some very common assumptions on both sides.

Possible Patient Assumptions	Possible Doctor Assumptions
• The doctor knows • The doctor is up on the latest research • The doctor is following best practices • The doctor is a scientist • The doctor cares about me • The doctor is motivated to get me well • The doctor understands what I mean • The doctor has control of the business aspects of the practice • Healthcare really should be free • The doctor should be able to understand what the problem is by looking at me	• Clinicians know what they are doing • Patients that talk too much waste time • The patient is starting with the most important problem • The patient is giving the most relevant information • The patient is telling the truth • The patient knows his or her own body and where the problem is • The patient wants to get better • If there are too many problems, then the patient is a hypochondriac

Patient–physician communication can be fraught with assumptions, and the above may not be all. Patients must understand how to communicate with their physicians if they are going to make progress.

Finding One's Advisor Physician

First, the patient must find a good doctor, and that is not always easy. "Good" means good for you, not necessarily good for others, even family members. Of course, one hopes his or her doctor is knowledgeable but also is someone that they can talk to and one who talks to them. If you want an advisor, then you shouldn't be meeting with an autocrat.

Dr. Dean always recommends that a person makes a "get acquainted" appointment before they need the doctor. This

ASK DR. DEAN:

Question 2: What "over-the-counter" medicines are useful for a patient and can thus help avoid un-needed expenses in visiting a doctor or emergency room?

When you go to a drug store/pharmacy looking for a medicine to treat a non-serious condition for you or a family member, there are a dizzying array of bottles, tubes, packets, bags, boxes, et cetera on the shelves for all kinds of conditions, diagnoses, and symptoms. How can you decide what to purchase from all these displays of products with so many different names?

The most important principle related to selecting an appropriate over-the-counter medicine for whatever problem you are trying to treat is to read the list of ingredients (active ingredients, not the inactive ingredients) and not the name of the product. The next principle of selecting based on the active ingredient(s) is to know what medicine in the product is likely to help relieve your symptom(s). A third idea is to have had experience with different medicines/products that have been effective in the past for similar symptoms. It is a much better method when you are dealing with the home treatment of symptoms to obtain medicines with only the individual active ingredient designed to treat the specific symptom from which you are suffering. Or, if you have more than one symptom, individual (active ingredient) medicines to treat individual symptoms. For example, if you have a cold and have a runny nose, sore throat, and cough, and if you take a "cold medicine" with multiple ingredients (such as acetaminophen, phenylephrine, dextromethorphan, diphenhydramine), you may be taking medicine for a symptom which you do not have.

Continuing with that theme, if you are feeling ill, think about the specific symptom, or symptoms, bothering you, then look on the list of active ingredients on the container of medicine you think might be a help for the symptom(s). Purchase the medicine with the one ingredient recommended for your symptom or additional medicines with the ingredient needed for other symptoms. (See list below)

Symptom	Ingredient to Look for	Additional Treatment
Pain (any)	acetaminophen, non-steroidal anti-inflammatory, aspirin	
Cough	dextromethorphan plus guaifenesin (these two ingredients are in all cough medicines; dextromethorphan is the ingredient that helps relieve cough)	cool mist humidifier
Runny nose	antihistamine (drowsy—chlorpheniramine, triprolidine, brompheniramine, diphenhydramine, doxylamine; non-drowsy—loratadine, cetirizine, fexofenadine)	drowsy antihistamines are good for nighttime, non-drowsy good for daytime
Stuffy nose	pseudoephedrine, phenylephrine	strips for nose, cool mist humidifier (especially at night)
Sore throat	benzocaine (most common ingredient in this remedy)	
Earache	treat with pain medicine (above)	apply warm cloth to ear (be careful about heat)

Sneezing	antihistamine (see in "Runny nose")	
Indigestion	calcium carbonate	
Itching rash (any)	hydrocortisone 1% cream (do not use more than seven days, then seek professional evaluation if rash does not clear or worsens)	
Minor cut		wash with soap and water, cover with bandage, change daily; do not use antibiotic or bandage with antibiotic as allergic reaction could occur
Toothache	see Pain list above	

There are some over-the-counter products (medicines?) that have a list of chemical names that you, and most others, know nothing about. My advice is to avoid any product like that, unless you know what those ingredients are.

It is a desirable plan to have several of the medicines that are useful for the most common symptoms in your medicine cabinet. Then, if symptoms occur at a time when it is inconvenient to leave home to purchase them, you are already prepared. Painful problems and ear, nose, and throat symptoms are likely the ones that are most common. Cuts and scratches are the most common injuries for most folks. The following is a list of items to have that deal with those issues:

Symptom treatment for ear, nose, and throat symptoms:

1. Earache treatment is pain medicine. If it worsens or persists for more than two days, seek professional evaluation and treatment.
2. Antihistamine for a runny nose or itching and/or sneezing
3. Throat spray for a sore throat
4. Cough medicine for a cough

Treatment for pain anywhere and from any cause:

1. Aspirin (all brands have the same ingredient, and none work better than any other)
2. Acetaminophen (any brand, see #1)
3. Non-steroidal anti-inflammatory (ibuprofen - avoid if you have problems with heartburn or a history of stomach ulcer)
4. Be sure to know of any allergies to any of the medicines for all family members before providing the medicine. A serious allergic reaction can occur as easily to one drop or part of a pill as a full dose.

My message for this section includes the following ideas:

1. You do not need to make a diagnosis to begin home treatment for symptoms. You only need to think about treating the symptom or symptoms until you either improve or get worse. If you get worse, you will need to seek professional evaluation and treatment.
2. If you have a non-emergency medical problem, you can treat symptoms at home by using single-ingredient medicines that are available for your symptoms. If the symptom(s) persist or worsen, you will need to seek professional attention.

3. Having the most common over-the-counter medicines in your medicine cabinet allows you to quickly deal with common symptoms and provide comfort.

4. It is important to use single-ingredient medicines for symptoms, since the multi-ingredient medicines may contain chemicals you do not need and therefore subject you to possible unnecessary side effects or allergic reaction. If you were to have an allergic reaction to a multi-ingredient medicine, it would not be possible to know which chemical you reacted to.

5. If you can treat and relieve a non-emergency medical problem with the advice above, you can avoid a time-consuming, expensive visit to an urgent care center, emergency room, or doctor's office.

Additional tips:

1. Most upper respiratory infections (90%) are due to viruses. Therefore, they will heal in several days without professional help. It is particularly important not to take an antibiotic for an infection caused by a virus, since viruses are not affected by any antibiotics. The too-frequent, inappropriate use of antibiotics, especially for virus infections over the years, has led to the serious problem of several formerly very useful antibiotics no longer being effective for certain infections caused by bacteria.

2. For upper respiratory infections, especially if accompanied by nasal stuffiness and cough, a cool mist humidifier (ultrasonic) used at night can provide a very important source of moisture for the sensitive linings of the nose, mouth, and throat and make sleeping more comfortable.

3. In addition to a humidifier, the nasal strips are very helpful in the presence of nasal stuffiness, again at night in particular. A significant point about this is that if one can increase the nasal passage by as little as 10%, there is a much better ability to nose breathe. That is indeed significant when swelling inside the nose causes a reduction in nose breathing.

4. Rest and hydration (drink more water) are often overlooked principles in the care of most illnesses. Upper respiratory infections are no exception.

5. I must address fever, even if it is repeated in other parts of this book. Fever is one of the body's defense mechanisms in dealing with infection. If you take medicine to reduce fever, you are removing one of the very important ways your body creates an environment that helps to kill germs (whether the "germ" is a virus or a bacteria). It is important to know and monitor body temperature during an infection; fever is not an illness. It is a symptom that does not specifically require treatment, as long as it is not excessive or long-lasting, especially if it is not associated with other persistent or worsening symptoms. And, by the way, fever is defined as a temperature of 100.4 degrees or more, regardless of what your "normal" temperature is and in spite of whether you take it under your tongue, from your ear canal or forehead, or any other location.

helps in finding out if you and your physician are compatible. Try to determine what your doctor's assumptions are of you. The person should be interested in you and your health. If he or she is abrupt, doesn't listen at all, doesn't look you in the eyes but rather is busy clicking on his or her electronic tablet, and seems uninterested in anything you say, then it might be best to find another advisor.

In your advisory session, realize that although smart and knowledgeable, the doctor does not know everything and cannot stay up on every research article on your problem. As you talk, if you know of well-done research in the field, let the doctor know about it.

Do not expect the doctor to talk to you about charges and billing—save those questions for the billing department. Do not expect that everything should be free for you—Ha! When did we ever expect that, as much as we might wish for it to be so! Don't think your doctor should be a mind reader, and for goodness sake, tell the truth about your symptoms.

Many PCPs are on a schedule that demand they see each patient for only five to seven minutes (Salgo, 2006, *https://www.nytimes.com/2006/03/22/opinion/the-doctor-will-see-you-for-exactly-seven-minutes.html*). Whatever problem you bring to your medical provider, your description of the problem must be short but as complete as possible. Initially in the visit, we have about 15 seconds to state our problem—but that time interval might have even shortened in recent years. Singh Ospina et al. (2018) said six seconds! That is the approximate length of time a doctor will listen before interrupting the patient. The provider has lots of patients to see and cannot waste time as someone goes off into tangents, but if your doctor never listens more than six seconds, that one might be too busy for you, and you might need to find another provider.

Regardless, out of respect for the provider's time, keep your problem statement focused on the most important thing and keep it short—if you get nervous, rehearse what you will say and time yourself—bring a piece of paper with the problem written down if necessary. (One would hope that over time, a patient would not continue to be nervous—over time, a positive relationship should develop—another indicator that you might need to find someone else.) The doctor should be happy to see you.

Here are some other practical hints (especially for those of you who hardly go to your doctor):

- Don't save up woes for your doctor and spring them all at once. Tell your doctor only the one or two problems that bother you the most. Try not to bring a laundry list of ills—see the doctor more often if necessary.
- By the same token, we should not be afraid of confronting our doctor when we think we are going down a wrong path (*https://www.everydayhealth.com/columns/ therese-borchard-sanity-break/dont-be-afraid-to-be-a-di fficult-patient/*). Make sure that you discuss what is wrong with you. Be honest and don't exaggerate. Don't underplay it either. The doctor won't know how much it hurts if you don't say. Again, they are not mind readers.
- Tell what you have done to alleviate the problem. Seek the provider's advice.
- Be respectful of the allied medical staff as well. Remember that they have many patients each day, so they are likely tired.
- Make sure that you do ask all the questions you have— take notes if you think you might not remember the answers. Remember, being assertive while respectful is not rude. If you have problems speaking with doctors, bring someone with you to help you.
- Later, visit your medical portal to see a summary of what was discussed and concluded in your visit.
- If you have more than one healthcare professional involved in the problem, make sure that the communication gets to both—literally carry your report to the other doctor to make sure it is done. Check your portal(s) to make sure both have the information. (Wouldn't it be wonderful if **portals were organized around the patient** so the patient only had one? The doctors could attach to the patient and then to one another.)
- Follow up—do not assume that no news is good news. It's your health, so inquire!

Two Special Areas of Concern for Patient Involvement in Healthcare Decisions

■ Parents' rights for decisions involving their children. Should doctors or insurance providers determine what should happen, or parents, or should it be the courts? Remember the UK court decision concerning little Charlie Gard when his parents wanted to bring him to the United States for treatment of his rare disease (*https://www.wa shingtonpost.com/news/worldviews/wp/2017/06/29/against- his-parents-wishes-this-terminally-ill-infant-will-be-allowe d-to-die/?noredirect=on&utm_term=.dea7f394ae2d*). How does a parent best become involved?

■ End of life—we need to think ahead of time as to what we want and what our loved ones want, in certain cir- cumstances. Do we want to be kept alive regardless of the cost, even if death seems imminent? We all, no doubt, remember when John McCain decided to receive no further treatment for his brain cancer. He died shortly thereafter. It was his decision how much treatment he received and for how long. Do we want to try all possible treatments, for example, for cancer, or do we want to bal- ance quality of life with or without extraordinary treat- ment? Advanced directives help to guide our caregivers in times when we cannot speak for ourselves. How about our parents and elderly relatives? Do they have advanced directives?

What Patient-Directed Medicine, CEOH, Is NOT

When we say to be a participant, we are NOT saying that you should completely ignore what your doctor says and demand what you want. Here is an example. Often patients go to the doctor with an upper respiratory infection thinking they need an antibiotic. Recognize that your doctor likely knows more

ASK DR. DEAN:

Question 3: When do I need to see a doctor?
There are times when you or a family member are not
feeling well or have specific symptoms that cause you to
wonder if the problem is severe enough that a doctor visit
is needed. There are symptoms that seem severe enough
to require a doctor visit, but that is not always the case.
Some mothers (or fathers) are more sensitive than others to
symptoms. There are some symptoms, such as the following—cough, nasal discharge, sore throat, earache, nausea,
reduced appetite, pain with no obvious injury—which
may not be reason enough to have a doctor visit. Some of
those symptoms can be observed for a time until you can
be confident that those problems will resolve with time
and home treatment. That assumes that there is no fever
(the definition of fever is a temperature of 100.4 degrees
or more) or the temperature rises and symptoms increase.
Whether you decide on a doctor visit or not depends on
your comfort with the decision and also the age and illness history of the ill person. I recommend that you have a
doctor with whom you have a relationship and trust. If you
do, then sometimes a call, seeking reassurance about an
office visit or "wait and see," may be appropriate. The bottom line on when you need to see your doctor depends on
your level of confidence about dealing with the illness and
previous health history.

In the event that the symptoms of a health issue are
severe, it is important that immediate medical care is
arranged. If the time of day or week is other than the family physician's office schedule, then an appropriate decision of where to seek care is important. Traumatic injuries,
depending on severity, should be taken to an emergency
room for care. It is a good idea for there to be someone in
the family who has had some training in the best way to

deal with traumatic injuries at the time they occur pending travel to a hospital.

Less severe health problems can be managed in your doctor's office (after a call) or, depending on the day or time of day, at an urgent care location. If the illness or injury is less severe, it is less complicated and time-consuming and less expensive to go to an urgent care than an emergency room.

Most illnesses can be managed by your family doctor and/or a specialist in the body system that is affected. Your family doctor can advise you on the necessity of a referral to an appropriate specialist in whom he/she has confidence.

There are other issues that sometimes require medical assistance. Mental health issues sometimes need attention at irregular times. If you are being treated by a therapist, you should make sure that person tells you what to do in the event of an occurrence at a time when they are unavailable. If you experience an emotional breakdown that is new, you can seek help with a therapist during regular office hours. If it occurs at a time other than that, depending on its severity, you can call your family doctor for advice or go to an urgent care or emergency room, depending on the severity.

Problems with drugs or alcohol should be attended to by the staff at an emergency room, due to their appropriate staffing and more effective methods of treatment.

than you do about most medical issues. If the doctor says you do not need an antibiotic, don't demand it.

As discussed in Chapter 5, we are overusing antibiotics in this country to the extent that we are reducing their effectiveness, and when a superbug comes along, we won't have anything to combat it. If we go home and develop a fever of over 101 degrees, then we should call the doctor again. We have a responsibility to know things like this. Being responsible is part of being the CEO of our healthcare.

If we truly have a disagreement with the physician, it is perfectly fine to seek a second or even a third opinion. But demanding the doctor give us whatever prescription we are wanting is bad form, unhealthy, and counterproductive. Many physicians have told me that patients come in with a prescription in mind and some demand to get it. Whether they heard about it on television or from a friend, they want it. In Winters-Miner et al. (2015), it was estimated that a third of those with a particular disease or disorder who see the ad get the drugs that are being advertised on television. Pharmaceutical companies know exactly what they are doing when they advertise. They advertise to patients, not to their doctors, when they put out their beautifully produced, often funny, commercials.

We should not be demanding to be our own physician—we need advice from those who know more than we do about a malady. You know the saying related to that—the person who treats himself has a fool for a doctor. However, you oversee the directions your healthcare takes. You are the CEO. The doctor is the advisor.

More examples of patient-directed medicine:

- Discussing preventive choices with one's doctor when an illness runs in the family, such as Alzheimer's, when one has a familial gene.
- Discussing decisions about what kind of treatment to try when several are possible. This is when one might do additional research and bring that research to the doctor to discuss.
- Determining for oneself if a medication has too many side effects given the benefits—weighing risks and benefits for oneself. A discussion with the doctor is also advisable. (I was prescribed an antibiotic for an infection. The antibiotic caused a terrible yeast infection on my tongue, and it was the weekend. I stopped the antibiotic and let

the doctor know on the portal. The next week, in communication with the doctor, we decided I should not take any more of it. The decision originated with me, but the physician agreed.)

■ Making one's own decisions when one has a chronic illness. Someone with type 1 diabetes must learn how to manage on his or her own and must make decisions sometimes many times a day. Discussions with one's physician serve to support and aid in self-management.

■ Medical devices can be a great help, and wearable devices potentially can give minute-to-minute information. If these devices are electronically connected to the patient's portal, then theoretically, an alarm could be sent to the physician as well as to the patient for quick problem resolution.

■ Patients will have access to all their medical information. We should have access to our lab results, to doctor's notes, and to health education. This can be accomplished on the portal. **We own our data!** Remember that—it is good to provide data to researchers, but make sure the data are not taken so that you have no control over how yours are used. As an aside, think thoroughly before sending your DNA lab kit—DNA is a tremendous amount of information about YOU. Do you really want a commercial entity to have that much information about you?

■ Patients need to have access to quality journals and research. Quality research articles can be placed on portals for all patients to access.

■ Patients should seek information concerning their illnesses from many sources and not simply from the doctor. Blogs with other patients with the same illness can be invaluable. The Internet, libraries, and online libraries are all beneficial in helping to learn more and in solving problems that might come up, particularly with chronic illnesses.

- Patients should be encouraged to self-manage and to know the sequence of progressive illnesses. Information can help with coping skills.
- Connecting with one's insurance plan often is helpful in self-management—often they have helplines and 24-hour physicians/nurses. Sometimes they charge for those services, such as a 24-hour physician, but the nurse's hotline might be part of the insurance program. Such additional help allows the patient to better direct his or her own healthcare.

Directing Our Health: Consumerism and Payment

Suppose you have insurance with a copay and you go for your appointment. Do you care how much it costs if you don't have to pay for it yourself? If so you are like most people. We tend not to care if we don't have to pay out of our own pockets. As mentioned above, you might want to treat the cost as though you are to pay for your X-rays, or a blood test, yourself. You might want to ask how much it will be. You might then want to shop around and see if you can get the same service for less. Being a consumer of medical care can help to keep costs down.

In Chapter 7 we provide information on various models for medical care. Some of those methods might be better than others in keeping costs down.

Directing Our Health: Education

The more we know, the more involved we can become in our care. There are so many places to get information these days—social media (who has experienced the same problem

ASK DR. DEAN:

Question 3: What can I, the average person, understand and do about blood pressure?

HIGH BLOOD PRESSURE (HYPERTENSION)

High blood pressure, or hypertension, is one of the most common health problems in the United States. According to the CDC (Communicable Disease Center, in Atlanta), 67 million Americans have high blood pressure. A significant number of those who have high blood pressure do not have it under control.

WHY DOES IT MATTER IF MY BLOOD PRESSURE IS HIGH?

The main reason for knowing whether you have high blood pressure and whether it is under control is that 1,000 people PER DAY, or almost 350,000 per year, die because of long-standing high blood pressure. High blood pressure is an underlying cause of heart attacks, strokes, heart failure, and kidney failure. Though high blood pressure is not the only cause of death, it is a strong contributing factor, and keeping it under control reduces that risk.

WHAT DOES HIGH BLOOD PRESSURE DO THAT MAKES IT SO DANGEROUS?

Blood circulates through your arteries to all parts of your body from your heart. In order for the blood to be able to get to all of the cells of your body to deliver nutrients and oxygen, it requires that the heart pumps at a high enough pressure so that the blood can do what it is designed to do. The normal pressure that is required does not damage any of the arteries through which the blood travels, and the arteries are designed to easily withstand that pressure.

Under certain circumstances, more pressure is required to get the blood everywhere in your body. The circumstances that cause the pressure to be higher than what is "normal" are caused by certain health conditions, by what you eat, by your weight, by how active you are, as well as what you inherit from your parents.

If a person has abnormalities in the factors above, then there may be a result of thickening of the arteries, or blockage of some very important arteries. Then, in order for the blood to be distributed as needed under those abnormal conditions, the heart may have to produce a higher pressure to make sure that the blood is delivered as required. That increased pressure causes stress on the walls of the arteries, and the arteries are damaged over time so that a heart attack, stroke, heart failure, or kidney disease could occur as a result.

It is important to recognize that the damage caused by high blood pressure takes place gradually over a period of time and is determined by the level of blood pressure over the normal pressure. So, if your blood pressure is 10% higher than normal, for example, the damage occurs over a longer period of time than if your blood pressure is 50% higher than normal, as another example.

An important point about the danger of high blood pressure that many people do not know is that it is called "the silent killer" because, in some people, no abnormal feelings are present, and therefore there are no warning signs of a problem. It is for that reason that it is important to have your blood pressure checked periodically, especially after age 45.

ARE THERE SPECIFIC PEOPLE WHO ARE MORE LIKELY TO HAVE HIGH BLOOD PRESSURE?

Blood pressure is more common in certain categories of folks, as follows:

- as you age, blood pressure gets higher
- African American men and women have high blood pressure at a younger age
- Hispanics have lower rates of high blood pressure than either whites or African-Americans
- all groups have high blood pressure more often as they get older, especially after 45
- your race or ethnic category is not the only thing that affects your likelihood of having high blood pressure or of keeping it under control, if you have it

What Can I Do to Deal with High Blood Pressure?
There are several things that you can do to make sure that your blood pressure is either normal, or that it is borderline high, to avoid high blood pressure—hypertension. The following list outlines some important things of which to be aware:

1. Periodically your blood pressure should be checked, especially after age 45, or younger if hypertension in a parent was diagnosed at an age younger than 45.
2. If your blood pressure is normal, then it does not need to be checked as often but should be checked at least yearly, or when you visit your doctor.
3. If your blood pressure is borderline high, it should be checked more often than yearly.
4. In order to diagnose hypertension, it is very important that the blood pressure is accurate.
5. If hypertension is diagnosed, then treatment with medicine to lower your blood pressure will be important, along with lifestyle changes.
6. Be sure to report to your doctor any uncomfortable feelings (medicine side effects) that occur soon after you begin taking your blood pressure medicine.

7. There are many different medicines to reduce your blood pressure. Since that is the case, if you have side effects to any of the blood pressure medicines, find one you can take that will not produce undesirable side effects.

8. Take your blood pressure medicine exactly the way that your doctor recommends. If you have a problem with following those recommendations, discuss them with your doctor so appropriate adjustments in treatment can be made that still work to reduce your blood pressure.

9. It is important also to keep track of your blood pressure readings outside your doctor's office. For that reason, you should have an appropriate blood pressure machine, one that your doctor recommends, and learn to use it.

10. Keep a written record of the readings you get at home, along with the date and time they were performed. Take it with you when you visit your doctor.

11. I do not recommend that you use the machine at the pharmacy or at any other location besides your doctor's office to measure blood pressure. Those machines are not necessarily accurate, and the readings are more consistent if measured on the same machine each time. Another device to avoid is the finger or wrist blood pressure machine, because they are not consistently accurate.

12. The lifestyle that helps reduce your blood pressure includes the following:
    - if you are overweight, it is important to get weight down to normal or near normal
    - regular exercise is a very good way to improve your blood pressure and help with
    - weight loss if that is needed. For example, 30 minutes of exercise per day five days per week is one recommendation (walking at a brisk pace is a good choice).

WHAT ARE THE "NORMAL," "BORDERLINE," AND "HIGH" BLOOD PRESSURES?

Normal Systolic: 120 mmHg
Normal Diastolic: 80 mmHg

At risk (prehypertension): Systolic: 120–139 mmHg
At risk (prehypertension): Diastolic: 80–90 mmHg

High risk Systolic: 140 mmHg or higher
High Diastolic: Higher than 90

as us, and what did they learn?), the Internet (one can find full texts of research articles on the Internet). You may not be able to evaluate all research, but if you read what was done, you can use common sense. Is someone trying to sell a product? (Likely that research has a bias.) How many people did the researcher enroll in the study? (Five people would not carry the weight of studying 500 people.) How long was the evaluation period for safety? (If the researchers studied the drug for six weeks and then put it on the market, that study would not reveal possible long-term problems as with a drug that was studied for years.) Was the study a case-controlled, double-blind study? (In such a study, the test group and the placebo group, for example, would have certain equivalencies—say, people with the disease at the same stage of disease, separated randomly between the study group and the control (placebo) group. Double-blind means that the evaluation of efficacy did not depend on the group one was in—the evaluator did not know if the person was in the experimental group or the control group) A double blind, case-control study is a type of traditional research one is apt to find in the literature at this time. One should try to find predictive analytical studies if they are available.

ASK DR. DEAN:

Question 4: What can I do at home, and when should I see a doctor, for various miscellaneous conditions, such as poison ivy, insect bites, and other types of skin issues?

POISON IVY

This aggravating plant is everywhere. If you develop an itching rash from this plant, it can be located anywhere on your body, and the itching is miserable. There are some points about it that are listed below:

1. You must have been in contact with the plant's oil (urushiol) in order to get the rash. You cannot get it by being in contact with someone else's skin or rash.
2. The rash does not "spread" to areas of skin that have not been in contact with the plant's oil. It seems to spread due to the fact that the rash does not develop on all the contacted areas at the same time. It develops over a period of a few days, and that makes it seem that it is spreading.
3. The offending oil can be present on clothes, gloves, tools, or pets, and if you come in contact with the oil because of any of those, you can develop the rash.
4. The reaction (rash) of poison ivy develops within several hours to a few days and may last from 7–10 days. In some cases, it can last considerably longer, but that is not usual.
5. The rash (and itching) is self-limiting; in other words, no matter what you do or do not do, it will resolve on its own.
6. Over-the-counter lotions are available to help reduce the itching.

7. If the rash covers a considerable area of your body, and/or if it is considerably uncomfortable, you may choose to receive treatment from your family doctor.

SPIDER BITES

Often, people have been seen with a complaint of having been bitten by a spider. They show a swollen, red, uncomfortable lesion on a hand, arm, or leg that is draining a small amount of pus. The first question is, what did the spider look like? Typically, no spider was seen. Almost without fail, the problem in this scenario is a local infection due to methicillin-resistant *Staphylococcus aureus* infection, or MRSA infection. That diagnosis can be proven by doing a bacterial culture, but the appearance of the lesion is so characteristic that doing a culture is not necessary and appropriate treatment could be provided immediately. On the other hand, if a person were to bring the spider (in a container and not alive), then it could be identified, and if a specific treatment or patient observation, based on the particular insect, was called for, that would be a different situation calling for a different approach.

SKIN RASH

A variety of skin conditions can occur, and they are very common. Some cause symptoms, such as itching, scaling, burning, blistering, chafing, pain, or infection. The rash may be unsightly, especially on the face, where it cannot be hidden by clothing. The causes are many, and the areas affected can be anywhere on the body. The first time you develop a rash, it is likely that home treatment with some over-the-counter cream or lotion can be used to treat it. If it resolves, then the problem is solved, at least for the time being. If it reoccurs or persists, you may want to have a professional evaluation. Your family doctor can suggest an appropriate first step for a possible diagnosis and treatment. A significant issue with skin rashes is that the skin has only a few reactions that are possible. Those include color change, blistering, swelling, bruising, bumps, pustules, and scaling, and the causes of those reactions are many. Initial treatment is usually simple. If a rash is recurrent or persistent and initial treatment is not effective, then it is necessary to have an evaluation by a skin specialist, a dermatologist. That specialist only treats medical problems related to the skin and has specific comprehensive training dealing with all the problems related to skin diseases and conditions. My previous comment about the importance of diagnosis is very applicable to skin problems.

We need to be smart when it comes to our healthcare. If we don't care, who will?

Directing Our Health: Future Trends

Devices are coming on the market every day! At the time of this writing, one could wear a tiny computer on one's wrist that would tell one's heartbeats, blood pressure, or whether the person was about to fall. An EKG device sold for under $100 that one could put two fingers on and get a readout sent to one's physician to tell if the person had atrial fibrillation. Glucose monitors have become quite sophisticated. Devices will become more prevalent and sophisticated. We can swallow pills that are nanomachines to hunt down and kill cancer cells. Perhaps we'll be able to place bio-hardware in our brains to maintain our memories.

Healthcare delivery is changing. Patient roles are changing drastically and will continue to change in the future with more innovations, with predictive analytics, and with greater uses of

ASK DR. DEAN:

Question 5: How can a person treat colds and upper respiratory infections at home? When should they consult a doctor?

Let me answer this by providing a series of sub-questions and answers:

Q: What are the symptoms of a cold?

A: Almost everyone knows the common feelings that they have when they have a "cold." Most of the time it starts with a scratchy feeling in the throat, or maybe a sore throat. Then one or two days later, other feelings include a runny nose, a stuffy feeling in the nose, and cough. Those feelings are not particularly a problem at first, but often get worse as days pass. The feelings that occur with colds might be different from one person to another, so if your feelings are more severe than someone else, that does not change the fact that you have a cold just the same.

Q: How long does a cold last?

A: Colds usually last seven days but can drag on for as much as three weeks.

Q: How can I know whether what I have is "just a cold" or something more serious for which I need to see a doctor for a diagnosis and treatment?

A: The most important way to tell whether you need to see a doctor or not depends on a few things. The most important is whether you have a fever. A mild increase in your normal temperature is certainly possible with a cold. However, it is important for you to know what temperature level means that you have a "fever"; that helps the doctor who is trying to make an accurate diagnosis. A temperature of 100.4 or higher is an important level to help the doctor understand more about your symptoms, along with other feelings that you report. I have seen many patients that tell me that they, or their child, has a fever. Then after I ask more questions, like, "what has your temperature been?", the patient might say, "I did have a fever because my temperature was 99.3 degrees and my normal temperature is 97 degrees." (See the next question about fever.) The reason that fever is important when you have symptoms of a cold is that colds are caused by viruses, and fever does not usually occur with a cold. On the other hand, if you have cold symptoms and also have a fever, there is the **possibility** that a "cold" is not the correct diagnosis. The higher the fever, the more likely that a complication of your cold is occurring and that you should see a doctor to correctly make a diagnosis and treat the complication. Therefore, checking the temperature of anyone with cold symptoms is an important thing to do in order to decide if your symptoms are due to a cold that will get better or might indicate that a more important diagnosis is occurring. *An important thing for you to remember is that treatment is very easy; it is making a diagnosis that is the hard part of medical care.*

Other things that might happen to suggest a diagnosis other than a cold and need a doctor's evaluation and/or treatment (including developing fever) are how long the symptoms have lasted, whether the symptoms are getting worse when they normally would be getting gradually better, or if you have a chronic or long-term illness like emphysema or another respiratory condition. Symptoms that are particularly important include increasing shortness of breath, coughing up more and more mucus, noticing blood mixed in with the mucus that comes up when you cough, and a feeling of congestion in your chest that does not get better with coughing it up. If you are a smoker, you are more likely to have a complication of colds or have more frequent colds than most people.

Most of the time, when you have a cold, the symptoms are uncomfortable and embarrassing in public but are not serious. The symptoms are treatable with medicines you can buy over the counter, and you get well over several days (or a week or so).

Q: What is important about body temperature and fever? The reason that a temperature may be lower than 98.6 degrees or a little higher than that is that there are things besides infection that can cause a mildly lower or higher temperature. The level of 98.6 is an average of many, many people who were not sick whose temperature was checked. Some of those people had a temperature a little lower than the average and some a little higher. The average of all was 98.6. So, in order to make a decision about what would be abnormal, the agreement of the experts was that fever would be defined as 100.4 or more. A temperature above the agreed upon 100.4 level would therefore be more likely to represent an important symptom rather than due to some random cause that was not important in making a diagnosis. In fact, a temperature of 100.4 degrees or more is necessary to know that fever is present, no matter what is "normal" for you or your child. So, if you have the symptoms of a cold and your temperature is 100.3 degrees or less, you do not have "fever" since the medical definition of fever is 100.4 degrees or more.

Q: Should I be worried about a very high fever? A: There are certain situations in which a very high fever for a long period of time could let you know that a doctor should evaluate you and establish a diagnosis. What is a "very high fever" and how long a period of time is important? My first comment about that is that the fever itself is not the problem. The *cause* of the fever must be determined so that the proper care and treatment can be given. If you look on the internet, you will find a large number of different opinions about fever and what is a dangerous temperature and what you should do. My advice depends on the situation that is present. A "very high temperature" that indicates a serious problem is different for a very young baby (1 to about 6 months of age) compared to a child (6 months to about 6 years), an older child (7 years to about 18 years), and an adult. There are other situations in which a doctor's evaluation must be done sooner. Those other situations are beyond the goals of this book.

In summary, regarding fever and how you can deal with it properly, the following will tell you the principles for dealing with fever:

1. Fever is not a disease or illness by itself. The cause of the fever is the important thing to deal with, especially if the fever is persistent, long-lasting (hours), and associated with symptoms that make the patient unable to function normally.
2. It is not necessary to treat a fever, with a few exceptions.
3. If a fever (temperature 100.4 degrees or higher) remains higher than a normal temperature for several hours, especially if there are also other symptoms that are not normal, then you should have a doctor perform an evaluation to establish a diagnosis that establishes the reason for the fever. Then the treatment that is ordered will help improve the cause of the fever and the patient will get well.
4. If you have fever that is getting higher and higher, or if you become especially worried about the symptoms that are present along with fever, then it is appropriate to contact your doctor or go to an urgent care or an emergency room so that a doctor can perform an evaluation and make a diagnosis and prescribe appropriate treatment.

5. Concern about fever, especially in children, has a long history that still affects people's action when it occurs. As a result, many people see their doctor when fever is present, for example, when they believe they have an infection that they think needs to be treated with an antibiotic. The origin of some of that concern, again, especially in children, was because the medical opinion in the past was that fever, especially a temperature higher than 102, was a cause of seizures. Years ago, if a child had a fever and developed a seizure, that child would be treated for "seizure disorder" for a year or more, and parents were cautioned to always give their child medicine to reduce the fever and avoid another seizure. More recent research has proven that there is not a connection between "high" fever and seizure disorder. A long-lasting fever is capable of causing a seizure, but in general treating fever is not necessary and may not be a good idea, since fever is one of the body's defense methods to help the body fight off infection by making the body a poor environment for the growth of viruses and bacteria and by causing the patient to remain at rest. Those ways of action, along with checking the temperature often to understand how the illness is doing, are better ways of dealing with a sick patient at home.

Q: If I don't go to a doctor for treatment when I have a cold, what is the best treatment to help me be more comfortable until I get well?
A: There are several medicines and procedures for home treatment of colds and some other common symptoms. Using these should help relieve the symptoms until the problem gets better and has the advantage of avoiding the inconvenience and expense of a doctor visit.

Most people go to a pharmacy and look at all the shelves full of all kinds of pills, syrups, and potions. The labels tell you what *diagnosis* each medicine is designed to treat. My suggestion is that what you really need is medicine to treat the *symptoms* you have, rather than trying to guess the diagnosis that is present. Then, if you treat the symptoms, as I will describe, and get better rather than worse, you will have properly dealt with your problem and avoided unnecessary expense.

Q: Okay, what should I do to follow your advice of treating the symptoms?

A: First, let me tell you what you should have available in your home medicine cabinet. These medicines and advice specifically apply to symptoms of the eyes, ears, nose, and mouth and include coughing. If you pay attention to what symptoms are present and match the medicine to the symptom or symptoms, then you can expect relief. They are as follows:

1. Cough

   It is especially bothersome to have a cough when you are trying to sleep, or if you are coughing frequently. The best and safest medicine is a syrup containing guaifenesin (for reducing cough) and dextromethorphan (for making the mucus in your chest easier to cough up). Always read the labels on the bottles. When you are deciding which brand of medicine to buy, look at the four ingredients. In the case of cough medicine, look for the two ingredients mentioned above and **only** those two ingredients. If you find the least expensive cough medicine that has only those two, you will save money and it will be just as effective as the most expensive. Another reason for knowing the ingredients, rather than just the name of the medicine, is that if you are taking other medicines, you need to avoid taking two or more medicines that have the same ingredients. If you do that, you might suffer an overdose and have a bad reaction that could have been avoided. The cough medicine can be taken every four hours if needed.

Be sure to carefully follow the dose instructions on the bottle in order to avoid any potential bad side effects.

2. Nose running

Many over-the-counter medicines have multiple ingredients, and you may not need all of those. If you take medicine with ingredients you do not need, you run the risk of bad side effects or possible allergic reaction. Therefore, you should only take what is necessary to give you some comfort from the symptoms you have.

In the case of a runny nose, an antihistamine is the proper treatment. Again, look at the ingredients and choose an antihistamine. Some common antihistamines include the following: chlorpheniramine (Chlor-Trimeton), brompheniramine (Dimetapp), and diphenhydramine (Benadryl). This medicine should be taken every four hours while the symptom is present.

These antihistamines can help reduce a runny nose, but they may produce drowsiness. They are to be taken several times a day, typically every four hours. Diphenhydramine (Benadryl) is the one most likely to cause drowsiness, so it is important to find out how these medicines affect you before you drive. There are other antihistamines that are made to not cause drowsiness, but they are not as effective for the runny nose of a cold or flu. Also, they are much more expensive.

3. Pain-body aches, headache, sore throat, muscle aches (along with cold or flu symptoms). There are two over-the-counter medicines for pain. These are

acetaminophen and ibuprofen. There are several
names for these two. Read the labels and look for
those two names. No matter what the cost of the trade
name, they are all the same and work equally well.
Acetaminophen (Tylenol) comes in 325 and 500 mg
strength. One tablet of either one should be given/
taken first, and the effect should be noted. If the pain
is not relieved, then the next dose can increase to
two tablets. (It is very important to check labels of
other medicines being taken to be sure whether one
of them also has acetaminophen as one of its ingredients. Prescribed pain medicines frequently do include
acetaminophen). Over-the-counter ibuprofen tablets
are 200 mg each. The appropriate dose is three tablets. These can be taken every four hours if needed for
pain/aching. (Do not take ibuprofen if you have heartburn or a stomach ulcer, and it is not a good idea to
take it daily for no more than 2 weeks.)
4. Nasal stuffiness/congestion/difficulty breathing through
your nose. This is a very common symptom of colds
and flu (allergy also). Treatment of this very bothersome symptom calls for a decongestant. The common
decongestants are pseudoephedrine and phenylephrine Both are effective. There are multiple products
that include one of these in over-the-counter pills. My
recommendation is to buy the pill that only has the
one ingredient.

Nasal sprays are very effective and quickly relieve nasal
stuffiness. The name of the medicine in the sprays is oxy-
metazoline hydrochloride (Afrin, Neo-Synephrine, Dristan,
Vicks Sinex, various store five brands). Always look at the
labels of medicine and choose the one with the chemical
name that has the important ingredient(s) rather than the

most frequently advertised name. The main concern about the nasal spray is that if it is used frequently or for a long period, it can lead to difficulty in stopping the use of it.

My recommendation is to use it only occasionally, such as at night when the nasal stuffiness can interfere with sleep. It can be used at other times also, but use it only occasionally.

The other method I recommend strongly is the nasal strips that stick on the outside of your nose and open it a little. If you can increase the opening of your nose by only 10%, there is a large improvement in your ability to breathe through your nose. [picture of Breathe Right on nose]

One other strong recommendation for improving cold/flu symptoms is to use an ultrasonic humidifier at night. It should be placed close to the bed and at a level that causes the visible mist from the humidifier to cover your face and head. My comment to patients is "when you use the humidifier, if you wake up in the morning and your blanket, your pajamas, the sheets, the pillow, and your hair are wet, that is perfect." One of the main functions of your nose is to moisten the air that you breathe. If you breathe through your mouth, the air does not get moistened, and the result is that your mouth and throat get dry, causing more coughing, sore throat, difficulty falling and staying asleep, and just general discomfort. If the air is moist, due to the humidifier, all of those symptoms are better. [picture of humidifier showing location and mist]

Another important treatment for the symptoms of a cold is to drink more water than would normally be the case. It is common for folks to not drink as much water as needed, especially when illness is present, such as with a cold or flu. The common recommendation is eight glasses per day. In general, that is a good recommendation when you are ill with symptoms such as a cold or flu.

SUMMARY

Upper respiratory infections caused by viruses, such as colds or the flu, can be treated at home until or unless complications or infection by other germs (bacteria) occur. Fever, especially if it occurs some days after symptoms begin, is the most important signal that a doctor should evaluate you and recommend treatment. Another occurrence that indicates that home treatment is no longer the right thing to do is if symptoms are getting more severe over time and in spite of home treatment.

Having certain over-the-counter medicines in your medicine cabinet will permit you to begin home treatment immediately, no matter what time of day or night symptoms begin. That treatment can begin even if you decide, based on the development of additional symptoms, that a physician's evaluation is necessary. Take the medicine as noted above, but only treat the symptoms you actually have. Many over-the-counter medicines have multiple medicines for different symptoms all in one bottle. If you take one of those "multi-symptom" medicines but only have one of the symptoms, you will be taking medicine you do not need and will risk a reaction or overdose of a medicine that you did not need. That is why I have recommended that you have several medicines that have only the one needed for your specific symptom. If you have more than one symptom, then you can take the additional medicine for that symptom as well. That method is the safest and most effective treatment for the illness you have without the risk of taking medicine you did not need.

List of Symptoms and Medicines/Supplies to Have Ready:

1. Cough medicine—one containing guaifenesin and dextromethorphan

2. Runny nose—antihistamine—pseudoephedrine or phenylephrine (tablets or liquid) 6
3. Stuffy nose—decongestant—pseudoephedrine or phenylephrine
4. Pain or aching—acetaminophen or ibuprofen
5. Ultrasonic humidifier to add needed moisture to your nose and throat and increase comfort
6. Nasal strips—for stuffy nose: to improve breathing through your nose
7. Thermometer—to allow you to watch the temperature and measure fever (if present)

Other Points to Remember:

1. Read labels and get over-the-counter medicines with only the one ingredient recommended above
2. Check temperature several times each day (two or three times) and record
3. Give/take only the medicines needed for the symptoms that are present
4. Take the medicines at regular times each day for several days, while the symptoms are present, based on the recommendations on the medicine containers; as symptoms improve, you can stop whichever medicine you were taking for that symptom
5. Watch for side effects of medicines (symptoms that are not related to the illness and begin soon after taking the medicine)
6. Drink at least eight glasses of water or other liquids per day (water is best)
7. Rest is important, especially when symptoms begin and depending on how severe they are
8. Frequent handwashing, by the sick person as well as everyone else in the house, is important to reduce the

likelihood of spread of the virus to others who live in
the same house
9. Spread of symptoms is most likely when symptoms
first begin and/or when fever is present

search engines on the Internet (Topol, 2015). We can take care
of many of our basic medical needs ourselves.

What we really need in this country are good models for
healthcare that are affordable and have the potential of including everyone.

References

Singh Ospina, N., Phillips, K.A., Rodriguez, R., Castaneda-
Guarderas, A., Gionfriddo, M.R., and Branda, M.E. (2018).
"Eliciting the patient's agenda-secondary analysis of recorded
clinical encounters." *Journal of General Internal Medicine*. DOI:
10.1007/s11606-018-4540-5

Topol, E. (2015). *The Patient Will See You Now*. New York: Basic
Books.

Verma, M. (2012). "Personalized medicine and cancer." *Journal of
Personalized Medicine*, 2(1), 1–14. Doi:10.3390/jpm2010001

Winters-Miner, L.A., Bolding, P.S., Hilbe, J.M., Goldstein, M., Hill,T.,
Nisbet, R., Walton, N., and Miner, G.D. (2015). *Practical
Predictive Analytics and Decisioning Systems for Medicine*.
Boston, MA: Elsevier/Academic Press.

Chapter 7

The *CURE*—SOLUTIONS to Make Healthcare Delivery in the USA ACCURATE, EFFECTIVE, and COST-EFFICIENT

> **"The ballooning costs of healthcare act as a hungry tapeworm on the American economy,"** Berkshire Hathaway CEO Warren Buffett said in a statement (*https://www.cnbc.com/2018/01/30/amazon-berkshire-hathaway-and-jpmorgan-chase-to-partner-on-us-employee-health-care.html*).

Americans are well aware that getting healthcare in the USA is an absolutely messy proposition. Americans clearly see what is going on. Unfortunately, even some of the early 2000s "alerts" (see Additional Resources at the end of this book for a listing of books published on the "healthcare mess" over the past 20 years) did little to bring about change, and we are about in the same situation in 2019 as we were back in

2009. Yes, some attempts at re-engineering healthcare delivery have been attempted here and there. Some have succeeded and some have failed. But none have been widely developed across the USA yet; those that are working, like the Oak Street model in Chicago, only affect tens of thousands of people or fewer.

Healthcare Information and Management Systems Society, or HIMSS, is one of the largest healthcare delivery organizations in the USA. Upwards of 50,000 people or more attend their annual meeting (usually held at the end of February or the beginning of March). Your senior writer of this book has given both invited and peer-reviewed selected talks at HIMSS in recent years and has observed and come to the opinion that HIMSS "lags behind" what really needs to be done in medicine. Yet, at HIMSS18 (March 2018) in Las Vegas, some of the keynote addresses done by some of the executives of HIMSS and associates were alerting all HIMSS members to the fact that ***action has to be taken ... and that those healthcare entities that DID not take action would be left behind, as changes are beginning to happen fast*** ... Thus, below we present some quotes from this recent HIMSS annual meeting to document that there is beginning to be wide acceptance in the USA that we can no longer talk about the need for change but that we must take action. These quotes were taken from the last print issue of the Healthcare IT News, March 2018, page 19 article titled "NEW PARADIGM—Why the Amazon, Berkshire and JPMorgan plans should inspire hospital IT shops to act fast," which came out at the time of the HIMSS meeting, as follows: (references: *https://www.healthcareitnews.com/himss-coverage; https://www.healthcareitnews.com/issue/march-2018-digital-edition-healthcare-it-news*)

"The entire ecosystem is changing, forcing smart CIOs to keep pace OR face significant disruption."

"... Amazon rattled the healthcare market on January 30, 2018, with their announcement ... creating a nonprofit healthcare company focusing on:

1. Cost Reduction
2. Increased Transparency
3. User Satisfaction

"We're starting to see a DISRUPTION MODEL take place .... This is not a one-and-done ... ALL HOSPITAL SYSTEMS have to FIGURE OUT 'How to Catch Up'"—as stated by HIMSS CEO Hal Wolfe.

But Wolfe continued to point out: "But more than one deal with ***Gigantic Disruption Potential*** is happening right now," like the following:

1. CVS announcing its intent to acquire AETNA for $69 billion;
2. DaVita selling its managed care group to OPTUM in a $5 billion deal;
3. Apple revealing its plans to add MEDICAL RECORDS to the iPhone

Wolfe continued: "'This is going to be a challenge to the (entire) ***Medical Model***. It's about ***thinking through the whole ecosystem***, which is changing ... this (probably) means that ***change*** will be ***faster*** and ***larger*** than what people would have liked ...'"

Rasu Shrestha, M.D., chief innovation officer of University of Pittsburgh Medical Center (UPMC) said: "Hanging on to today's ways of doing business only makes hospitals ***vulnerable to failure*** and, ultimately, being ***rendered irrelevant*** ... I am excited about the waves of possible ***disruption***, if they are based on ***substance*** (and not hype) ... Therein lies the opportunity for ***forward-thinking health systems***" ... "Health systems ***must be proactive*** in their approach to not just tackle the everyday challenges of what we know as health and care today, but to ***redefine the very notion of healthcare*** in the bold new world ahead."

Nick Patel, M.D., executive medical director of clinical infor-matics at Palmetto Health-USC Medical Group said: "It's not just Amazon, either... JPMorgan and Berkshire Hathaway have the potential to advance transparency, leverage economies of scale, and bring expenses down to revolutionize cost-savings."

Patel continued: "With Apple improving how patients' records are accessed and shared, duplication of labs and other tests will hopefully be reduced ... ***companies are fed up with rising costs and lack of improvements in patient care and safety to show for it***."

Wolfe focused on three action items for ***how*** hospital and IT executives could make this disruption happen:

1. STRATEGIC CONNECTIVITY
2. THINK on a NETWORK BASIS
3. WORKFORCE TRAINING

Bill Russell, CEO of Health Lyrics (former CEO of St. Joseph Health) said: "hospitals have to start cultivating the ***necessary skills*** for the ***rise of consumerism*** in healthcare."

Will Weider (longtime healthcare CIO) said: "The tec-tonic shifts (that will happen) should also include

***making it easier for patients to do business
with you*** .... We need to recognize that our customers (i.e. patients) do not want to be restricted
to business hours that do not fit their schedule, or
having to make phone calls to conduct business
(healthcare delivery) ... even seemingly simple
tasks, such as registering to use or re-setting patient
portal passwords and scheduling are often difficult,
today, in healthcare portals and systems."

Weider continued: "Amazon did not become the leading
retailer because of price or selection—but it is a
leader because it is so damn easy to buy things from
them!!! ... When it becomes easier to do business
(healthcare delivery) with someone else, there will
be no loyalty to a previous 'healthcare provider'" ...
period!!!!!

Shrestha continued: "[we have to] reimagine new care models, embrace what has worked, and rethink products,
services, and culture across healthcare in ways that
have never been done before ... we must be bold, we
must be steadfast, and we must be intelligent in our
approaches."

Wolfe continued: "**Interoperability** has to happen almost
immediately."

*AND to this, this book's senior author, Dr. GARY MINER,
wrote:* "And there has to be an intersection back to
the medical model for whatever virtual ideas that
are developed to sit on the outside ... the outside and the inside (medical care) must connect
***(seamlessly, instantly, and accurately, with
security)***."

THE "CURES"—GOOD SOLUTIONS—GOOD MODELS for Re-Engineering Healthcare Delivery in the USA:

There appear to be at least five possible solutions ("Cures"!!!!) to the "sickness in today's US healthcare delivery systems":

1. Single-payer system for all of the USA's citizens' healthcare
2. Direct care for routine "everyday primary care health issues," PLUS low-cost catastrophic insurance for the rare expensive health crisis
3. Corporate takeover of healthcare—the *Amazon—JPMorgan—Berkshire Hathaway* corporate plan to take care of their employees all the way (plan of early 2018 where the "corporation" will take care of all health needs, from production of drugs, to patient care, to payer provisions)
4. A system like the **Oak Street Model** (which started in Chicago and is now expanding—but this is just for seniors—Medicare—Medicare Advantage patients) … that could be expanded to the entire population
5. A "hybrid system" distilled from the chaotic mixture of systems currently intermingling in US payment for healthcare (because of the unique way that the USA has developed over the past 100 years in healthcare—thus many diverse/conflicting ideas and political interests and a "hybrid system" may be the only type of system that is possible (e.g. realistic) to obtain)

To be truly successful, whichever model is adopted from the above must take into account the "disruptive/turned upside down" model presented as the main thesis of this book as illustrated in Figure 7.1.

In this chapter we will discuss in a bit more detail these five types of "DELIVERY MODELS for HEALTHCARE," any one of which could be successful in the USA in the future, if it was developed cleanly without any kinds of "governmental and bureaucratical" tangents.

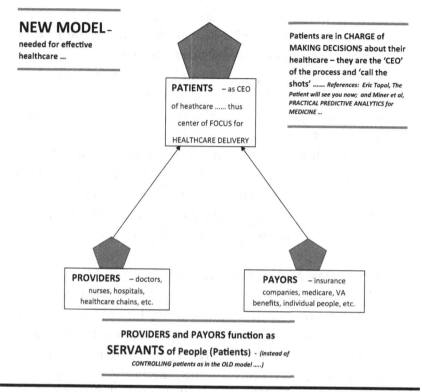

NEW MODEL-

needed for effective healthcare ...

PATIENTS – as CEO

of heathcare ...... thus

center of FOCUS for

HEALTHCARE DELIVERY

Patients are in CHARGE of MAKING DECISIONS about their healthcare – they are the 'CEO' of the process and 'call the shots' ...... *References: Eric Topol, The Patient will see you now; and Miner et al, PRACTICAL PREDICTIVE ANALYTICS for MEDICINE ...*

PROVIDERS – doctors, nurses, hospitals, healthcare chains, etc.

PAYORS – insurance companies, medicare, VA benefits, individual people, etc.

PROVIDERS and PAYORS function as

SERVANTS of People (Patients) - *(instead of CONTROLLING patients as in the OLD model .....)*

Figure 7.1   New Model: Umbrella philosophy of effective healthcare solutions for the USA. (Model by Gary Miner.)

1. Single-Payer Model

In this model, the government would provide healthcare for all citizens of the United States, and it would work quite a lot like Medicare, but for all. The healthcare providers could be either public or private. Remember that in the models from other countries, providers can be either private or public. In all those countries, single-payer healthcare was able to limit the costs only if the prices for all services and medications were negotiated and standardized. There was a strictly followed price list for all procedures and medications. If we were to follow the German model, public health could be refused by an individual, and private healthcare could be privately purchased, as Germany also has private hospitals that cater to the wealthy. ***The secret to keeping the prices down is the negotiation part.*** At present, the United States has no good mechanism for negotiating prices, and the proverbial foxes look after the hen houses with pricing according to what the market will bear. We have to decide if the market is free if someone's life is on the line. Deciding on a life-saving medication is not quite like picking a loaf a bread. One might rather go bankrupt than die. The free market can work quite well for competing products, but not for those that are life-saving and have patents for exclusive sales (Figure 7.2).

2. Direct Pay Model for Basic Care

This mode for basic care uses a free market system. The direct pay method is being used by a growing number of doctors and clinics around the country. Doctors in this model run their own businesses. They do not file insurance or take insurance. Rather, patients pay a monthly fee, say $50 per month for an adult and $25 per

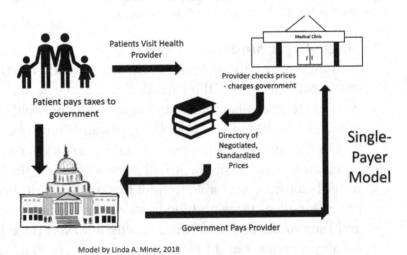

Model by Linda A. Miner, 2018

Figure 7.2 The Single-Payer Model—works like Medicare, except that all prices are negotiated and standardized to keep down costs. (Model by Linda Miner.)

month per child under 18, to subscribe to the service. The fee pays for office visits, phone calls, and emails. Use of portals would also be used. The fee paid would cover all basic care, including common lab tests and X-rays, and basic shots. Specialized and emergency care would need to be covered by a catastrophic insurance policy, which would cost less because it would be used less often. Generic drugs in the direct care model often are sold for cost plus a small percentage.

Catastrophic insurance is very much less expensive than traditional insurance because the copays are huge—perhaps $20,000 to $25,000. Most people don't use catastrophic insurance, but if one starts when young with this system, he or she would be able to put the savings into a health-care savings account (HSA). One is allowed a little over $6,000 per year tax-free. Over the years, if not needed, this sum could amount to a sizeable savings account, well able to cover a copay if needed (Goldhill, 2013).

In the direct care model, patients would find their own doctors, and doctors would then compete for patients until they had enough—enough for the individual doctor. It is conceivable that doctors that were considered "good" by patients might garner more patients than doctors that patients did not really like. Of course, if the popular doctors should become so busy as not to be able to help patients in a timely fashion, patients might leave and find another physician (Figure 7.3).

To include everyone in this model, the government would pay for poor citizens, so that all could find doctors. If doctors could decide when they had enough patients, then one thing to consider by law would be the question of pre-existing conditions. In a fair system, everyone should be able to subscribe. Perhaps everyone would be accepted by law, up to a certain number set by each doctor.

The costs of such a direct care model for a family of four could be as low as about $100 for catastrophic care and $140 a month for the direct pay part—a total of under $250 per

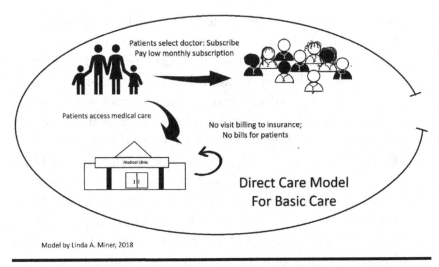

Model by Linda A. Miner, 2018

Figure 7.3   The Direct Care Model for Basic Care—This model is used with the purchase of catastrophic insurance. It is self-contained except that the doctor must obtain medicine, labs and/or materials and devices from outside. (Model by Linda Miner.)

month. In an article by Guy Boulton, published June 7, 2018, in USA Today:

> "The total costs for a typical family of four insured by the most common health plan offered by employers will average $28,166 this year, according to the annual Milliman Medical Index." (par. 1 *https://www. usatoday.com/story/money/business/2018/06/06/ health-care-costs-price-family-four/676046002/*)

The total of $28,166 per year would amount to about $2,248 per month, nearly ten times as much as the direct pay model. And of course, that $2,248 does not include what the family would pay for copays, lab tests, and basic medications, which would be included in the Direct Care Model. Employers that provide healthcare could pay for the direct pay subscription cost for the family and then sock the rest away in the employees' health savings accounts. Families that did not have employer-sponsored healthcare could better afford the direct care subscription plus catastrophic care more than they could foot the bill for regular insurance, which could cost ten times the direct care+catastrophic model.

Physicians would not have to use insurance companies, therefore saving money, and if they jacked their prices up too much, patients would find other doctors. Doctors could also control the number of patients they would like to treat and could thus have some control over their stress levels. In this model, the physicians would still negotiate pricing with the drug companies for the basic generic drugs needed for their clinics, as well as the basic technologies they would need, such as X-ray machines and lab equipment for blood and urine testing.

Interoperability might become more of a problem under this model, unless there was some basic kind of record keeping that individual clinics would like to use—something that did not interfere with their practices and would allow for a more personalized experience for their patients. Perhaps there could be a portal system that worked, kind of like Siri works in the home, with the electronic listening device writing up the visit directly into the patient's portal and possibly even connecting with the patient's home Siri that could keep track of health issues at home. Privacy might be a problem for older people; however, many millennials and younger generations do not seem to mind, as they prefer working with their devices, which seem to require all their data. What might not be possible today might be possible tomorrow.

3. Corporate takeover of Healthcare—the "Amazon/ JPMorgan/Berkshire Hathaway" corporate plan example:

Healthcare professionals in the USA received almost an "earthquake type jolt" on January 30, 2018, with the press release that Amazon, Berkshire Hathaway, and JPMorgan Chase & Co. were going to partner to develop their own healthcare for their employees. The stated mission and goals were to "improve employee satisfaction and reduce costs. The three companies, which bring their scale and complementary expertise to this long-term effort, will pursue this objective through an independent company that is free from profit-making incentives and constraints. The initial focus of the new company will be on technology solutions that will provide U.S. employees and their families with simplified, high-quality and transparent healthcare at a reasonable cost..." (*https://www.business-wire.com/news/home/20180130005676/en/Amazon-Berkshire-Hathaway-JPMorgan-Chase-partner-U.S*).

The January 30, 2018 press release was followed by several others during 2018, as this partnership developed:

- May 5, 2018: Berkshire Hathaway, Amazon and JPMorgan are close to hiring a CEO for their healthcare venture (*http://fortune.com/2018/05/05/warren-buffett-berkshire-hathaway-amazon-jmorgan-healthcare/*).
- June 20, 2018: Amazon, JPMorgan, and Berkshire Hathaway have picked the CEO to run their health venture (*https://www.businessinsider.com/amazon-jpmorgan-and-berkshire-hathaway-health-joint-venture-ceo-pick-2018-6*). This person is Dr. Atul Gawande, a surgeon who is also a professor at the Harvard T.H. Chan School of Public Health and Harvard Medical School. *This work will take time but must be done*, Gawande said in the companies' news release. ***The system is broken, and better is possible***.
- June 24, 2018: CEO's goal: "Take some of the middlemen out of the system" (*https://www.bloomberg.com/news/articles/2018-06-24/amazon-berkshire-jpmorgan-health-venture-takes-aim-at-middlemen*).
- June 25, 2018: Dr. Atul Gawande: Amazon-Berkshire-JPMorgan venture will tackle three types of healthcare waste. These are 1) to figure out ways that will drive better outcomes, 2) better patient satisfaction with care,

and 3) better cost-efficiency with new models that can be used by others (*https://www.beckershospitalreview.com/hospital-management-administration/dr-atul-gawande-amazon-berkshire-jpmorgan-venture-will-tackle-3-types-of-healthcare-waste.html*).

■ July 9, 2018: Atul Gawande starts his first day as CEO of Amazon, Berkshire Hathaway, and JPMorgan health venture (*https://www.geekwire.com/2018/atul-gawande-starts-first-day-ceo-amazon-berkshire-hathaway-jpmorgan-health-venture/*).

■ Atul Gawande will give the opening **KEYNOTE address for HIMSS19 on February 12, 2019** at 8:30 am at the Orange County Convention Center in Orlando, Florida (*https://www.himssconference.org/education/keynote-speaker-atul-gawande*).

Additionally, at least one other group announced plans to do something similar—BLOCKCHAIN HEALTH ALLIANCE (*https://www.investors.com/news/blockchain-health-alliance-follows-amazon-berkshire-jpmorgan-pact/*). This one, announced on April 2, 2018, stated that the goals were to "develop a pilot program to use blockchain to improve data quality and reduce administrative costs associated with changes to health care and provide demographic data," according to the press release. The groups involved include Humana, Quest Diagnostics, Multiplan, UnitedHealth Group's Optum, and other UnitedHealthcare units.

And Amazon itself has gotten into the drug selling/distribution business during the latter part of 2018 by purchasing PillPack (*https://www.nytimes.com/2018/06/28/business/dealbook/amazon-buying-pillpack-as-it-moves-into-pharmacies.html*). It would only take "one more step" for Amazon, as part of the Amazon–JPMorgan–Berkshire Hathaway endeavor, to start manufacturing their own drugs, thus offering the possibility of even greatly reducing healthcare costs more for the consumer, the patient.

I think we can clearly see that the Amazon–JPMorgan– Berkshire Hathaway model could be extended beyond its own corporate employees to a much larger segment of the population, if not everyone in the USA (Figure 7.4).

What if more huge corporations decided to use the same model? What if not so huge corporations decided to use the same model? What could we have? Patients would be like the serfs of yore, working for the lord of the manor and running to the castle for medical protection. Hmm (Figure 7.5).

We are almost at the point now when people are working and choosing a job primarily for the healthcare benefits.

4. A system like the OAK STREET MODEL ... a Personalized, Value-Based Model

"OAK STREET HEALTH SYSTEM" (*https://www.oak-streethealth.com/*)

The primary goal of the Oak Street Health system is primary care for seniors in a value-based model (*https://catalyst. nejm.org/caring-for-older-adults-in-a-value-based-model/; 2016*). Others have called it "Rebuilding healthcare 'as it should be'" (Myers, G., *http://annual.hfma.org/2018/Custom/ Handout/Speaker0_Session12_1.pdf; 2018*).

Oak Street Health started in the Chicago area in 2013. They opened their first center in Chicago's Edgewater neighborhood. Oak Street Health continues to expand to new cities and states and seems to be further expanding as we authors write this last chapter of this book during August, 2018— currently there are 40 locations and growing.

One of the slogans of Oak Street Health is: "Every visit to the doctor should be a great experience"—they proclaim that "Oak Street Health is unlike any doctor's office you have experienced before." Some of the specifics that go into making it such are:

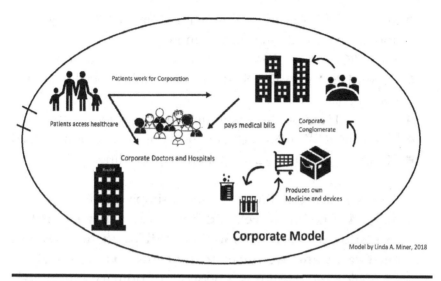

Figure 7.4 The Corporate Model, such as the Amazon–JPMorgan–Berkshire Hathaway Plan. Note that the model is self-contained, except there could be a gate (hatch marks on left) to allow patients from outside the employee base. (Model by Linda Miner.)

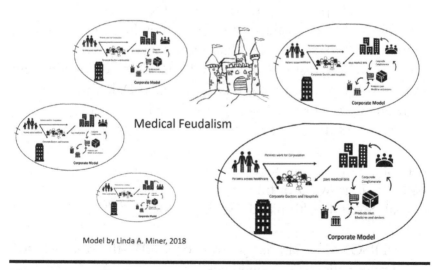

Figure 7.5 Medical Feudalism: Something to think about—not that we think it would be bad; just gives us a bit of a different picture of what medicine could look like.

- MORE TIME—2× more time with your doctor (every appointment is 20 minutes or more)
- EASY SCHEDULING—see your doctor today or tomorrow
- COMMUNITY EVENTS—take classes plus social activities and events
- LESS WAITING—short wait times to see your doctor
- TRANSPORTATION—rides to and from the doctor if needed
- PHONE SUPPORT—24/7 patient support line

The mission of Oak Street Health is simply put in one sentence: **"A mission to rebuild healthcare as it should be—traditional healthcare makes it difficult to truly put patient health and wellness at the center. Our model does."** "Oak Street Health is a network of primary care practices for adults on Medicare. Our approach is well care, not sick care. By keeping thousands of patients happy, healthy and out of the hospital, we've built a healthcare model that works."

To be more specific about a healthcare model that works, here is how Oak Street Health judges the success and the impact they are having: Oak Street talks about keeping patients happy, healthy, and out of the hospital. They are doing all three of those things: (1) they have a 92% Net Promoter Score, so they feel like their patients are happy; (2) they are a five-star practice on the Healthcare Effectiveness Data and Information Set (HEDIS) scale, so Oak Street is a high-quality practice delivering evidence-based care; and (3) they have cut the hospital admission rate by over 40%. That's not only good for patients, but those savings then are what Oak Street is using to invest in making the model bigger and better as it grows over time.

Oak Street Health has three major goals:

1. PERSONAL—Care is "person-centered"—the staff gets to know patients as individuals.

2. EQUITABLE—Everyone should have access to care no matter where they live.
3. ACCOUNTABLE—Oak Street Health holds themselves accountable for their patients' care by taking on the risk and cost of their care.

The above major goals were addressed in much more detail in an interview on August 3, 2018 (*https://catalyst.nejm.org/ rebuilding-health-care-oak-street-health/*); for readers of this book who want to know more, we suggest you go to this link to learn more and then google "Oak Street Health" to see what has happened between the time we completed this book (August 2018) and the time you are reading it!!!

In one sense, a ***patient-first healthcare system*** is here with the Oak Street model. Although it may not meet all of this book's author's goals and their disruptive model with the "patient as CEO" of their care, it meets many and has the potential for meeting them all, we think (Figure 7.6).

The Oak Street model, as is currently running in Chicago and other locations, is only for seniors, patients on Medicare/

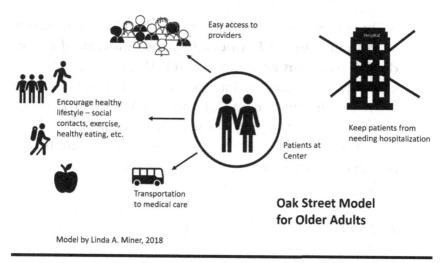

Easy access to providers

Encourage healthy lifestyle – social contacts, exercise, healthy eating, etc.

Transportation to medical care

Patients at Center

Keep patients from needing hospitalization

Oak Street Model for Older Adults

Model by Linda A. Miner, 2018

Figure 7.6 Oak Street Model for Adults on Medicare. (Model by Linda Miner.)

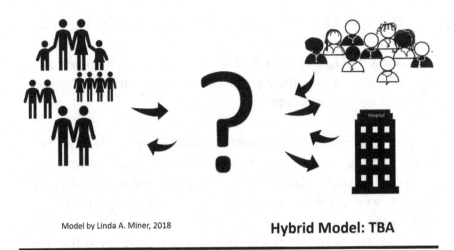

Model by Linda A. Miner, 2018   **Hybrid Model: TBA**

Figure 7.7   The Hybrid Model is not known at present, but the solution model very well could be a hybrid. (Model by Linda Miner.)

Medicare Advantage. So to work for the entire population, the Oak Street model would have to be expanded to cover everyone in the USA, from birth to death. Thus, this system might turn out identical or almost identical to the first model we presented above (the "single-payer" model).

5. **A "hybrid system" distilled from the chaotic mixture of systems currently operating and intermingling in the US payment and care models** (Figure 7.7).

   In the USA today, we have a somewhat chaotic mixture of systems for healthcare that currently exist either side by side or in "intermingling messes" that are called healthcare. There are primarily four models of healthcare that are used in other countries of the world (Reid, T.R, 2010).

These are:

1. The BISMARCK MODEL: found in Germany, Japan, Belgium, Switzerland, and to a degree in Latin America. Both providers and payers are private entities. But unlike

US health insurance, they are basically charities that cover everyone; there is not a profit. The hospitals and doctors are private businesses—privately owned. Tight regulation of services and fees gives much of the cost-control "clout."

2. The BEVERIDGE MODEL British Medical System: financed/provided by government, through tax payments. No medical bills, instead medical treatment is a public service, like the fire department or the public library. Hospitals and clinics are owned by government; some doctors are government employees, but there are also private doctors who get their fees paid by the government. Low costs per capita; government controls what doctors can do and also what they can charge. In addition to the UK, the Beveridge Model is also in ITALY, SPAIN, and most of SCANDINAVIA. HONG KONG still has its own version of this beveridge system. (This model is probably what americans have in mind when they think of "Socialized medicine".) The two purest examples of this BEVERIDGE MODEL are found in CUBA and the US DEPARTMENT OF VETERANS AFFAIRS.

3. The NATIONAL HEALTH INSURANCE MODEL: This has elements of both the Bismarck and the Beveridge systems: providers are private, but the payer is a government-run insurance program that citizens pay into. There is no need for marketing, no expensive underwriting offices, and no profit. This becomes a single payer covering everyone—thus they have the ***power*** to negotiate for ***lower prices***. The best example, maybe only one, is CANADA.

4. The OUT-OF-POCKET MODEL: Only about 40 of the world's countries, industrialized nations, have an established healthcare system. Most nations are too poor and too disorganized to provide mass care. This rule is simple and brutal: The rich get medical care, the poor stay sick or die. Areas that have this are: rural regions of AFRICA, INDIA, CHINA, and SOUTH AMERICA

ASK DR. DEAN:

Question 1: What is an example of the ultimate VALUE of DOCTORS to a PATIENT?

One of the most difficult and unpleasant tasks of a physician is helping patients and families face the death of a family member.

A 59-year-old electronics technician patient of mine complained of vague abdominal pain. He had had very little illness in his life and was definitely not a complainer. Blood count, urinalysis, biochemical profile, and X-rays were all normal. There was no hint of a specific abnormality or specific diagnosis. The pain continued, and even with thorough questioning and careful examination, the problem eluded detection. The next step was admission to the hospital, along with a CT scan and consultation with specialists. Still no diagnosis could be made, and with a sense of frustration felt by all, abdominal surgery was scheduled. Surgery provided not only the diagnosis but also despair. The diagnosis was cancer of the pancreas.

It is interesting how a person's mind will deal with unpleasant news. The surgeon informed him of the diagnosis, yet when I made my rounds and inquired what he understood about his problem, he did not know what he had been told. We then discussed the diagnosis, and the following day he learned about the dismal prognosis.

His hospital stay was seven days, and during that time he recovered from the surgery uneventfully. At home, pain was the most distressing symptom, but nausea and poor appetite were significant symptoms as well.

My mind was constantly going over, "what do I do now?" I decided that now was an excellent opportunity to put into practice my belief that terminal patients have a right to know their diagnosis, participate in plans for terminal care, and be in a position to take care of their own affairs. Calling on my psychologist friend, we made a house call and met with the patient and his wife. This patient was clearly informed of his prognosis, again, in terms that were simple and clear. He was given time to consider that and ask any questions. Then the psychologist led him through the process of considering how he wanted to deal with his family, being sure his will was in order, and verbalizing what his fears and desires were about medical care.

Over some time, the symptoms worsened, and hospital readmission became necessary. A tube was inserted into his stomach to remove excess fluid and intravenous fluids and pain control medicine were provided. Pain control was the patient's chief concern.

Now, another problem surfaced. Two relatives were scheduled to arrive for a visit on or about Christmas Day, and December 25th was four weeks away. His condition was steadily deteriorating. As the days passed, the real-ization dawned on me that his conversation comments represented his conviction that it was his destiny to die on Christmas Day. His wife and I then began to work on creating a goal and increasing hope in his mind. We began talking about him going home for Christmas and spend-ing the day with the family and grandchildren. Plans were under way to make sure we could deliver on this plan. As we encouraged him, it began to take effect! He indeed caught some interest and excitement. On Christmas Day an ambulance came, and the suction machine, intravenous fluids, and other paraphernalia were packaged up and he went home one last time. The day was beautiful. He held his grandchildren on his lap, had a small eggnog (spiked!), and said afterward that he had never had a more wonderful and meaningful day. He returned to the hospital and gradu-ally deteriorated over the next ten days and died quietly in his sleep. The last days were not marked by increasing pain and suffering. Instead, he gradually became less and less aware and slipped into a coma.

The two events that had the most impact in this case were the confrontation by me and the psychologist with the truth, listening to the patient's wishes, and making arrangements for his one last Christmas Day at home.

(hundreds of millions of people go all their lives without *ever* seeing a doctor ...). All of this is *paid out of pocket*. Out-of-pocket payments also account for 91% of total healthcare spending in CAMBODIA, 85% in INDIA, and 73% in EGYPT. (In contrast, the figure in the UK is 3%; in the USA, 17%.)

For the USA, we have elements of *all four of these models* in our American "Convoluted National Healthcare Apparatus":

- For US working people under 65—we are "GERMANY or JAPAN," Bismarck model fashion
- For US Native Americans, military personnel, and veterans—we are "BRITAIN or CUBA"
- For USA over 65—we are CANADA
- For the 45 million uninsured Americans—we are CAMBODIA (or Burkina Faso, or rural India)

AND yet the USA is **like no other country** ... because it maintains separate systems for separate classes of people, and relies heavily on for-profit private insurance plans to pay the bills. With its fragmented array of providers and payers and overlapping systems, the US healthcare system does *not* fit into any of the four recognized models ...

AMERICA IS RESISTANT TO CHANGE: ... the VESTED INTERESTS are doing well in healthcare now!!!:

- Insurance Companies
- Hospital Chains
- Pharma companies

But these three "vested interests" have also blocked any significant re-engineering of the American healthcare system ...

Thus, for the USA (be it via the federal government/congress and/or private entities), we have to come up with a plan that is *disruptive* (more than what is going on currently ...) and that *un-blocks* these three "vested interests" so that the goals presented in this book can be met and the USA can have the quality and cost-effectiveness of healthcare that is found in most if not all of the industrialized nations of the world.

But what will be finally arranged for the USA is a "big question"—one that Congress, Washington, DC, and private providers will have to grapple with during 2019 and the years ahead if a "solution" is not adopted in 2019.

Evidence-Based Medicine (EBM)

We talked about EBM earlier in the book. For the past 20 years or so, EBM was the next best idea. Truly, it sounded great. Find out what works best and do it! What works best was determined by using large group studies and p-value statistics. The goal was noble, and methods came from the research that was determined to be the "gold standards." How could one go wrong? And we addressed how things could and do go wrong. The patient receiving the gold standard for medicine and treatment might not be like the mean of the group being tested. Individual patients might fit best in the "tail" of the distribution, as can be seen in Chapter 1. Something else might work best for that individual person. Hickey and Roberts (2011 pp. 4–5) stated it clearly in their preface:

> "Even the simplest experiment is difficult to ana-
> lyze with EBM (Evidence-Based Medicine) standard

"frequentist" statistics. We suggest the use of Bayesian, Trees, and Heuristics ("Rules of Thumb" ... it is becoming increasingly clear that EBM based on meta-analysis is junk science ... EBM harms patients and suppresses medical progress."

Until we can accurately say what works for individuals, we continue in the realm of trial and error and the intuition of doctors who know their patients well. We should all try to find Dr. Eicare, of Chapter 1, in our physicians, and strive to take care of ourselves so that we don't need to be treated and don't need medications. Or we can focus our research resources on determining what works for individuals, through predictive analytics.

Predictive Analytics

Regardless of what "curatory system" is adopted to solve the USA's healthcare delivery issues, predictive analytics will have to be front and center for all aspects of this solution in order to iron out all of the rough edges of the current healthcare delivery mess ... in order to have a "cure that will work," bringing the changes needed for:

- Cost-effectiveness,
- Accuracy,
- A truly *best predictable benefit* to both society and to the individual person in our society.

In all of this, the patient must return to being at the center of all these efforts—in other words, the patient is the CEO of their diagnosis and treatments, and payers and providers must return to being servants of the patients; e.g., the healthcare delivery is for the patients' well-being and payers and providers need to act with a mindset of the patient as the most important aspect of all transactions.

Minimum of four essentials needed for an Excellent Healthcare Delivery System in the USA (whichever "solution model" is adopted):

1. INTEROPERABILITY ... of patient medical records among all/any providers—***ABSOLUTELY ESSENTIAL***
2. PREDICTIVE DATA ANALYTICS used correctly among providers and payers—***ABSOLUTELY ESSENTIAL***
3. TRANSPARENCY—of costs, treatments pros/cons, all aspects of treatment and recovery needs—***ABSOLUTELY ESSENTIAL***
4. COSTS brought back down to what they would have been if they only increased with the "costs of living index" of the past few decades—to rectify the "runaway beyond inflation costs of healthcare of past decades"—***ABSOLUTELY ESSENTIAL***

In Conclusion

We have presented five possible solutions to healthcare in this chapter; we have presented predictive analytics as a modern methodology that allows for higher accuracy in anything from diagnosis to treatment to business operations; and we have presented a "disruptive model" that puts the patient at the center as the CEO of their healthcare with the payers and providers as servants of the patient (*kind of like "back to the future"—e.g., the way healthcare was decades/centuries ago, maybe*).

So we are "after the BIG GAME" ... it is up to YOU, the reader, and a group of readers, and the American Public to "bag the GAME," so to speak.

Using the *New York Times* bestseller *The Black Swan: The Impact of the Highly Improbable* (Taleb, 2007), and the ideas presented therein, maybe we can get into a mood that will allow the USA to "bag this BIG GAME." After all, BLACK SWANS underlie almost everything of importance in our world.

As Taleb points out, "humans are hardwired to learn specifics (e.g. details) when they should be focused on generalities"; "humans concentrate on things we already know and time and time again fail to take into consideration what we DON'T KNOW ... and therefore we are truly unable to ESTIMATE OPPORTUNITIES ... we are too vulnerable to the impulse to SIMPLIFY, NARRATE, and CATEGORIZE, and not open enough to reward those who can imagine the 'IMPOSSIBLE,'" thus, we FOOL OURSELVES ... and are surprised when "BIG EVENTS" (like the Internet, Google, 9/11, the election of Trump in 2016, etc.) re-shape our world ... when we could have been part of the "NEXT BIG EVENT" ...

So, readers of this book, it is up to you ... maybe we need a ***Black Swan of Healthcare*** to become the "best answer," the "best solution" to the issues presented in this book ... again, it is UP TO YOU ...

Many medical doctors, even in the younger generation, who are friends of the authors and also express the issues presented in this book, will say, "But, we just *cannot* do it and be as *cost-effective* as some of these other industrial nations .... Because our society is 'so much more complicated'...."

... To which we authors say: "Rubbish." This is just a *push back* and reflects attitudes and indoctrination in medical school and residency training indicating that they do not want to embrace the changes needed. The changes can be made—it is a matter of attitude change first before the mechanics of change can be applied.

BUT TO BE PRECISE—so there is no misunderstanding what the authors of this book are stating—TO BE SUCCESSFUL in a RE-ENGINEERED HEALTHCARE DELIVERY SYSTEM for the USA, all of the following must be met:

1. Meet ALL aspects of this books' model (e.g., a return to servanthood healthcare);
2. EVERYONE in the population (citizens) must be included;

3. PRE-EXISTING CONDITIONS must be covered;
4. COMPLETE TRANSPARENCY in COSTS (for all parts/ aspects of healthcare delivery)— so that doctors and patients can both easily understand AND both doctors and patients can easily talk about before deciding on treatments (analogous to most other aspects of society, such as "buying a car," "purchasing a home," etc.).

If America opens itself up to these four needs and opens itself for the "black swan" solution, it can have the most exceptional healthcare in the world.

If what is worked out does *not* have all of these aspects, it will:

■ NOT be successful;
■ NOT meet the needs of America;
■ NOT be a true re-engineering or "black swan" advancement.

SO, READERS: Be vigilant and look for and support the "black swan" when it presents itself!!!!!!!

References

Goldhill, D. (2013). *Catastrophic Care*. New York: Knopf.

Reid, T.R. (2010). *The Healing of America: A Global Quest for Better, Cheaper, and Fairer Health Care*. New York: Penguin Books http://https://www.amazon.com/Healing-America-Global-Better-Cheaper/dp/0143118218/.

Taleb, N.N. (2007). *The Black Swan—The Impact of the Highly Improbable*. New York: Random House.

Topol, E. (2012). *The Creative Destruction of Medicine: How the Digital Revolution Will Create Better Health Care*. New York: Basic Books.

Winters-Miner, L.A., Bolding, P.S., Hilbe, J.M., Goldstein, M., Hill, T., Nisbet, R., Walton, N., Miner, and G.D. (2015). *Practical Predictive Analytics and Decisioning Systems for Medicine*. Boston, MA: Elsevier/Academic Press.

Additional Resources for All 7 Chapters of this Book

HEALTHCARE ISSUES—GENERAL REFERENCE/ RESOURCE LIST of BOOKS and PAPERS published over the past 20 years that are concerned with the problems with US healthcare delivery and how to solve these problems; many of these were read by this book's authors as background and influenced the authors of this book, leading them to write HEALTHCARE'S OUT SICK—PREDICTING A CURE:

Agus, D.B. (2011). *The End of Illness*. New York: Free Press – A Division of Simon & Schuster, Inc.

Berry, L. L., and Seltman, K.D. (2008). *Management Lessons from Mayo Clinic – Inside One of the World's Most Admired Service Organizations*. New York: McGraw Hill.

Cleverley, W.O., Song, P.H., and Cleverley, J.O. (2011). *Essentials of Health Care Finance*, 7th Edition. Sudbury, MA: Jones and Barlett Learning.

Christensen, C.M., Grossman, J.H., and Hwang, J. (2009). *The Innovator's Prescription: A Disruptive Solution for Health Care*. New York: McGraw Hill Education.

Elton, J. and O'Riordan, A. (2016). *Healthcare Disrupted: Next Generation Business Models and Strategies*. Hoboken, NJ: John Wiley & Sons, Inc.

Halvorson, G.C. (2009). *Health Care Will Not Reform Itself: A User's Guide to Refocusing and Reforming American Health Care.* New York & Boca Raton, FL: CRC Press – A Productivity Press Book.

Heineman, M., and Froemke, S. (2012, October 5). *Escape Fire – The Fight to Rescue American Healthcare.* Los Angeles, CA: Roadside Attractions/Lionsgate (Feature-length documentary film; January 19, 2012 (Sundance Film Festival)).

Hickey, S., and Roberts, H. (2011). *Tarnished Gold: The Sickness of Evidence-Based Medicine.* Scotts Valley, CA: CreateSpace Independent Publishing Platform.

Jeff Hayes Films. (2012). *Doctored: Your Food, Your Medicine, Your Healthcare.* http://jeffhaysfilms.com/doctored/, https://www.facebook.com/DoctoredTheMovie/.

Kinney, C. (2011). *Transforming Health Care: Virginia Mason Medical Center's Pursuit of the Perfect Patient Experience.* New York & Boca Raton, FL: CRC Press – A Productivity Press Book.

Makary, M. (2012). *Unaccountable: What Hospitals Won't Tell You and How Transparency Can Revolutionize Health Care.* New York: Bloomsbury Press.

Moriates, C., Arora, V., and Shah, N. (2015). *Understanding Value-Based Healthcare.* New York: McGraw Hill Education.

Munro, D. (2016). *Casino Healthcare: The Health of a Nation – America's Biggest Gamble.* Pennsauken, NJ: BookBaby.

Porter, M.E., and Teisberg, E.O. (2006). *Redefining Health Care: Creating Value-Based Competition on Results.* Boston, MA: Harvard Business School Press.

Protzman, C., Mayzell, G., and Kerpchar, J. (2011). *Leveraging Lean in Healthcare – Transforming Your Enterprise into a High Quality Patient Care Delivery System.* New York & Boca Raton, FL: CRC Press – A Productivity Press Book.

Reid, T. R. (2010). *The Healing of America – A Global Quest for Better, Cheaper, and Fairer Health Care.* London, UK: Penguin Books.

Rosenthal, E. (2017). *An American Sickness – How Healthcare Became Big Business and How You Can Take It Back.* New York: Penguin Press.

Sterling, R.B. (2010). *Keys to EMR/Her Success – Selecting and Implementing an Electronic Medical Record,* 2nd Edition. Phoenix, MD: Greenbranch Publishing.

Topol, E. (2015). *The Patient Will See You Now – The Future of Medicine is in Your Hands.* New York: Basic Books.

PREDICTIVE ANALYTICS—GENERAL REFERENCE/ RESOURCE LIST of BOOKS and PAPERS published over the past 15 years; most of these have been read by the authors *(and the 2009 book by some of this book's authors became the "Bible of Predictive Analytics," an awarded book and the bestseller in that type of book during 2009–2015):*

Books Written Previously by the Authors of This Book

Miner, G. et al. (2012). *Practical Text Mining and Statistical Analysis for Non-Structured Text Data Applications.* Boston, MA: Elsevier/Academic Press.

Miner, G., Winters-Miner, L. et al. (1989). *Caring for Alzheimer's Patients: A Guide for Family & Healthcare Providers.* New York: Plenum Press-Insight Books.

Miner, G. et al. (1989). *Familial Alzheimer's Disease: Molecular Genetics and Clinical Perspectives (Series on Neurological Disease & Therapy).* New York: Dekker, Inc.

Nisbet, R., Miner, G., and Yale, K. (2018). *Handbook of Statistical Analysis and Data Mining Applications,* 2nd Edition. Boston, MA: Elsevier/Academic Press.

Nisbet, R., Elder, J., and Miner, G. (2009). *Handbook of Statistical Analysis and Data Mining Applications,* 1st Edition. Boston, MA: Elsevier/Academic Press.

Winters-Miner, L., et al. (2015). *PRACTICAL PREDICTIVE ANALYTICS & DECISIONING SYSTEMS FOR MEDICINE: Informatics Accuracy and Cost-Effectiveness for Healthcare Administration and Delivery Including Medical Research;* Boston: Elsevier – Academic Press.

Books and Papers by Others on Predictive Analytics

Abbott, D. (2014). *Applied Predictive Analytics – Principles and Techniques for the Professional Data Analyst.* Indianapolis, IN: John Wiley & Sons.

Bari, A., Chaouchi, M., and Jung, T. (2017). *Predictive Analytics for Dummies,* 2nd Edition. Hoboken, NJ: John Wiley & Sons, Inc.

Burke, J. (2013). *Health Analytics – Gaining the Insights to Transform Health Care.* Hoboken, NJ: John Wiley and Sons, Inc.

Carey, R.G. and Loyd, R.C. (2001). *Measuring Quality Improvement in Healthcare – A Guide to Statistical Process Control Applications.* Milwaukee, Wisconsin: Quality Press of ASQ (American Society for Quality).

Duncan, I. (2011). *Healthcare Risk Adjustment and Predictive Modeling*. Winsted, CT: ACTEX Publications, Inc.

Fayyad, U., Grinstein G. G., and Wierese, A., editors. (2002). *Information Visualization in Data Mining and Knowledge Discovery*. San Diego, CA: Academic Press.

Francis, B. (2016). *Data Analytics – The Complete Beginner's Guide*. San Bernardino, CA: CreateSpace Independent Publishing Platform.

Kudyba, S.P. (2010). *Healthcare Informatics – Improving Efficiency and Productivity*. New York & Boca Raton, FL: CRC Press – Anerbach Book.

Lewis, A. (2012). *Why Nobody Believes the Numbers – Distinguishing Fact from Fiction in Population Health Management*. Hoboken, NJ: John Wiley & Sons.

Minelli, M., Chambers, M., and Dhiraj, A. (2013). *Big Data Analytics – Emerging Business Intelligence and Analytic Trends for Today's Businesses*. Hoboken, NJ: John Wiley & Sons, Inc.

McNeill, D., editor. (2013). *ANALYTICS IN HEALTHCARE and the LIFE SCIENCES – Strategies, Implementation Methods, and Best Practices*. Upper Saddle River, New Jersey:PEARSON EDUCATION-Pearson FT Press.

Patterson, J. and Gibson, A. (2017). *Deep Learning – A Practitioner's Approach*. Sebastopol, CA, & Boston, MA: O'Reilly Media, Inc.

Riffenburgh, R.H. (2006). *Statistica In Medicine*, 2nd Edition. Boston, MA: Elsevier/Academic Press.

Siegel, E. (2013). *Predictive Analytics: The Power to Predict Who Will Click, Buy, Lie, or Die*, 1st Edition. Hoboken, NJ: John Wiley & Sons, Inc.

Siegel, E. (2016). *Predictive Analytics: The Power to Predict Who Will Click, Buy, Lie, or Die*, 2nd Edition. Hoboken, NJ: John Wiley & Sons, Inc.

Speed, T. (2003). *Statistical Analysis of Gene Expression Microarray Data*. New York & Boca Raton, FL: Chapman & Hall/CRC – CRC Press LLC.

Srivastava, A. and Shami, M. (2009). *Text Mining – Classification, Clustering and Applications*. New York & Boca Raton, FL: CRC Press – A Chapman & Hall Book.

Strite, S.A. and Stuart, M.E. (2013). *Basics for Evaluating Medical Research Studies – A Simplified Approach (And Why Your Patients Need to Know This)*. Delfini Group LLC. http://www.delfinigrouppublishing.com/.

Weiss, S. M., and Indurkhya, N. (1998). *Predictive Data Mining – Practical Guide*. San Francisco, CA: Morgan Kaufmann Publishers, Inc.

Yang, H., and Lee, E.K., eds. (2016). *Healthcare Analytics: From Data to Knowledge to Healthcare Improvement (Wiley Series in Operations Research and Management Science)*. Hoboken, NJ: John Wiley and Sons, Inc.

Appendix

Appendix: Dr. Dean's HOME HEALTHCARE KIT

ASK DR. DEAN: What should I include in a very complete "home healthcare kit"?

HOME HEALTH KIT
1. Ultrasonic cool mist humidifier
   Use this for colds or any upper respiratory condition (especially at night, but continuously for an adult, baby, or young child if he/she is in bed all the time). Place the humidifier at bed height and close to the patient's head so that the moisture is inhaled with breathing.
2. Thermometer (any brand or type)
   Temperature should be taken with any illness. Fever is defined as a temperature of 100.4 or more. When the temperature is taken, enter the result in your paper pad along with symptoms and any other information you might want to share with your doctor, or to refer to later during the illness.
3. Elastic bandage, at least 2-inch and 3-inch sizes
   An elastic bandage is used for such issues as a sprain of a joint. The size depends on the size of the injured joint. It should be applied continuously a short distance above and below the joint. Be careful not to apply it too tight. If, after the application, the extremity below the bandage

269

changes color or swells, the elastic bandage is too tight and should be loosened somewhat.

4. Triple antibiotic ointment (Neosporin ointment sometimes causes an allergic reaction)

   This ointment is used for application on skin burns, scrapes, or minor injuries. The area should be cleansed first, dried gently, and applied with a light application of ointment. Whether to apply a gauze pad, Band-Aid®, or other dressing depends on the size of the injury and your preference. Leaving it without a dressing, especially if it is relatively small, will hasten healing. If a dressing is applied, it is a good idea to remove it as soon as practical.

5. Gauze rolls, 2-inch size

   Gauze is a bandage frequently used for such injuries as burns, scrapes, and other significant injuries that require a larger dressing due to their size. The main issue with this dressing is that, if there is bleeding or draining, the gauze will stick to the skin unless there the area is covered with a telfa dressing or similar.

6. Scissors (preferably bandage scissors)

   This is an obvious inclusion. The main issue with scissors being in the kit is that if someone removes them from the kit (because they cannot find a pair otherwise) and fails to replace them, they won't be there when needed.

7. Stopwatch for counting pulse rate

8. Gauze pads (they do not have to be sterile)

   Some injuries are not severe but need to be covered for protection and/or to keep clean. Other injuries need more coverage due to more drainage, pus, or blood. The plain gauze pads can be used on top of the dressing that prevents adhesion to the skin.

9. Chlorhexidine gluconate for cleansing skin injuries

   Cleaning can be done with soap and water or chlorhexidine, an antiseptic that removes germs. Either one can be used, but one or the other should be used initially after an injury and with bandage changes.

10. Band-Aids (strips of different sizes and spot sizes)
11. Tape (half-inch and two-inch sizes)
    Tape is obviously used to secure bandages that have no adhesive. The main issue to remember is to not secure it too tightly around an extremity. That can cause a reduction in blood circulation below the bandage. Just apply tape firmly enough to hold a dressing in place.
12. Cough medicine (any that includes only dextromethorphan), with measuring device
    Any cough that occurs frequently and is uncomfortable can be reduced by an appropriate dose of cough syrup. Avoid a cough syrup that includes several different chemicals besides dextromethorphan, which is the medicine that helps reduce the cough, along with the syrup. Other symptoms besides the cough should be treated with medicine that is specifically made for the additional symptom(s).
13. Decongestant (Sudafed generic, 30 mg tablet or liquid)
    This medicine is used for nasal congestion. It is useful to reduce nasal swelling and is especially useful before sleeping so that a person can sleep more comfortably when nasal congestion is present and causing sleeping difficulty. It is important when taking this medicine to follow the dosage instructions on the bottle.
14. Antihistamine (chlorpheniramine and/or non-drowsy type)
    This medicine is for the purpose of reducing nasal discharge, such as occurs during a cold. There are specific instructions on the bottle that should be followed. It is important to understand that a common effect of this medicine is drowsiness. Therefore, it is a good idea to understand that effect in relation to driving and other activities that require alertness.
15. Ibuprofen tablets
    This medicine is available over the counter and is used to reduce pain of any source. This medicine is an anti-inflammatory, which means that it reduces

inflammation. Inflammation causes pain. There are other medicines (with various trade names) that have the same effect. While ibuprofen is short-acting and other similar medicines may be longer acting, if the pain is much improved with ibuprofen, then the longer effect of the longer acting medicines is not necessary and could cause other symptoms. The main issues with ibuprofen are that 1) it may cause indigestion, and 2) depending on what dose you take and how long you take it, you could develop a stomach ulcer. If you already have a problem with heartburn or indigestion, it would be better to avoid any anti-inflammatory medicine due to those side effects.

16. Acetaminophen tablets (350 mg or 500 mg)
Obviously, this medicine is used to reduce pain. It is used for any pain and is generally safe to take, though it is wise to follow the specific instructions for dosing on the container.

17. Nasal spray
This spray is very useful for nose stuffiness, mainly due to colds and other upper respiratory conditions. Nasal stuffiness can make trying to sleep difficult. Using a nasal spray can reduce that unpleasant symptom. The main issue with this medicine is that, if used too often for too long, the stuffiness can become chronic, and that then becomes a worse issue than the original stuffiness.

18. Face masks (to prevent the spread of viruses)
This suggestion is potentially useful, especially during flu season, but also at any time a family member has a viral illness (viruses are the most common causes of upper respiratory symptoms).

19. Gloves (latex or vinyl)
Wearing gloves when attending to another person who is sneezing, coughing, and/or vomiting can reduce the likelihood of catching the condition of the other person.

20. Nasal strips (medium size)

    This is an additional product that is very effective for treating nasal stuffiness. It can be used any time a person has nasal stuffiness but is especially useful at night when you are trying to sleep. In addition, if you have nasal stuffiness due to a cold or other upper respiratory condition, applying a nasal strip at bedtime can make a significant improvement in nighttime comfort. While it does not open your nasal passages a large amount, the reason it helps is that if you increase the nasal capacity by 10–15%, which the strip does, you will notice a significant improvement of your breathing. With that help, you can breathe just better enough that you do not have to mouth breathe.

21. Lozenges (containing benzocaine, a topical anesthetic)

    This medicine is specifically used for a sore throat from any cause. It can be used as needed with no specific restrictions. However, if your sore throat is no longer present, do not use this remedy.

22. Orajel or Anbesol (for a toothache)

    One of the common discomforts one can have is a toothache. It seems to come at a most inconvenient time, such as at night, on a weekend, or at another time when your dentist is unavailable or does not have an appointment time immediately. These medicines, basically ointments, can reduce the pain of a toothache when applied. An additional treatment could include aspirin or Tylenol.

    The information above is for you to be able to treat some health occurrences that do not necessarily require a doctor visit. You will need to make that decision, but this information may be helpful in making that decision. You should review the list and decide what you believe you need to include. Then obtain a container for all the items and store the container in a location known by everyone in the family.

Index

Printed in the United States
by Baker & Taylor Publisher Services